Philippa Hanna is led by a heart devoted to God. She shows this in her music, her voice to speak up for the poor through her work with Compassion, and now through her new book, *Amazing You*. This 365-day devotional will inspire anyone who has dreams to chase them relentlessly as unto the Lord. We are proud and thankful to call Philippa our friend and Artist in Residence.

—MARK HANLON, senior vice president, Compassion International

Just a few years back, I had the incredible privilege of writing music and performing with Philippa Hanna. I was inspired and encouraged by her talents, as well as her depth of insight and humanity. She is that rare type of artist who can blend her faith and life experiences in a way that can bring about change in others.

—KEVIN MAX, artist and member of DC Talk

Philippa is amazingly gifted as a singer, musician, and writer. *Amazing You* will encourage you to never give up on what God has uniquely called you to do for his kingdom purpose.

—BRENDA CROUCH, author, speaker, singer, and television co-host

With engaging honesty and vulnerability, Philippa's passion for God and his kingdom shine though on every page in *Amazing You*. Let her unique insights and experiences draw you closer to him and his unique plans for you.

—STUART TOWNEND, writer of *In Christ Alone*

Philippa's wisdom, vulnerability, and heart will encourage you to not give up and to live out the unique dreams that God has placed inside of you.

—MASEY MCLAIN, actor, speaker, and author of *It's Worth It*

From struggles with self-esteem to dealing with online bullies, to romance, ambition, and anxiety, *Amazing You* emerges from the place where faith meets daily life. Life is done a day at a time, and out of her own journey, Philippa offers daily doses of practical wisdom, insight, life lessons, and prayer. I believe this book will enrich many lives.

—GRAHAM KENDRICK, songwriter and worship leader

Philippa is always uplifting and authentic. *Amazing You* is full of timely, relevant words to keep us focused on what matters most in life. It's a daily dose of inspiration that keeps you thinking and motivated toward your dreams.

—PAUL BALOCHE, worship leader and songwriter

Amazing You is an invaluable tool for the rushed and the weary, providing a practical focus for thought and a place to pause and pray.

—REV. KATE BOTTLEY, Church of England priest and BBC Radio 2 presenter

Philippa has given us a daily devotional that captures her creativity and experience. We're all dreamers, but in today's challenging culture, it's easy to become discouraged while pursuing those dreams. Let this devotional help inform and encourage your life to make God's best dream come true for you.

—KATHLEEN COOKE, co-founder of Cooke Pictures, The Influence Lab, and author of *Hope 4 Today: Stay Connected to God in Distracted Culture*

When I read Philippa's book, I was blown away. It is so simple... simply profound. That only happens when God is holding the pen and the writer writes. That impossible-to-describe feeling wells up inside of you and you know you're loved by God.

—MICHELE PILLAR, speaker, author of *Untangled, The Truth Will Set You Free*, and three-time Grammy nominated singer

Amazing You

You

365 DEVOTIONS FOR DREAMERS

BY
PHILIPPA HANNA

BroadStreet
PUBLISHING

BroadStreet Publishing® Group, LLC
Savage, Minnesota, USA
BroadStreetPublishing.com

Amazing You: 365 Devotions for Dreamers

Stock or custom editions of BroadStreet Publishing titles may be purchased in bulk for educational, business, ministry, fundraising, or sales promotional use. For information, please email info@broadstreetpublishing.com.

Represented in the UK by Storm5 Management
Cover design and typesetting by GarborgDesign.com

Printed in China
19 20 21 22 23 5 4 3 2 1

Contents

For Lucy, Lily, Grace, Keziah, Cerys, and Phoebe, my six beautiful nieces. You are so precious and powerful. Every day I pray for you to fully know and live out your value, beauty, purpose, and unique God-given destiny.

Love always, Philippa

Dreamers Change the World

Some may believe that dreams are a trivial distraction, but let's be real—dreamers change the world. Every great leader, entertainer, explorer, and inventor in history began with a dream. From Thomas Edison to Martin Luther King, dreamers are game-changing revolutionaries. They don't just see what is, but what can be. I've come to view dreams not as fantasies but as blueprints for our purpose in the world. If you want to leave a positive imprint on this world during your brief stay, you need a dream. A dream will direct the course of your life. It will cause you make the most of your gifts and talents. Dreams give birth to hope, giving us passion and focus in even the hardest times.

This year I'm celebrating my tenth year as an independent recording artist. I have traveled the world and experienced the great honor of people connecting with my art and my story. I have even had the unrivalled joy of watching that story unlock people from their sorrows. I feel above and beyond blessed to do what I love—and more importantly, what I feel I was *made* to do.

But it hasn't been an easy ride. Being an independent artist makes every day an exercise in faith. My husband, Joel, and I believe daily for God's provision, both for our personal and business needs. There have been financial, relational, spiritual, and physical trials at every juncture. Recently someone asked me via Facebook Messenger, *Do you ever feel like giving up?*

Only a few times a week, I replied. The truth is, I can't even count the number of times where I've felt like hanging up my guitar forever. But when you feel *called* to something, you quickly realize that giving up is not an option. If this dream of yours has truly come from heaven, then it's your duty to pursue it faithfully. Remaining steadfast in that purpose is an act of obedience. So…

- How do we stay strong and motivated on the journey?
- How can we fight fear and fatigue?
- How can we get back up when we have fallen or failed?
- When it comes to our future—and our relationships and ambitions—how can we remain hopeful in troubled times?

I have asked all of these questions along the way. On the journey to the life of my dreams, I have experienced relationship breakdowns, seasons of despair, and even depression. I have struggled to separate myself from my works and not to measure my worth by accomplishments. But I've reached a place in my life where I consider myself an overcomer. With God's daily help I found the tools and the supernatural strength to keep straining toward the goal.

In order to keep going, I found myself reaching into heaven for strength and inspiration. I've been amazed to find that through prayer, reflection, and reaching into heaven, *every* day something encouraging has fallen into my spirit like manna. I began sharing these thoughts via social media about three years ago, and the more thoughts I shared, the more I was inspired. People in my world who were also reaching for their best life in God began to respond to those posts and journey alongside me. Many suggested I organize these musings into a book. So by God's grace I did just that! I have collected 365 inspiring thoughts that I hope will be daily fuel for you as they have been for me.

These thoughts are not only for those pursuing a ministry or career goal. I have purposed these writings for anyone needing encouragement to fight the good fight of faith in their daily lives. I have included encouragement on love, peace, managing relationships, insecurity, self-esteem, fear, discouragement, and much more.

I have planned out these daily readings in an order that makes sense as we journey through the year. But I have also organized them into monthly themes so you can find the readings most helpful for you at any time. You can journey with me daily, or you can move from section to section. You can simply let the book fall open, or you can search for the monthly theme that most applies to where you are in the journey right now. It's entirely up to you! Please personalize this journey as you desire.

Each reading is accompanied by a Scripture passage, a reflection, and a prayer, intended as light suggestions to guide and inspire you. But feel free to respond as you choose. I encourage you to scribble, doodle, circle, outline, and make this book your own!

However you choose to enjoy this work, I pray with all my heart that it spurs you on. I also pray that you can look back over this year and see both wonderful progress and God's fingerprints on everything. Feel free to quote and share these thoughts with the people in your world using the hashtags #AmazingYou and #inspiration365.

Love and blessings,
Philippa

Surrender

Then Jesus said to his disciples, "Whoever wants to be my disciple must deny themselves and take up their cross and follow me. For whoever wants to save their life will lose it, but whoever loses their life for me will find it."

MATTHEW 16:24–25

We will approach innumerable doors as we pursue our dreams in life. But before we go any further, there is one door we must go through for ourselves. I believe that everything good, right, and necessary in life is beyond it. This is the door of surrender to God. There will be many gatekeepers whom we will strive to charm and influence, but God is above all of them, and the key to surrender is entirely in *our* hands.

Back in early 2004 I was doing a vocal session for a university student named Andy Baker. He was a Christian and therefore a completely alien species to me. I was a young agnostic struggling with my music dreams and ambitions. Andy believed God has a plan for our lives. The session went well, and I noticed that Andy had become quite emotional as I finished my last take. He called me into the control room, where I found him in tears. Surprised and shocked, I asked what was wrong. He sat me down, and this is what he said: "I believe you have the gift of reaching people emotionally. But Philippa, I really feel you need to give your gifts to God because he can do more with them than you can ever do alone."

It was a couple of months later that everything began to change. I went to a church gathering, and during the worship I found myself praying. I was depressed, defeated, and desperate for God to show up in my life. I realized I had to let go of *all* of it.

I had to put all my dreams and gifts before God and relinquish ownership. It was scary and strange. But I honestly believe that without this commitment, none of the doors that followed would have opened. By God's grace I was slowly released into the life of purpose, one I identified in my spirit.

As a reader, you may not be ready to make that commitment. That's okay. But I needed to share at the outset what I believe will help you most. As for the rest, I pray you'll find something in each passage that helps you to keep moving and keep believing.

REFLECTION

If there's something you want to lay down right now, here's your chance. Write down your dream in just a few words and, if you feel brave enough, hand it completely to God. Let me encourage you, the adventure starts here.

Lord, I surrender all the desires of my heart because I trust you. I know that whatever I have planned is nothing compared to your plan, Lord. Take my life, my gifts, and all my desires and have your way. May your will be done and your kingdom come through my time here on earth. In Jesus' name, amen.

Upgrade Your Dream

As the heavens are higher than the earth, so are my ways higher
than your ways and my thoughts than your thoughts.

Isaiah 55:9 KJV

When I was little, I liked to play with flour. I guess I discovered it
while baking with Mum. When she saw me playing with the flour,
she asked if she could use it to make homemade Play-Doh. If I
would let her add water and food coloring, we could build things
together and have so much more fun. But I was content to make
patterns with the flour and didn't want my happy little situation
to change. One day Mum went ahead and made the Play-Doh
without telling me, and I discovered a whole new world. I could
actually sculpt my favorite shapes and animals! I realized that if
I'd trusted her sooner, I could have been building and making
things the whole time.

I have to trust God in a similar way when it comes to certain
things in my life. He sees more clearly than I do what will fulfill
me. If I can trust him to take away what I have, he's sure to return
with something better—just like my mum did that day.

REFLECTION

Take a moment today to look at your heart and ask what is in
there that really matters to you. What do you hold onto most
tightly: marriage, children, a dream? Take a moment to write
down what is most dear to you and entrust it to God.

Lord, you know what is most dear to me. But I trust that you
will always do a better job than me at deciding my path. Though
it's not easy, I now hand over my deepest desires, knowing that
you will always have what is best in mind. In Jesus' name, amen.

Delight Yourself in the Lord

Delight yourself in the LORD;
and He will give you the desires of your heart.

PSALM 37:4 NASB

God did some truly incredible things in my life as a new Christian. He led me out of a long season of anxiety and depression. He made it possible for me to break free from relationships that were destroying me because I no longer needed to fear being alone. As this spiritual awakening happened, my dreams began to evolve. As I focused on God's goodness in my life, my dreams became less about my own success and more about introducing others to this great Savior. As I reflected on what I'd overcome by only his strength and the elusive peace I'd found only in his arms, my dreams evolved and my prayers did too. I began to see answers to those prayers right away.

When we delight in his goodness, his sovereignty, and his love, when we long to see his goodness prevail in our lives and the lives of others, when we realize that he *never* gets it wrong and that his agenda is perfect, our dreams will begin to align with *his* plan.

REFLECTION

Today let's just think about how awesome our God is. In your journal use the space to focus on something that inspires you about him. It could be a thought, a Scripture passage, or even a sketch of the sunset. Remind yourself why he is so awesome!

Lord, help me to become more and more amazed by you. Help me to delight in nothing more than I delight in who you are. In Jesus' name, amen.

The Kingdom Filter

"But seek first his kingdom and his righteousness, and all these things will be given to you as well."

MATTHEW 6:33

There is a filter that I put my dreams and plans through: Am I doing this because it pleases me, or because it's right? Am I being selfish, or considering others first? Can the outcome of this dream have positive effects for God's family? I've come to refer to this as my "kingdom filter."

Some years ago I was offered a job in a church. It was a tempting offer that promised a decent salary for doing what I enjoy. But after praying about it, I felt a conviction I would be more fruitful doing outreach. I knew in my spirit that although it would be harder financially, my reach for God would be wider by going out into the world and sharing music beyond the walls of a church. For me, this was seeking first God's kingdom on earth. It was a tough call at the time, but favor seemed to follow. I now travel full-time with my husband, reaching people in unusual places every day.

REFLECTION

What opportunities are presenting themselves to you right now? Do you have a tough decision to make about your future? Or are you confused about how to best use your talents? Today take a moment to examine your dreams and opportunities under a "kingdom microscope" and put it though the "kingdom filter."

Lord, help me always to seek you first. Although it's hard, let me choose what is truly good over what feels good in the moment. Let me make decisions that build your kingdom and benefit those around me. In Jesus' name, amen.

Your Dreams Are a Map for Your Future

Then the LORD told me: "I will give you my message in the form of a vision. Write it clearly enough to be read at a glance."

HABAKKUK 2:2 CEV

I was speaking to a medical student recently who was telling me about her dreams to practice medicine in the developing world. "I'm not sure it'll work out," she said. "It's so competitive."

Listening to her, I realized this dream of hers was a divine one. The idea of doing something like that was so specific to her and alien to me that it could only be something imprinted in her DNA somewhere. In that moment I had what I believe was a God thought: *maybe the desires of our hearts are roadmaps for the fulfillment of God's purpose in our lives.*

A lot of people think those with big dreams need to simply "get real" or pursue a "sensible career." But if you've been born with a dream you can't shake, there is *every* chance that the dream is a signpost for your destiny. In the same way your looks, strengths, and preferences are a part of you, so are those dreams. Instead of calling them dreams, begin to call them roadmaps.

REFLECTION

Do you have a dream in your heart that you believe is from God? Take a moment today to write it down and put it somewhere you can see it. You can keep it simple or even draw it out as a map and then commit that map to God.

Lord, thank you for the way you have made me. Thank you that along with my physical and intellectual attributes, you have also placed dreams within me. Today help me to consider those dreams as signposts for my destiny in you. Help me to have faith in what you've placed in my heart. In Jesus' name, amen.

Submit Your Plans

Commit to the LORD whatever you do,
and he will establish your plans.

PROVERBS 16:3

I would love for God to show me his plan at every turn, but often I am pretty clueless as to what he has in store. If we want to see the outworking of our dreams, it usually begins with *us* making a plan. Whether we dream of starting a business, traveling, having a family, or buying a house, it helps to put pen to paper and map things out. Keeping track of appointments, making lists, and plotting out a timeframe really helps things to progress.

God promises to bless our plans when we submit them to him. So if you're about to begin something, pray, plan, and then pray over the plan. Make your plans prayerfully, hand them to God, and cast off all worry. He promises to bless blueprints drawn up in faith.

REFLECTION

If there's something you're planning right now—an event, a career move, even a wedding—take this moment to submit your plan to God.

Lord, I am making this decision with you in mind. I want this decision to honor you and benefit everyone involved. I ask that you would take this plan and pour your blessings over it. May your will be done. In Jesus' name, amen.

Amateurs Built the Ark

But God chose the foolish things of the world to shame the wise;
God chose the weak things of the world to shame the strong.

1 CORINTHIANS 1:27

So you have a dream, you've made a plan, and now you're realizing you feel wildly underqualified. But someone once said, "Don't be afraid to try new things. Remember amateurs built the ark; professionals built the *Titanic*." I love this quote because it reminds me that God's presence and wisdom far outplay expertise, experience, and even ability.

I can witness to this in my own journey. After years in the music industry, I've seen people with decades of expertise fail to hit the mark while a beginner with faith creates huge waves with their creative efforts. In the end it isn't about being an expert but about having the right idea at the right time—and God's favor.

REFLECTION

If you feel overwhelmed today, remember Noah and the ark he was asked to build. When the dream in your heart is God given, he can work through your limited ability and experience to make it a reality.

Dear Lord, my need is great, but so are you. I trust you with the journey ahead, knowing that where I lack you will provide and where I am weak you will be strong. In Jesus' name, amen.

Step Beyond Your Comfort Zone

"Come," he said. Then Peter got down out of the boat, walked on the water and came toward Jesus.

MATTHEW 14:29

The saying, "Life begins at the end of your comfort zone" is beautiful and true. In the early days of my performing career, I forgot to book a guitarist to accompany me for a show. I presumed we would have to cancel. But my manager, Andy, knew I had written the songs on my guitar and could play them. Andy refused to cancel the show, so I had little choice but to play. As I stood, guitar in hand, in front of a packed hall, I realized I was being kicked out of the nest. I was plummeting toward the ground and had to flap my little wings or I would crash. Today I play up to 150 shows a year with a guitar in my hand. I never do a show without it, and I've never looked back.

In the beginning I wanted a career in music that was entirely on my terms. I only wanted to do what was comfortable for me, but this mind-set was limiting what I could accomplish. If you're not willing to do things that terrify you, you're unlikely to learn what you're really capable of. Step out of the nest, and there's no telling how far you'll fly!

REFLECTION

What gifts are you not using because you're afraid to stand up and share? Perhaps it's time to step out of the boat.

Lord, give me courage to go where you send me and do things that scare me, knowing that you're right beside me every step of the way. Let me never allow fear to prevent me from learning and becoming all that I can in you. In Jesus' name, amen.

God Will Equip You

And God is able to make all grace abound to you, so that always having all sufficiency in everything, you may have an abundance for every good deed.

2 Corinthians 9:8 nasb

Stepping outside your comfort zone often leads to doing things you don't have the skills or money for. When you realize that what you're attempting can't be achieved with the resources you have, it can be quite daunting. Remember this: *What God has asked you to do, he will equip you to do.* He won't leave you to perish in the middle of his mission. You don't need to worry about your age, skill level, background, or resources.

When I first got the call to join Lionel Richie on tour, I was hesitant to say yes. We were going need a lot of resources we didn't have at that time. But when I felt the nudge so deeply in my spirit that I should take the opportunity, I agreed. Within forty-eight hours, we'd managed to find everything we required. And we were blessed beyond measure through the tour and today, six years later I still meet people who stumbled upon us there and were deeply impacted by what was shared.

Reflection

If there are things you need in order to go forward in your journey, don't fear! God has promised provision for every good work. Take a moment to detail what you need and bring it to God today in prayer.

Lord, some of the tasks ahead of me are beyond what I feel I can do. But I trust you'll provide the resources and the strength I need to see it through. Thank you for the miracles you are about to do, Lord. In Jesus' name, amen.

Keep on Driving

"Go in peace," the priest replied. "For the Lord is
watching over your journey."

JUDGES 18:6 NLT

Life really is a journey. It requires daily movement, change, and
challenge. It's full of twists and turns (some of them wrong
ones). And we all know that travel ranges anywhere from exciting
and scenic to straight-up tedious and exhausting. Some days you
want to open the window, belt out your favorite song, and enjoy
the view. Other days it's all you can do to keep the tank full and
keep the vehicle in a forward motion.

I'm destination focused and love finished products. But not
all days are destination days. Not all days involve arriving somewhere beautiful. Most days are travel days. Although travel days
can really take it out of you, they're essential if you want to see a
new horizon. You'll *never* arrive anywhere without travel days.

So today, enjoy the journey in whatever way you can. Throw
your all into the email messages you need to write, the bills
you need to pay, and the preparations you need to make. When
you're losing motivation because nothing "great" happened, take
a moment to remind yourself, *Today is a travel day. I'm headed
somewhere.* Bon voyage!

REFLECTION

Today, write down one mundane thing you did that has been an
essential part of your journey to beautiful horizons.

Thank you, Lord, that you are watching over every element of
this journey. I know that not every day will be a destination day,
so I simply ask for the patience and the endurance to do today's
travel well. In Jesus' name, amen.

Character Outweighs Talent

Do not think of yourself more highly than you ought, but rather think of yourself with sober judgment, in accordance with the faith God has distributed to each of you.

ROMANS 12:3

Talent is everywhere. It's so plentiful that it's easy to fall into the snare of comparing yourself to others and becoming discouraged. But let me encourage you. Talent is a very small component of success. Character far outweighs talent. Some of the most gifted people end up throwing away their shot at success because their character isn't strong enough to carry the gift.

Character is more important than money, fame position, or status. Because without good character, it's impossible to carry any of those other things. Every time you survive a trial, you grow a little stronger. The setbacks, delays, and disappointments we face on our journey serve at least one great purpose—they help refine our character. My setbacks have helped me to be hardworking, tenacious, and well prepared (none of which I was by nature). They have armed me with material and experience for the next stage of my career or ministry.

REFLECTION

Thank God for the difficulties you're facing. They'll prepare you for the blessings to come. And you'll emerge from those challenges stronger and wiser—and more patient.

Lord, I'm grateful for the challenges I'm facing because I know you're preparing me for what's to come. These trials are a priceless gift because all the gold in all the world can't buy good character! Please make sure I'm ready to carry whatever blessing you have for me. In Jesus' name, amen.

Steady and Slow Wins the Race

And let us run with perseverance the race marked out for us.

HEBREWS 12:1

Most people take themselves out of the race by simply giving up. If you really love what you do, keep doing it. If the song didn't impress, write another. If your singing needs work, get lessons. If you can't get a job writing for a magazine, start a blog of your own. Most artists write hundreds of songs before any of them reach a large audience. Comedian Drew Lynch played five hundred shows the year before he landed his golden buzzer audition for *America's Got Talent*. If you're really determined to reach that finish line, you won't mind taking the slower mode of transport.

You may not be the most talented person on planet earth. But while others are procrastinating, living it up, or simply giving up, keep going. In the story of the tortoise and the hare, out there on the track the hare had the advantage. But the tortoise, who kept going while the hare wasted time, crossed the finish line first. Steady and slow wins the race.

REFLECTION

Do you feel that you're losing focus on the race marked out for you? Do you feel that moving slowly is causing you to become discouraged? Today, let's take this to God in prayer and simply ask for his renewed focus and strength.

Lord, help me to be someone who perseveres. When those around me appear to be stronger or more capable, let me focus on my own journey. Help me to bravely and consistently place one foot before the other and keep moving, knowing that you'll help me to keep running the race marked out for me. In Jesus' name, amen.

Your Destiny Rests on God

The LORD is my light and my salvation—whom shall I fear? The
LORD is the stronghold of my life—of whom shall I be afraid?

PSALM 27:1

We can get pretty hung up on impressing the right people. We
dream of bumping into that one person who could open all the
right doors for our next chapter. It's easy to place all our hope in
regular humans who are likely to disappoint us.

I used to get hugely anxious about meeting with investors,
agents for record labels, and so on. But it took a number of
victories (and knockbacks) for me to realize that my destiny
wasn't going to rest in any one person's hands. Looking back
over a decade of full-time music career and ministry, I can see
that although key figures came and went, my purpose remained.
God's presence and favor never for a moment wavered.

It's good to reach a point where the outcome of a meeting
doesn't threaten our joy and faith. We must learn to trust that
the wrong doors close and the right ones open. If one gatekeeper
doesn't connect with us, there'll be another who does. No one
person decides your destiny. When you entrust your future to
God, he ultimately rules proceedings.

REFLECTION

Remember that God is the real boss, and that he already approves
of you! He will align the right people at the right time to make
sure you move forward.

Lord, help me to have complete peace in my interactions with in-
fluencers I encounter. Help me to conduct myself as someone who
knows where true help and provision comes from. It all comes
from you, Lord! Thank you for your favor. In Jesus' name, amen.

Progress Is Painful

Count it all joy, my brothers, when you meet trials of various kinds.
JAMES 1:2 ESV

Moving forward can hurt like crazy. When my team and I
were preparing for our first big tour, there were disagreements,
setbacks, and even tears. The stakes in my career were
getting higher. The risks were becoming greater and it was
uncomfortable, even painful. But it was healthy and it was
necessary.

If you were in labor but didn't know you were expecting,
you'd probably fear for your life. But as labor so beautifully
reminds us, *pain doesn't always mean things are going wrong.*
Sometimes pain is an indication that things are moving in exactly
the right direction. Growth is painful. Expansion is painful. But
I've never seen a new mother with a baby in her arms that didn't
think the pain was worth it. So keep going, keep breathing, and—
dare I say it?—keep pushing.

REFLECTION

Have things become more difficult in your dream journey
recently? Take a moment to look behind you and see how far you
have already come. Don't presume that things are going wrong
just because they're becoming less comfortable.

Lord, thank you for this process that I'm in. Just as a child has a
growth spurt, my growth as a dreamer can likewise be painful.
Help me to deal with the pain that comes from progress and to
know that it's an encouraging sort of pain. Thank you finally for
the delivery of this dream that someday will come as I have faith
in you. In Jesus' name, amen.

Make the Most of Every Opportunity

"He who is faithful in a very little thing is faithful also in much."
LUKE 16:10 NASB

A little while ago I felt a strong desire to branch out and write for other artists, but it didn't seem that any new doors were opening. Then one day these questions fell into my spirit: *Am I overlooking the opportunities that are right in front of me? Are there people close to home that I could reach out to and connect with?*

So I made a list of all the great people I was already in touch with and began to write some emails. Pretty soon I had a bunch of appointments scheduled, and within a few months, doors beyond my network were opening. I realized that I'd become so focused on my bigger goals that I'd forgotten to see and seize the opportunities God had already blessed me with.

Sometimes we have to ask ourselves, *Am I making the most of what God has already put in my life?* Your current life might not seem as exciting as the one you're praying to live, but some of your greatest accomplishments might be right where you are. Perhaps God is waiting for you to "use up" what he has given you before he replenishes you with new opportunities!

REFLECTION

Try to think of some opportunities you might be missing. Are there any ways you can serve with your gift that you haven't already tried? Are there people you can help and mentor? Take time to consider this and make some notes.

Lord, help me to make the most of everything you've given to me. If there is anything you would have me do that I'm overlooking please show that to me as I pray. I want to be faithful with everything you've given to me. In Jesus' name, amen.

Not Everyone Will "Get" You

And this is love: that we walk in obedience to his commands.
As you have heard from the beginning, his command is
that you walk in love.

2 JOHN 1:6

In the years since I began singing in both church and mainstream settings, I've had all sorts of criticism. Some people have questioned my faith because not all my songs mention Jesus, and others have said my music would never appeal to the mainstream because of its faith content. But I cannot change what my heart beats for, and I decided not to try. My mission is to reach and bless people where they are.

I recently received a message from a Yorkshire-based school teacher and it made my heart overflow:

Hi Philippa,

I thought I would message you because I have had one of the most amazing days today and it's thanks to you. I work in a highly deprived school and one of my responsibilities is to conduct the school singing assembly (which is unfortunate as I can't sing to save my life!). Anyway, each week after practicing our school song I play the children a music video with a good message. This week I decided to play your new song 'arrow'. I was completely blown away with their response. 300+ children sat in silence (which is unknown) and the moment it had finished hands were raised: 'Who was that again?' 'Can we hear it again?' Then at playtime a group of girls approached me: 'Can you write down the name of that singer, please?' I never could have imagined that a song would have got such a positive reaction from such a lot of children. So thank you for your vision. I wish you all the best with your music. You really are an inspiration.

In these moments, I realize the importance of being obedient to your unique call. You never know what God will do with it!

REFLECTION

Take a moment to look inside your heart and ask, *Heart, what makes you beat faster? What are you passionate about?* Those things may be a little out of the box, and that's okay. If you have one, write your unique vision below. In times where you're being pulled in different directions, go back and take a look at what you wrote.

Lord, help me to identify how I can love people in my own unique way. Thank you that your call on my life is custom designed. Help me to tune in better to what makes me tick and to be obedient to that in times of distraction. In Jesus' name, amen.

There Is Only One Yes You Need

What, then, shall we say in response to these things?
If God is for us, who can be against us?

ROMANS 8:31

In the pursuit of your dreams you're likely to hear the word *no* a thousand times. There will be people who don't believe in you and don't see your value. There'll be well-meaning friends who don't see the point in your venture because it doesn't make sense on paper. This is when you have to hold on to the God-vision within. God's plans don't always make sense on paper, and that's why faith is required to stick to them.

When God says yes, it doesn't matter who says no. When I made my first record, a certain radio station wouldn't play it. The head of programming thought it was too artsy for their usual playlist. I was discouraged by their feedback but believed in the songs with all my heart. I knew that they needed to reach people and knew that God was bigger than this decision. Just a matter of weeks later, the head of programming moved on and several of my songs were playlisted. Not only will God go around people, he will sometimes wait until they are moved aside.

REFLECTION

Has the word *no* been spoken over you one too many times? If this word now is causing you to doubt your calling, and even your value, it's time to remember that God's promises nullify the noes.

Lord, I thank you that your yes is final. I thank you that no matter who is against me, you are for me. Help me to accept the rejections and decisions of others graciously and patiently, knowing that you have a plan for me and it's perfect. Amen.

The Long Road Has More Treasure

The LORD is my shepherd, I lack nothing. He makes me lie down in green pastures, he leads me beside quiet waters, he refreshes my soul. He guides me along the right paths for his name's sake.

PSALM 23:1–3

Sometimes it can feel as if we're being made to take the scenic route with our dreams. We wonder why so many others seem to arrive at their dream job, marriage, or family before we do. We work hard, pray hard, and prepare, yet we *still* wait for a breakthrough. But be encouraged. As you walk this long road, you're collecting treasure. There are twice the number of jewels on the scenic route.

In the beginning of my career, my only goal was to get a record deal. Years later I can see how I've been doubly blessed by staying independent. I've been able to keep hold of my true self, my original vision, and my focus on God. Being involved in every aspect of the journey has given me invaluable skills I never thought I'd have.

If your dreams are taking forever to come true, take heart. God wants you to be more than just another person praying for a yes. He wants you to be your own *yes* and eventually a *yes* for others.

REFLECTION

What has the scenic route taught you? Make a list of some of the treasures you've picked up on the journey so far.

Lord, thank you for what you are teaching me on this journey. I know you are blessing me through these extra miles. What I encounter on the way will refresh my soul and the souls I come into fellowship with. Help me to absorb and embrace all that you have for me. In Jesus' name, amen.

Get Better at What You Do

Do you see a man skillful in his work? He will stand before kings.
PROVERBS 22:29 ESV

I'm a self-taught musician, and I've always found sight-reading nearly impossible. I used to sit by my frustrated piano teacher, picking out one painful note at a time, my cheeks hotter by the moment. I took other lessons, but formal training didn't work well for me. So when it came to singing, I avoided training. I associated singing with freedom and learning with failure, so I didn't imagine how the two could combine.

But then I began singing full-time and started to feel limited. I was losing my voice every weekend and struggling to fully express myself onstage because of vocal fatigue. So I bit the bullet and bought some learning materials. When I improved, I became hungry for more, so I found myself a teacher. Today I credit that teacher for my career, because without her I don't think I'd have a voice left. My one regret was not finding her sooner. Now I'm hooked on improving and eager to *never* stop learning.

REFLECTION

How can you invest into what you do? Writing classes? Singing lessons? An online course? Dream new ways to improve today.

Lord, thank you for what you've given me already. I so appreciate the raw materials you've blessed me with. Help me to make something with those materials. Help me to invest in sharpening my tools. And help me achieve excellence with my natural abilities. May I never take those things for granted. In Jesus' name, amen.

Chip Away at the Big Stuff

The plans of the diligent lead to profit.
PROVERBS 21:5

Big dreams take a lot of work, which can be very intimidating. But the great thing is, you don't have to achieve everything today. If you commit to doing *something* each day, you will begin to look behind you and see lots of progress.

When you have a large project you're keen to undertake—a book you want to write, an album you want to make, or perhaps a house you want to renovate—it's easy to keep putting off the task because it's so big. But here's the thing: a little effort every day will eventually amount to a finished project. It's not always about how productive you can be, but rather how consistent. If all you can manage is a tiny step per day, even those steps will eventually get you somewhere.

Don't distract yourself with how fast and fruitful other people's lives are. If you just faithfully put one foot in front of the other, you can do anything.

REFLECTION

Set yourself an easy goal for something you want to accomplish. Commit to sitting down for just half an hour a day to invest in it. It's okay if that half hour isn't the most productive. The habit will help you to find momentum, and you'll begin to see results.

Lord, when I'm overwhelmed, help me to simply do a little at a time. Thank you that you have provided sufficient time and that I don't need to squash everything into a single day. Instead of leaving things till the eleventh hour, help me to begin on time and work slowly. In Jesus' name, amen.

Share Your Story

Oh give thanks to the LORD, call upon His name; make known
His deeds among the peoples.

1 CHRONICLES 16:8 NASB

So you're working on your skills; that's great. But don't ever
forget that those skills are secondary to who you are. If the skills
are a glove, the heart that beats within you is the hand.

*What is your story and message? If the spotlight were on you,
what would you say? Who are you beneath your gift?* It's important to consider these things because these are what people
truly connect with. There is a lot of emphasis on being the best,
the richest, the fastest, and the most popular. There is a lot of
pressure to be the best singer or the painter with the most prefect
brush strokes. But this way of measuring our worth as artists is
flawed. If we're talking about vocal dexterity or speed of playing,
then there can only ever be one "best."

Where does that leave the rest of us? The truth is, it's not
always the best singers that most move us. A singer who puts her
heart into a melody and best delivers truth that we remember.

REFLECTION

Can you tell your story within a few minutes? Can you pull out
the key themes of your life that share a specific message? If you
don't know where to start, begin by sharing where you came
from and how you arrived at your current beliefs or way of life.

Lord, thank you that my story is entirely unique. You have given
me plenty to share. Please help me to find my unique voice and
message so I can share something meaningful with the world. In
Jesus' name, amen.

Use It

> "And who knows but that you have come to your royal position for such a time as this?"
>
> ESTHER 4:14

Achievement is awesome. Winning is awesome. But perhaps more inspiring than both is trying. There is nothing more inspiring than someone who will take a risk and try something new. God sees a winner when he sees someone trying. So whether you're stepping into a gym for the first time, putting on a suit for a job interview after years of unemployment, asking someone out, or singing a first choir solo—high five! Being prepared to try is a winning state of mind. Don't be afraid; give it a try.

We could waste our whole lives being quiet, not daring to act, speak, write, or draw because we don't feel good enough. But guess what? An average singer who sings will move a thousand more hearts than a virtuoso who stays silent. So paint, sing, write. You can't control the talents you're born with, but you *can* rock what you have.

REFLECTION

You probably have more talents than you know. Take a moment to write down *all* of the things you know you might be good at. From writing to sewing, write them down. You don't have to spend your life doing one thing. Just because you're a keen scientist doesn't mean you can't pick up a paint brush and paint the sunset. Use it. Use it all!

Lord, help me to step up and use what I have. I may not be the brightest or the most able, but you, Lord, are able. Help me to bring out everything I can while I'm alive. In Jesus' name, amen.

Count the Cost

"Suppose one of you wants to build a tower.
Won't you first sit down and estimate the cost
to see if you have enough money to complete it?"

Luke 14:28

When we catch that wave of inspiration to do something great, we often throw ourselves in headfirst. When I began my daily YouTube uploads, I vastly underestimated the time I would have to spend on it each day. What I should have done was time myself filming, editing, and uploading, multiply that by 365, and figure out how much of my year would be spent on it. Instead, I looked at the idea of 365 two-minute videos and thought it sounded easy. How wrong I was. I'm more than halfway through the commitment now, and while I'm surviving, it has been one heck of a sacrifice of time, energy, and sleep!

It's great to have a big dream, but preparation is vital, and that means calculating the cost on every level. The last thing you want is to run out of steam or resources at the midpoint.

REFLECTION

Today is the day to get realistic about your dream. Don't be discouraged—God can do anything! But it's important to know what your needs are, how to prepare, and even what to pray for as you move forward.

Lord, I come to you asking you to show me what I'll need for this next season. Help me to be sober minded and realistic about the sacrifices I'll have to make. Give me the discernment to know whether or not I'm truly ready to make these commitments. Finally, Lord, thank you that you're able to provide for these needs should I decide I'm ready to go. In Jesus' name, amen.

The Depth of God's Love for You

And I pray that you, being rooted and established in love, may have power, together with all the Lord's holy people, to grasp how wide and long and high and deep is the love of Christ, and to know this love that surpasses knowledge—that you may be filled to the measure of all the fullness of God.

EPHESIANS 3:17–19

It's easy to measure your success by how many people you're reaching—how many friends you have, how many people attend your church, how many customers visit your store. If you're a creative, you may start to stress about how many people are watching your YouTube videos, attending your shows, or buying your records. But it's so much more valuable to have a deep impact on a few than to have a superficial impact on millions. In fact, the greatest impact you have in this lifetime may be on the people you're with right now—your family, your friends, or your partner. Because it's not how broadly you're celebrated that truly matters. It's how deeply you're prepared to love those God gives you. Rest assured, you *are* deeply loved, indeed.

REFLECTION

The world runs on numbers, but God is in control of who you're able to reach. He is far more concerned that you make a valuable impact than a large one. Remember that Jesus only had twelve disciples in the beginning.

Lord, help me not to compare my achievements with other's and to be truly thankful for the people in my life I can impact. Help me to love and bless them deeply, so they can impact others. And above all, to you be the glory in all of this. In Jesus' name, amen.

Dream Big, Start Small

"Though your beginning was insignificant,
yet your end will increase greatly."

JOB 8:7 NASB

Nothing big starts big. Trees start as acorns. Elephants start as a handful of cells. Platinum-selling recording artists must learn their craft and do a bunch of shows before they reach the masses. Although artists like Foo Fighters now sell out stadiums they began in tiny clubs. The key to growing beyond a small beginning is treating that small opportunity like a big one.

Some of the keys to the biggest careers were hiding somewhere in a small crowd. The people who have invested in my music have appeared in the most humble and unexpected settings, standing in the wings on what might have otherwise been a very average night for me. Never be afraid or ashamed to picture an awesome future. But don't be ashamed to start small. Never be afraid to picture the most outlandishly positive outcome for your career, ministry, or family, but don't shy away from the smaller opportunities. There are no limits to what God can do through you if you're willing to dream big and start small.

REFLECTION

The most noble tree springs from the smallest seed. Do your best with every opportunity, and treat today's appointments like royal appointments, no matter how humble they may seem.

Lord, please help me to keep my wits about me and to treat every opportunity as though it's the opportunity of a lifetime. Thank you that you are with me and that with your help my dreams will flourish. In Jesus' name, amen.

Don't Look at the Clouds

Whoever watches the wind will not plant;
whoever looks at the clouds will not reap.

ECCLESIASTES 11:4

If you're waiting for the perfect conditions to begin living out your dreams, you could be waiting forever. As anyone who lives in the UK will know, we'd never plan an outdoor trip or festival if the weather dictated our plans. There is no "perfect time" to begin. If I had waited for the perfect time to release music or write a book, I'd never have done anything at all. I've never had the perfect financial situation, the ideal size of team, or even the perfect content.

Thank God that by his grace he is able to use our imperfect works to bless others. Thank goodness … because that's all we have. In fact, I've found that people connect more with my unpolished recordings than the best productions. Your imperfection has appeal, so don't let perfectionism prevent you creating. People will be blessed by your work in progress.

REFLECTION

Have you been waiting for the perfect moment to begin planting something new in your life? Be careful. Perfect weather will never come. Settle for what you have and get to work.

Lord, I thank you that you are able to work through even our imperfect efforts. Thank you that you can be present even in stormy weather and cause things to grow even throughout a terribly rainy season. Give me the strength and the courage to step out today and sow the seed you've blessed me with. In Jesus' name, amen.

Wait Actively

Wait for the LORD; be strong and take heart and wait for the LORD.
PSALM 27:14

The most amazing things happen while we wait. I used to rely on other people to organize my career for me. But now, while I engage the help of others, I *always* help myself in the meantime. Even when I have a great agent, manager, or publicist, I actively seek work and opportunities. I never wait for someone else to fix everything into place. Think of the helpers in your life as extra pairs of hands and never let yours become idle. It would be tragic to clock-watch your way through life, waiting for the phone to ring. I've trained myself to get on with something useful while I'm waiting for that elusive good news. Very often I become so busy actively waiting that I forget I'm even waiting for a call!

REFLECTION

Waiting can be frustrating, but remaining active is a great way to pass the time. Today why not find a way to occupy yourself during the waiting period? Perhaps you can offer help to someone else or volunteer somewhere. You might well find you're very blessed in doing so, and that new opportunities arise as a result.

Lord, there are many things I can't do right now. Please show me what I can do. Please help me to put my time, energy, and talents into something meaningful while I'm waiting for you to move in another area of my life. Lord, please give me patience and faith in the waiting. Amen.

You Are Qualified

Not that we are competent in ourselves to claim anything for ourselves, but our competence comes from God.

2 CORINTHIANS 3:5

People seem to best connect with my songs about personal struggle. Setting my tough experiences to music seems to be a strength I have. It occurred to me recently that this strength actually comes from weakness. The reason I'm able to articulate pain is because I've experienced it. The reason I can speak about healthy self-esteem and confidence is because I know what it's like not to have those things. It occurred to me that although I don't have many formal qualifications, I'm certainly qualified in the art of finding my true confidence.

One way to learn a whole lot about something is to go through it. The things in life we battle *can* become our areas of expertise. Our survival can teach others how to survive. This is a beautiful example of how God can use the bad things we've been through as blessings. It's a way that darkness can become light. If you suffered in any way and survived, congratulations. You are fully qualified to console and comfort others. What a gift.

REFLECTION

Take a moment to write down an experience that has caused you to grow—perhaps something that could help you help others.

Lord, thank you for the unique things I've been through. I thank you that you've uniquely qualified me to help others. Today I ask you for the wisdom to take what I've learned and give life to others through those valuable lessons. Teach me how to apply what you've shown and taught me so that through my pain others will be comforted. In Jesus' name, amen.

Faith Doesn't Use a Safety Net

God will make this happen, for he who calls you is faithful.

1 THESSALONIANS 5:24 NLT

I saw a lovely German proverb recently that said, "Begin to weave and God will give you the thread." Often we're waiting for some form of provision before we step out in faith. Often we want materials, resources, money, or time before we're willing to do what's been asked of us. But God requires our faith. When he calls us to step out of the boat, he doesn't hand us a safety net. We can waste a lot of time peering over the side looking for it, asking, *Will you really take care of me, Lord? Can I trust you? Perhaps I'll wait until I have something more secure in place…*

It's time to stop looking for the invisible. It's not until we step out in faith that the miracle happens. From planning weddings, to raising a family, to going out on missions, we first *commit*, and then he gives us what we need. Go ahead—step out and watch what happens! *Begin to weave.*

REFLECTION

Have you been waiting for God to provide before you begin something? Have you been looking for a green light or a safety net that will make a certain transition that bit easier? Take a moment today to pray about this. God might be waiting for you to step out of the boat before he comes up to meet you with his miraculous hand.

Lord, thank you for all of your provision. Help me to be both wise and full of faith. Guide my hand to do what you've asked of me and increase my faith to move forward when circumstances tell me I should stop. In Jesus' name, amen.

Focus on What You Bring

To them God has chosen to make known
among the Gentiles the glorious riches of this mystery,
which is Christ in you, the hope of glory.

COLOSSIANS 1:27

I've auditioned in lots of offices. At some time or other, you may be required to do something similar, and it can be the hardest kind of performance to deliver. You might be asked to speak in front of your peers, share a testimony, or give a presentation. If you're a little unnerved by that prospect, there is a simple transaction that can turn the whole ordeal on its head: *Make the decision not to focus on what the room has to offer you.* Don't think about the approval, the promotion, the deal, or the grade that might come as a result of your performance. Focus instead on what you're taking *into* that room: *You're an answer to prayer. You're a light in the darkness. You're blessed to be a blessing.*

Today, with the light running through your veins, you have the opportunity to be part of heaven's glorious invasion. As a child of the Most High, you are never a side thought and you are never incidental. You are "the hope of glory" (Colossians 1:27).

REFLECTION

Do you have something ahead that you're a little nervous about? Absorb this truth into your soul today: You're the hope of glory in that situation! God is sending you there.

Lord, thank you that you have placed your amazing hope in me. It's incredible that you have called and chosen me to shine your light. Help me to have confidence in this and to know it with all my heart. Fill my heart with your peace as I go into situations that could intimidate me. In Jesus' precious name. Amen.

You're Here for a Reason

"You did not choose me, but I chose you and appointed you so
that you might go and bear fruit—fruit that will last."

JOHN 15:16

My husband doesn't use many words, but they're usually perfect.
Whenever I feel out of my depth, he will say to me, "There's a
reason you're here." So simple, so truthful.

He says:

"There's a reason you've been given this job."

"There's a reason you're singing in this venue."

"There's a reason you're spending time with that person."

It always changes my perspective and my attitude. Look
around you. If you've prayed to be in the center of God's will,
there's a reason you are where you are.

REFLECTION

Today let's ask God to give us eyes to see the spiritual. If we can
begin to seek God's purpose for us in every circumstance, we will
become more and more attuned to the works he has planned for
us. Let's ask him to show us what our purpose is in this place and
in this season.

Lord, I thank you for bringing me into this situation. I trust that
you have a purpose for me here and for such a time as this. Give
me eyes to see what you would have me do here today. If there
is someone here I need to reach out to, please make that clear in
my heart. If that ever overwhelms me, help me to overcome my
fear and simply be the salt and light in this situation. In Jesus'
name, amen.

Rome Wasn't Built in a Day

"For the revelation awaits an appointed time; it speaks of the end and will not prove false. Though it linger, wait for it; it will certainly come and will not delay."

HABAKKUK 2:3

We are a generation that likes to move and achieve things quickly. Everything happens at the click of a button. We can have our purchases next day without even leaving the house. We have the power to create content that goes viral without a penny spent on marketing.

But some things cannot be rushed. You might be able to throw together a fast-food restaurant overnight, but there is no quick way to build a cathedral. Beautiful art cannot be rushed. Building a great relationship can't be rushed. A medical degree can't be rushed. Recovering from an illness can't be rushed. Growing a child in your womb can't be rushed. It's easy to become restless when our efforts don't produce fruit overnight. But for some things there really is no shortcut. Take heart. Building anything truly meaningful takes time.

REFLECTION

Write about something beautiful that took a long time to build. Every time you feel frustrated by how long your dreams are taking to come true, think of this amazing thing and take a deep breath.

God, thank you for the many beautiful things in my life that have taken time to grow. Help me to be patient through this next building phase in my life. I want what we build together to be strong and to last. Thank you that you are taking enough time to create something meaningful. In Jesus' name, amen.

Rethink the Way You Measure Success

Whoever loves money never has enough; whoever loves wealth is never satisfied with their income. This too is meaningless.

Ecclesiastes 5:10

Before you can achieve success, you first need to identify what success really is to you. Money—something that flows in and out of our lives—is transient in nature and certainly can't be taken with us beyond this life. So is having lots of money really a measure of success? Or will knowing that the world is a little better because you were here give you a greater sense of achievement?

God calls us to bear fruit—fruit that will last. In other words, he asks us to use our gifts and our lives to bring others to Christ and ultimately to heaven. On those days where your peers are getting promotions, better opportunities, and bigger paychecks, it's good to hold on to what you know is really a measure of success for *you*.

Reflection

The lie that you're unsuccessful because you're not rich and famous is a very broad reaching and damaging one. There is every chance that you've been living with this deception to some degree, even if it's only through the subtle language of social media likes and shares. Today, take a moment to intentionally shake off this lie before God so he can refocus you on what is truly important.

Lord, thank you that you have called us to bear fruit. Thank you that you've given us the tools to be satisfied and fulfilled with whatever we have materially. Help us always to focus on what success is in your eyes, Lord. In Jesus' name, amen.

Don't Compromise

"What good is it for someone to gain the whole world,
yet forfeit their soul?"

MARK 8:36

When we begin to operate in our gifting, all kinds of temptations come our way. We may be tempted to water down our message or our brand. We may be invited to work with or for people who don't share our core values. We may even be tempted to acquire materials or wealth by means that aren't legal or ethical. But wealth is worthless when we compromise our beliefs to acquire it.

In the beginning of my career as a Christian artist, I won a competition to sing at Glastonbury Festival. But when I went to rehearsals, I found that the band I'd be fronting had songs with drug-related themes. It was hard, but I turned down the opportunity. I really believe that God has opened extraordinary doors since then that wouldn't have opened had I compromised.

Keep your eyes open and always be prepared to walk away from something that conflicts with what you know is right. If you have to become someone else to reach your goals, your goals will evaporate and you'll lose sight of why you began.

REFLECTION

If you've resolved not to compromise on the path of your dreams, you can look forward to a career filled with blessing. Hard as it may be in the moment, set today's questionable opportunity aside in readiness for something better.

Lord, give me strength to make good choices. When opportunities arise that look good but may compromise my values, give me the courage and the faith to turn them down. Thank you that you only have something better in mind. In Jesus' name, amen.

Breakthroughs Are Small

Blessed is the one who perseveres under trial because, having stood the test, that person will receive the crown of life that the Lord has promised to those who love him.

JAMES 1:12

We have this vision of "breakthrough" that looks like the swinging of a hammer through glass. But honestly, it's more like crawling through thorny, tangled grass. Step by step, we claw our way toward the clearing. The breakthrough doesn't come by chance. It comes by moving tirelessly forward. Sometimes it helps to make a little list of these smaller breakthroughs so you can see just how far you've come. Whether it's a new responsibility you've been given, a good grade, a publication, or even just an encouraging message from someone you've blessed, keep them all and count them often.

REFLECTION

Today, encourage yourself by writing a little list of your recent achievements, however small. Remember to include the things you've overcome and survived. You're persevering, and you're standing the test.

Lord, thank you for giving me strength to persevere under trial. Although sometimes it feels as though I'm crawling along, I thank you for your promise that I'll receive the crown of life. In Jesus' name, amen.

Forget the Odds

Jesus looked at them and said, "With man this is impossible, but with God all things are possible."

MATTHEW 19:26

When I began my career, I had many conversations about my chances of success. Lots of people wanted to tell me the odds were stacked against me as a Christian in the UK music industry. But I knew God had given me something to share, and the odds were irrelevant.

I wonder how the odds stacked against David as he faced Goliath. I wonder what the odds were of Elizabeth conceiving John the Baptist when she was barren and in her later years. I wonder what the odds were of a man being born of the Holy Spirit, crucified for my sins, and raised from the dead.

If we were to act on the odds in life, we'd never do anything. The odds are against our health, our successes, our marriages, and certainly our dreams. But all that those variables decide is what our victories will look like! Every hero in history defied great odds to win. So today I choose not to let statistics limit my confidence. Instead, I will focus on the miracle that I even exist. We are chosen and called, and by the power of the Spirit we may achieve the impossible.

REFLECTION

Today, let's thank God that he is above the odds. He orders the universe, and he can turn it upside down at any moment.

Lord, thank you that for what you've intended in my life, the odds are irrelevant. Help me to be gracious when others cast doubt over my acts of faith and to remain focused on you. In Jesus' name, amen.

Love Is the Greatest Achievement

If I have the gift of prophecy and can fathom all mysteries and all knowledge, and if I have a faith that can move mountains, but do not have love, I am nothing.

1 Corinthians 13:2

It's easy to become focused on the things we're achieving. We get fixated on ministry milestones and promotion. We do this in part because we fall prey to the untruth that our works determine how valuable we are to God. But the real truth is that nothing we do matters a jot without love as the sole focus. I've made the mistake of thinking what I achieve is what gives me value.

I've measured my worth in CD sales, Facebook likes, and even the number of people I'm reaching with my ministry. But in truth, I've felt most fulfilled, most whole, and most beautiful when there were no music, lyrics, or mirrors involved. One trip with the leprosy mission reminded me that all it takes for life to be amazing is to *love someone who's desperate for love*. The incredible news is we can *all* do that. Whether we're rich or poor, young or old, strong or weak, sick or well, we can always have the greatest ministry there is—to *love one another*.

REFLECTION

Ask God to readjust your focus. If your've become preoccupied with doing and achieving rather than loving and believing, re-center around God's truth. God puts love above everything else. Seek the opportunity to love others today.

Lord, when it comes to my life and my dreams, help me to love above all else. Thank you that by loving others I can always be fruitful and enjoy a sense of purpose. In Jesus' name, amen.

All Our Heroes Experience Rejection

For the LORD will not reject his people;
he will never forsake his inheritance.

PSALM 94:14

In this life, you will experience discouragement and rejection. It's not a question of *if* but *when*. Don't worry, though. If you've been told you'll never make it, you're in good company. Just about all your heroes had to overcome rejection in order to impact the world. Steven Spielberg was rejected by the University of Southern California School of Cinematic Arts multiple times. Oprah Winfrey was fired from her first job for caring too much about the stories. Walt Disney was fired from his first job because he lacked imagination.

Maybe the world wasn't ready to recognize the gifts of these now-revered and even iconic people, but thank goodness they didn't give it up. If you have a dream or vision, don't wait for anyone else to validate you. There's a good chance you've been given a revelation that the world is yet to have. Work hard, be kind, and never give up.

REFLECTION

Rejection is not a signal to quit. It is often a sign that you're present in your purpose and taking healthy risks. Focus today on the truth that God will never reject you. Bask and soak in his amazing love and acceptance.

Lord, thank you for this journey that I'm on. I am so thankful that you have promised not to reject me. You loved me even before I loved you, and that is amazing. Help me to shoulder rejection with courage and assurance in you. In Jesus' name, amen.

Don't Dull Your Sparkle

He has made everything beautiful in its time. He has also set eternity in the human heart; yet no one can fathom what God has done from beginning to end.

ECCLESIASTES 3:11

Did you notice what all of the heroes from yesterday's reading have in common? *They were all rejected for very qualities that made them great.* When you fully commit to being who you are, you will stand out. Your unique DNA will be a challenge to some of the people who are around you because no one has quite forged the path that you were born to. A unique person voyaging through unchartered territory is a bit of a mystery. Not everyone wants to venture into the unknown with you, but don't let that put you off or tempt you to change course.

As a very wise and successful artist manager once said to me, "Being unique is not your best shot at success; it's your *only* shot at success." In an overcrowded and noisy world, your unique sparkle might be the only thing people will remember. The world may be hesitant to embrace it at first, but don't lose it! It's your sparkle.

REFLECTION

Take a moment to write down some of your unique qualities. Are you aloof? Mysterious? Thoughtful? Funny? Imaginative? Emotional? Do you love to wear a certain style or drink a certain tea? All of these things are interesting. Jot them down.

Lord, thank you that you made only one of me. I am as unique as a falling snowflake but infinitely more precious to you. Thank you that you designed me with this moment in mind. Let me never despise what you've so loved. In Jesus' name, amen.

Our Heroes Work Hard

Never be lazy, but work hard and serve the Lord
enthusiastically. Rejoice in our confident hope.
Be patient in trouble, and keep on praying.
ROMANS 12:11–12 NLT

Making an honest appraisal of your abilities can be discouraging.
In comparison to our heroes we often fall way short in the talent
department. But don't worry—very few great people were born
great. Ed Sheeran said in a recent TV interview that his early
recordings were "really bad" and that he wasn't born with natural
talent. My favorite photographer, Rosie Hardy, says she didn't
start out a great photographer and that she wasn't born knowing
how to take a good picture. Great work comes from hard work.
Of course, some people are endowed with what seems like
buckets of natural ability. But many of our biggest heroes put
their success down to passion, hard work, and availability over
all else. Be encouraged. You can take your gift a long way with
dedication and perseverance.

REFLECTION

Spend time on your passion today—a few minutes writing,
practicing, watching something on YouTube that might help you.
God may well have placed great ability in your DNA, but it's up
to you to work it. Write some notes.

Lord, thank you for the gifts you've placed in me. Thank you for
trusting me with them. Let me be a good steward of what you've
given me; help me to work it hard. Help me to become all that I
can be for you. In Jesus' name, amen.

God Knows Rejection

He was despised and rejected by mankind, a man of suffering, and familiar with pain. Like one from whom people hide their faces he was despised, and we held him in low esteem.

Isaiah 53:3

I once heard a preacher describe a traumatic teenage experience of being rejected by a pretty girl at a school dance. He had walked across the dance floor in front of all his friends, reached out a hand, and simply asked, "Would you dance with me?"

To his dismay, the object of his affections said, "No, thank you." Disappointed, hurt, and humiliated, he walked away vowing *never* to take such a risk again. Just when he was about to build a wall around his aching heart forever, he had this thought: life is a little like a dance, where every day God crosses the floor, reaches out his hand, and asks us to dance with him. No matter how many times we might say no, he will always cross that floor and ask again. Because to dance with him is life and he won't ever give up on us.

REFLECTION

By giving us the free will to choose him, God faces rejection all day, every day, and still he loves each one of us. He never gives up. In the same way, even after another rejection, we carry on. We keep crossing that dance floor and asking the world to dance.

Lord, I cannot even fathom the depths of your love for me. To think that you, the King of kings, would humble yourself to rejection, even death upon a cross, just blows my mind. Thank you for your humility and your enduring love. Please help me to become more like you—prepared to risk rejection for the love of others and of course for my love for you. In Jesus' name, amen.

Rejection Is Not a Measure of Your Worth

She is more precious than rubies;
nothing you desire can compare with her.
PROVERBS 3:15

Your heroes have all been rejected. Even the Master of the universe knows what rejection feels like. So clearly, rejection is no reflection of value. Whenever you begin to feel worthless, you have to remember that you are not what you do, nor are you what others think of you. You have gifts and you have a purpose, but you are always more than your achievements. You win and you lose, but you are not the measure of your battle outcomes. God doesn't hold a score card up to decide how loved you are. You are always his most precious treasure.

REFLECTION

Today, take a moment to lay aside everything you're doing to consider what you mean to God. He loves you because you're *his*, not because of what you can do. I find it helpful to remind myself that even if I never sing another note in my life, I am a beloved child of the Most High. That is what gives me my worth. The rest is simply part of my journey, my service to him, and my human experience.

Lord, I know that I am truly precious in your sight. I know that you loved me so much that you gave your only Son to have a relationship with me. Help me to hold up my head today, knowing just how adored and valued I am by you, my Father in heaven. In Jesus' name, amen.

Loving Those Haters, Part 1

"But I tell you, love your enemies and pray for those who persecute you, that you may be children of your Father in heaven."

MATTHEW 5:44–45

I first experienced online criticism after releasing my debut album, and it was very difficult for me. Going public with your labor of love is a scary process. My music is very personal to me and, as a newcomer, I took negative comments to heart. But after a few implosions over bad comments or reviews, I realized I had to toughen up if my kingdom dream was going to survive. Here are some lessons about criticism I've learned along the way. I've identified five main types of haters and five ways to deal with them.

Hater #1: The critic. This person may be making a valid assessment of your work, although it's not up their street, not their cup of tea, not their bowl of granola. Of course it stings when people don't enjoy what you create, but nonetheless you should take their comments as a compliment. Reviews, however negative, are a sign that you have joined the world of creators and your work is reaching a new audience. Honest review is a form of validation. It says you're contributing and therefore deserve to be critiqued like any other artist.

Response. Let it be. Everybody is entitled to an opinion. You may want to take some of their critique on board. For example, if they commented "cheap production," you may want to save enough money to raise your game next time. But if the production style was exactly your intention, then simply conclude that they didn't get where you were coming from and move on. Take comfort in knowing that while not everyone loves your stuff, some people will.

Hater #2: The troll. These people really have nothing against you; they just find cruelty entertaining. It's something they do for pleasure, and you're very likely to be one of many, many people they target.

Response. Ignore. You may as well imagine them wearing a Joker costume and rubbing their hands together. It's a hobby. Use whatever blocking methods you can and don't respond; *don't feed the trolls.*

REFLECTION

Do you have any haters in your life? How have you responded to them in the past? How do you want to respond to them in the future?

Father, I need your help. My heart is sensitive, and I can't help feeling hurt when people go out of their way to be cruel to me. Help me, God, to filter out all hatred. Help me to know when to respond and to always respond in love where a response is called for. In Jesus' name, amen.

Loving Those Haters, Part 2

"But to you who are listening I say: Love your enemies,
do good to those who hate you, bless those who curse you,
pray for those who mistreat you."

LUKE 6:27–28

Hater #3: The one with the grievance. This is someone who has an issue with your behavior, content, or character. This could also be someone with a personal grievance—someone who is threatened by you in your workplace or whose phone call you forgot to return. People may harshly challenge your views and choices. As a Christian artist I've had harsh criticism concerning song content and even wardrobe choices. It can be very hurtful, especially if you take care over these things.

Response. You may be able to redeem such a person's view of you, or you may not. You can apologize or even try to explain your choices. But if the person is unwilling to hear you, then it's important for you to know that you are not the problem. People with good motives will always offer advice rather than unkind words. If you're troubled by what they're accusing you of, take a moment to check your own heart and motives. Ask the opinion of those close to you, whom you trust. Ask God to deal with anything that you may have done mistakenly and move on.

Hater #4: The bully. It's one thing to find a horrible comment on your YouTube post. It's quite another to find that the same person has commented on every video or post you've ever made. This person is targeting you.

Response. You may also try sending the person a direct message to discuss what the problem is. I once did this. I sent an apology to the person, and it seemed to work. If that doesn't work, it's time to use the block function. All social media, email, and phones have block functions. You can usually notify the platform team itself and, if they agree that you are being targeted, they may suspend the perpetrator's account. If you feel you're in any danger, collect the correspondence and speak to the police.

REFLECTION

Cursing someone who has cursed you just puts their hate into your heart. Blessing those who've cursed you and praying for those who have mistreated you keeps your heart clean and open to the blessings God has for you.

Lord, today I'm lifting up my enemies to you in prayer. I don't understand why anyone would want to hurt me or mistreat me. But I do know that you can break through in their hearts. Lord, please speak to my enemies. Call their hearts to turn from hatred and toward you. If they have been hurt and have mistreated me out of brokenness, please bring them the healing they need. In Jesus' name, amen.

Loving Those Haters, Part 3

"No weapon that is fashioned against you shall succeed, and you shall refute every tongue that rises against you in judgment. This is the heritage of the servants of the LORD and their vindication from me, declares the LORD."

ISAIAH 54:17 ESV

Hater #5: The spiritual attacker. At nearly every important spiritual juncture in my life, I've had random hate mail from somewhere, from poisoned-pen letters threatening to curse me to strange email messages from distant acquaintances. I've learned to identify these spontaneous attacks as spiritual. There seems to be no basis for them, and there's an extra kick of venom that may be quite out of character, a deeper level of nastiness.

REFLECTION

It's important to see through these acts of hate for what they are—a good sign that God is doing something very positive in your life. Lift up the perpetrator in prayer and pray that no weapon forged against you (or them) will prosper.

Lord, when darkness comes against me, I'm very aware of the enemy. I feel that I'm under attack, and sometimes I even feel afraid. Today I hold to this great promise—that you won't allow anyone who comes against me to be successful in their attempts to destroy me. Thank you that you promise vindication protection and success for me. In Jesus' name, amen.

Our Heroes Receive Criticism

Do not be quickly provoked in your spirit, for anger resides in the lap of fools.

ECCLESIASTES 9:9

No matter what your age or status, you will encounter criticism. You will encounter criticism even when you're doing your best. Even when your heart is in the right place, someone will find a reason to berate or insult you, and it's unlikely that you will ever truly learn not to be affected by it. As the biggest celebrities have proven, being loved by millions doesn't make you immune. In fact, the more loved you are by strangers, the more likely you are to collect haters too. It's best to accept this an inevitable part of stepping out in faith. Don't allow it to make you aggressive. It's not worth the energy.

REFLECTION

Decide today: *I will not let the voices of my enemies dictate my confidence, rob me of my joy, or prevent me from blessing others. I will not become bitter, and I will not make their job easier by hating myself or hiding away.*

Lord, help me to keep control of my emotions. When it comes to being criticized, please help me to keep things in perspective and to have a gentle nature. In Jesus' name, amen.

Live to Bless, Not to Impress

But just as we have been approved by God
to be entrusted with the gospel, so we speak, not
as pleasing men, but God who examines our hearts.

1 Thessalonians 2:4 nasb

I'd been feeling sorry for myself, super discouraged by the industry reaction to the "Daffodil Song," a song I'd written about being yourself and enjoying life. I was even made fun of on national radio. But a few weeks later, four hundred children put me back in my place. After finding out they loved to use the song in their assembly time, I was invited to a local school to perform it live. I must admit I wasn't keen on the idea after my public humiliation, but agreed to go nonetheless. With their loud, proud, joyful voices, those children all but blew out my eardrums singing along! They knew every word, and a song I'd intended to encourage others with became an encouragement to me.

If you live your life to impress people, you'll always feel inadequate. If you live to bless people, your heart will always be full. You're making the world a more beautiful place.

REFLECTION

Who is being blessed by your life right now? Who *could* you bless with your life? Remind yourself of who you want to help in life; that way you can bring them to mind when discouragement comes.

Lord, thank you for the people in my life who are being blessed because I'm around. From family to friends and beyond I'm so grateful for the opportunity to be a positive influence in the lives of others. Lord, if I can be more of a blessing, please make me so. Please help me to be the best that I can be, for the good of others and for your glory. In Jesus' name, amen.

The Faith Workout

Consider it pure joy, my brothers, whenever you face trials of
many kinds, because you know that the testing of your faith
develops perseverance.

JAMES 1:2–3

Missionary and evangelist Heidi Baker was once asked, "Why
did you move to the poorest part of Africa to do ministry?" She
answered, "Because I wanted to see what only God can do."

As much as we don't enjoy them at the time, our seasons of
need are the ones that truly increase our faith, because we get
to see the miracle in motion. Seasons of plenty are good for the
soul and always a great reminder of God's incredible power to
provide. But it has been in those times where I've truly *needed*
God to move that I've seen his hand in things and felt my faith
grow exponentially.

Every trial is an opportunity for the Lord to increase and
inspire greater faith within us. As my lovely mother-in-law,
Yvonne, once told me, "You can't have the testimony without the
test!" So today, hard as it may be, let's bring our faith test to God
and thank him for what he is about to do.

REFLECTION
Bring to mind the things are testing your faith right now and
write them down in your journal. Lift them up in prayer today
and look forward to reflecting in future months how God has
worked in and through them.

Lord, thank you that the trials I'm facing give me a tremendous
opportunity to see you at work. Although it isn't easy right now,
I'm excited to see what you're capable of. I really want to see
what you will do! Amen.

Rejection Is Better than Regret

"Be strong and courageous, and do the work. Do not be afraid or
discouraged, for the Lord God, my God, is with you."

1 Chronicles 28:20

Fear of rejection can cause you to stand on the sidelines,
watching. It can cause you not to give your all. It can cause you
to stay silent when you know you should ask for an opportunity.
Rejection never feels good, but it's far better than missing out on
something great because you didn't step out. When it comes to
pursuing purpose, there are many anxieties we face. It's easy to
become anxious about failure or what people might think of us.
But some of the worst anxiety comes from the feeling that you're
holding *yourself* back. I've come to the realization that I would
rather hear the word *no* a hundred times than the sound of my
own conscience asking, *Why didn't you just ask?* So ask. Ask again
and ask some more.

REFLECTION

Have you been waiting for an opportunity to come to you? Are
you hoping that someone will invite you to be involved at their
event? Or have you been hoping someone will ask you to join
a team? Today I'm challenging you to put yourself forward. It
isn't arrogant to make yourself available. A simple "If you need
an extra pair of hands …" or "I'd love to be involved; how can I
help?" could be the start of something really important.

Lord, give me the courage to step out in faith for you, even if it
means I risk rejection. Help me to overcome the pride and fear
that can so often stand in the way of progress in life. In Jesus'
name, amen.

It's Not Over

"I will refresh the weary and satisfy the faint."
JEREMIAH 31:25

It's still early in this year, but you may be feeling a little tired already. When we add the pursuit of a new dream to the existing busyness of our lives, things can get a bit hectic. If the initial sheen of this adventure has begun to dim, don't worry—God has you. The weight of the dream might be starting to feel heavy on your shoulders, but you're not carrying it alone. You may even have been wondering if you're doing the right thing by seeking out God's call on your life. But don't worry—God's call is God's concern as much as it is yours.

When we partner with God in his purposes, he promises to refresh us. He gives us his word that he will hold us up when we feel faint and renew our strength. Renewed strength is not just topped-up strength—it's *brand-new* strength! Don't despair. You're about to get your second wind.

REFLECTION

If you're already feeling weary trying to identify and pursue your purpose, take a moment today to refuel yourself in God. Just kick back and spend a few hours in his presence. You need strength for this journey, so don't forget to plug back into the source.

Lord, I come to you today to find my rest. I trust that you will renew me! Thank you that you will give me a brand-new surge of energy for the things I love and the adventure you're taking me on. In Jesus' name, amen.

Being Proactive

"For truly I say to you, if you have faith the size of a mustard
seed, you will say to this mountain, 'Move from here to there,'
and it will move; and nothing will be impossible to you."

MATTHEW 17:20 NASB

Once I asked God to do something. And he didn't do it. So I did
it myself. And you know what? I think that was God's plan all
along. You might be waiting for an answer to prayer right now.
You might be hoping for a break or opportunity that just doesn't
seem to be coming. You might be waiting for a reason to travel
or for someone to put your painting in an art gallery. Maybe it's
time to take things into your own hands.

Sometimes God moves the mountains, parts the oceans, and
heals the wounds in our lives. Other times he does something
miraculous in us that causes us to rise up and scale that
mountain, swim the ocean, or step into wholeness ourselves.
By his grace we don't need to be perfect to begin making that
journey, and we can triumph even while we're still hurting.

REFLECTION

Have you been praying for God to do something and yet not
seen any movement? It might be time to begin moving yourself.
Today, pray. Ask God if it's time for you to take things into your
own hands.

Lord, today I pray you would give me the wisdom to know when
it's my time to act. I thank you that you've given me the tools
and the authority to speak to the mountains in my life! Let me
not fall into the habit of simply waiting for you to fix everything. In Jesus' name, amen.

Flipping Criticism

When they hurled their insults at him, he did not retaliate; when he suffered, he made no threats. Instead, he entrusted himself to him who judges justly.

1 PETER 2:23

You absolutely will not please all of the people all of the time. If you're doing your best to be a positive and loving voice in the darkness, then hold your head high! Don't use up your energy responding to negative comments. Keep yourself busy doing good. The last thing you should do is allow negativity to distract you from your positivity. That's exactly what the darkness would want. I used to spend hours constructing responses on social media to defend myself against criticism. Then one day I realized that I could have spent that time writing something like this, something to help others.

These days I like to keep myself too busy to respond to critics. While others are wasting their time trying to drag you down, spend yours building people up. As Jesus did, you can trust the Father to deal with people who mistreat you.

REFLECTION

If you've been criticized today, flip it around and find someone to encourage. Take that emotion and turn it into something positive for someone else to draw from.

Lord, help me to wear the blinders of faith, which block out the negativity around me and enable me to fix my gaze on you. Thank you that you can use me as a light. Help me to entrust dealing with my abusers to you. You are a righteous and just God, and you have this under control. In Jesus' name, amen.

Rocky Start

"For I know the plans I have for you," declares the LORD, "plans to prosper you and not to harm you, plans to give you hope and a future."
JEREMIAH 29:11

One of my most memorable stage disasters was at the iconic O2 Arena in London. My job was to open up for the headline band. You can imagine my horror when I walked out in front of thousands of excited music fans, attempted to plug in my guitar, and the sound of broken cable filled the room. It was a hideous, deafening sound followed by complete silence. The room fell still and my guitar wouldn't work. An engineer came to my rescue and we were back on within a few moments. But those moments seemed like decades.

My first words were, "You know that nightmare you have where you turn up at work and realize you forgot your trousers? That's what this just felt like." Thousands of people laughed and clapped in support, and I went on to have one of the best shows of my life. Some of the best times of my life—best days, best shows, even best friendships— have had a rocky-as-anything start. Here's praying that the tough times you're in are the beginning of something so great it blows your mind.

REFLECTION

Take a moment to release all anxiety about something that has started badly. Let it go and recognize that this could be the beginning of something truly wonderful.

Lord, thank you for your amazing plan. Today, I'm choosing to take these early-days setbacks and view them as a huge encouragement. I know that you will see this through and bring it into a positive outcome In Jesus' name, amen.

It's Not about How Perfect Your Song Is

"For the eyes of the LORD range throughout the earth to strengthen those whose hearts are fully committed to him."

2 CHRONICLES 16:9

We were in Norway on what had already been a difficult tour, and the week was topped off with the worst transport meltdown we've ever seen. After a frozen fog cloud grounded all flights, we did a three-hour drive to another airport, an hour-long trip on an express train, and finally another car ride. Eventually we ran through the venue doors and directly onstage, out of breath and exhausted. Then we did as we always do—we played our songs. In hindsight I don't know how we managed to continue. With lost luggage and broken instruments, the whole Norway tour had a theme for me: *Will I keep going when I'm out of my comfort zone, without the things that make me feel secure, when it's not the way I want it to look?*

The answer? Yes, I will. Because in the end our lives won't be measured by how perfect our song was, but by the moments where we felt like giving up, yet somehow kept singing.

REFLECTION

No matter how hard we try, things will go wrong in our work. The question is, What will be our attitude when things aren't as we'd hoped? Our challenge will be to remain fully committed to *God* and not merely the quality of what we produce.

Lord, I always want to do a great job. But help me never to forget that you come first. Help me to be committed to serving you even if what I share with the world isn't as perfect as I'd like it to be. I want my heart to be one of the hearts you see turned fully toward you. In Jesus' name, amen.

Bring Your Best

When the disciples saw this, they were indignant. "Why this waste?" they asked. "This perfume could have been sold at a high price and the money given to the poor." Aware of this, Jesus said to them, "Why are you bothering this woman? She has done a beautiful thing to me."

MATTHEW 26:8–10

When you love what you do and want to honor God, you endeavor to give your best work at all times. You might feel a little down if it's not seen or appreciated by many people. This could cause you to feel you wasted your time. But here's the thing— keep bringing your best. Bring the most beautiful, precious thing you have to God. The best you can do, the most you can offer even when others don't see or celebrate you. Spend hours on it. Spend a lifetime. Spend yourself. Don't concern yourself with the praises of others … or the criticism. Pour out your best perfume for Jesus, because this is true worship.

REFLECTION

No amount of effort, no amount of honor, is ever too much for the King of kings. We should always bring the very best of what we have. Take a healthy pride in pouring out your best for him, even it appears decadent to others. Jesus sees the degree of your sacrifice. He sees when he's first in your heart.

Lord, let my lifestyle be this kind of offering to you. Let it be fragrant and extravagant. Let people look on in puzzlement at the sheer level of sacrifice, because you are more than worth the very best I have to offer. My work, my relationships, my art, my song—let me bring them all to you. In Jesus' name, amen.

Be Your Own Biggest Fan

Therefore, my dear brothers and sisters, stand firm. Let nothing
move you. Always give yourself fully to the work of the Lord,
because you know that your labor in the Lord is not in vain.

1 CORINTHIANS 15:58

"Glory supporters" only cheer for their team when their team
is winning. Fickle people jump on board with something when
it's working and skulk off without paying the bill when it's not.
The same can happen with friendships. Many will flock when life
is rosy, but few will stick around when things turn sour. Don't
be surprised or discouraged by this. Not everyone is fickle. True
fans cheer you on during good and bad seasons. And whatever
happens, make sure that *you* remain a true fan of you. Remain
devoted to your progress. Agree with yourself today that you're a
diehard mega fan of what you do. You will wear your team colors
wherever they sit on the leaderboard because that is what a true
fan does.

REFLECTION

I believe that something divine happens when you say the words
"I'm not giving up." So say it. Say it again and again. Folks may
have given up on you or your dream, doctors may have given up
on your health, but guess what? You don't have that luxury. So
say it with me now: "I'm not giving up."

Lord, help me to hold form to my purpose when others give
up on me. You promise me that my efforts for you are never in
vain. So help me remain steadfast when others lose faith in the
mission. In Jesus' name, amen.

Declare Your Worth

No, in all these things we are more than conquerors through him who loved us. For I am convinced that neither death nor life, neither angels nor demons, neither the present nor the future, nor any powers, neither height nor depth, nor anything else in all creation, will be able to separate us from the love of God that is in Christ Jesus our Lord.

ROMANS 8:37–39

If you feel like a loser, it's time for a pep talk. You may be feeling wounded or defeated right now. The words of the enemy may be ringing in your ears. You open your mouth to speak, and before the words come out, you've already decided your words are worthless. You pick up your pen to write, and before the ink hits the page, you've already decided it's nonsense. It's time to stage your own intervention. Your enemies are working hard to destroy you. Don't help them. You have already decided to be your own biggest fan, so don't be distracted by the negative chants of the opposing team.

People may have put you down, written you off, and shattered your confidence. Maybe they've even cast doubt over your authenticity as a Christian or caused you to question God's love for you. But are you going to let them dictate your future, steal your joy, and keep you paralyzed? Get up! Take back your destiny! You have a right to be yourself, to be happy, and to fulfill your purpose.

REFLECTION

Take a moment today to make some strong declarative statements about your worth and victory in God. You could write them down, or even dare to go somewhere private and say them aloud as a prayer. Sometimes we have to get a little scrappy in order to deal with being trampled, both by other people and by unseen spiritual forces. Above all, know today that you are more than a conqueror through Jesus (Romans 8:37).

Lord, thank you that nothing can ever separate me from you, King of the world! Thank you that in you I am a victor, a winner surrounded by an army of angels and filled with a Spirit of power. You have forever given me a place on the winning team and no amount of mockery or self-doubt can change that. Help me to be strong in this truth and to stand confidently in the presence of my enemies, always knowing that darkness is forever defeated. In Jesus' name, amen.

Take a Bird's-Eye View of Your Life

When I look at your heavens, the work of your fingers, the moon and the stars, which you have set in place, what is man that you are mindful of him, and the son of man that you care for him?

PSALM 8:3–4 ESV

I love to fly, because for just a moment everything down on the earth has some perspective. We live linear lives. We move from past to future, yesterday to today. We can only see what is immediately around us and what the moment and immediate future hold. This limited perspective brings rejection, discouragement, and criticism, which can be overwhelming. In these times, it's helpful to try to take a bird's-eye view of our lives. We can't always hop on a plane to see how small everything is. But we can take a moment to rise above our setbacks, look at the big picture, and remember how big God is. If he can put together the whole world, he can surely hold your world together too. He is good and faithful. He hasn't forgotten you.

REFLECTION

Take some time out today and consider the big picture of your life. Try to think outside of your current location, passions, friendships, and places of work, because your story is so much bigger than those things. What do you think God sees when he looks across the full story of your life?

God, you are so big, so powerful, and so very good. You see and care for every aspect of my life. You even know the number of hairs on my head. How amazing you are! Help me to rest today in the knowledge that there is nothing too big for you to deal with and nothing too small for me to bring to you. In Jesus' name, amen.

All Things Are Possible

Jesus looked at them and said, "With man this is impossible, but with God all things are possible."

MATTHEW 19:26

It's amazing how many times you'll hear the word *impossible*. People love to remind you of your cultural and physical limitations. Even people of faith make the mistake of speaking doubt into your faith. But the truth is, nothing is impossible with God. When deep down you know that something will work, don't let anyone discourage you. Hold onto God's promise and keep moving.

REFLECTION

Don't worry about being strong or capable enough to achieve the impossible, because you can't achieve the impossible in your own strength. Rather, God achieves these things through us.

Lord, help me to ignore the word impossible. I know that however unlikely they may be, with you all things are possible. Today I am resting in this truth. In Jesus' name, amen.

Ignore the Barking Dogs

"If any household or town refuses to welcome you or listen to your message, shake its dust from your feet as you leave."
MATTHEW 10:14 NLT

One of my greatest mentors is a former youth leader named Andy Rushworth. He gave me a heart to reach people from every walk of life with the living hope of Jesus. From early on I felt called to leave the church walls and go to where those people could be found. Sadly, and much to my surprise, I faced scrutiny from other Christians. They questioned my motives and expressed concern for my spiritual safety. But Andy Rushworth encouraged me greatly when he told me, "If a postman stopped at every barking dog, he'd never deliver the news."

Many may try to dissuade you from stepping beyond the church walls. But we have a message to deliver. There will always be naysayers who criticize our methods and question our motives. Quite honestly, we don't have to time to stop and calm everyone down. Keep moving and keep delivering, come what may.

REFLECTION
The battle against our own doubts in life is hard enough. We don't have time for anyone else's unbelief! So today, make the decision not to give precious airtime in your thoughts to the voice of discouragement.

Lord, thank you that you've given me a job to do. You know that it isn't easy, but my desire is to do what you've called me to. I want to reach the lost and do the uncomfortable things that make all the difference. Please help me to walk past those barking dogs and simply get on with delivering the news! In Jesus' name, amen.

Steps Make Strides

"Arise, walk about the land through its length and breadth;
for I will give it to you."
GENESIS 13:17 NASB

We can pray for God to open doors of favor that accelerate our success, and sometimes he does! But sometimes there is simply no shortcut up the mountain. At that point, you have a choice. You can stand around waiting for God to send you a taxi, or you can put one foot in front of the other and begin walking. Doing things the slow way might seem like the tough and uninspiring option. But start walking today, and you'll be amazed how far you can go.

REFLECTION

Begin now. If you've always dreamed of learning a language, look into it today. If you need new materials for your art project, start saving today. If you want to find yourself in a new destination in life, begin walking in faith today. It might take a little longer than you'd hoped, but by the end of this year, you'll be amazed at what you can achieve.

Lord, thank you that as I begin walking today, you are helping me to claim the land beneath my feet. You're helping me to move forward one step at a time all the while bestowing your favor on my path. When the road gets long, help me simply to keep putting one foot in front of the other. In Jesus' name, amen.

Save Your Breath

For it is God's will that by doing good you should silence the
ignorant talk of foolish people.

1 Peter 2:15

There are times in our lives where it's right to speak up in defense
of others or ourselves. But if we spend our lives arguing with
those who come against our efforts, we're often wasting breath
that could be used to speak life and light into lives. When those
unhelpful voices come in force, it's important to take a quiet
moment to discern, *Is this argument constructive? Could I be using
my words better elsewhere?*

When a person's motive is to abuse or discredit us, our
attempts to reason with them are often wasted. We risk becoming
so wrapped up defending ourselves we become totally distracted
from our calling. Continue to be obedient to what God has asked
of you, and the good fruit you bear will speak up loud and clear.

REFLECTION

Today, take a moment to pray about whether your efforts to
defend yourself or reason with someone are being wasted. Would
your words better spent elsewhere?

Lord, I need your perfect wisdom in this area of my life. I want
my words to be useful and I want to display both strength and
confidence. Please help me to discern when response is called for
and when silence would speak louder. In Jesus' precious name.
Amen.

Sticks and Stones

"As for you, you meant evil against me,
but God meant it for good."

GENESIS 50:20 NASB

There's a great scene in the first *Hunger Games* movie. Lead character Katniss Everdeen has arrived on the battlefield with no weapons and no armor. The enemy is in hot pursuit, and as she runs for her life, she feels the impact of a knife. Thankfully she is shielded by her backpack, and as she pulls out the blade, she shouts behind her, "Thanks for the knife!" Her attacker had armed her for the fight that was to come.

This spoke to me profoundly about how God can use our trials for our good. Whatever ammunition the enemy throws at us, temptations, disaster, sickness, and betrayal, God can give us the strength to reach for that knife, pull it out, and use it as a weapon against the enemy's schemes. God can take the rocks thrown at you and use them as building blocks for your future and for his kingdom.

REFLECTION

If life has thrown something tough at you recently, take a moment to thank God for this potential building block. Ask him to take whatever has been used against you and use for good.

Lord, thank you that what the enemy intends for my destruction you can use for construction. You can take everything that was intended to destroy me and build beautiful things. Thank you that every day you are using the fiery arrows of the enemy to sharpen and strengthen me and that your kingdom can grow as a result. In Jesus' name, amen.

The Power of Persistence

"Will not God bring about justice for his chosen ones, who cry out to him day and night? Will he keep putting them off? I tell you, he will see that they get justice, and quickly."

LUKE 18:7–8

At the beginning of 2018, I decided to upload an inspiring video to YouTube every day. But the daily schedule of uploads was grueling and on the rough days barely seemed worth it.

Then one day, a video I'd made of a pop song given a gospel lyric makeover went viral across the globe. My mind was blown! At that point I'd made over a hundred videos since the start of the project. Aside from those, I'd made a dozen music videos through my career that had taken time, a team, and lots of artistic energy. Then, this one video caught the wind and flew. Was it better than the rest? I don't know. But all I know is that showing up day after day, trying everything, had somehow paid off.

It got me thinking about the persistent widow. The Bible says that eventually she got what she was asking for because she simply would not give up. Did she get better at asking? Did she become more convincing? Was the persistence simply enough to demonstrate that her heart was truly fixed on her goal? I wasn't there so I don't know. But this I do know: it pays to persist.

REFLECTION

What prayer do you constantly pray? Well, pray again right now.

Lord, I bring my request to you once again today. You can do it! Although I'm tested as I wait to see breakthrough in this area, I haven't lost faith. Please come through. You are good and you know my heart. Please bring about this miracle so I can testify once again of your faithfulness. I believe. In Jesus' name, amen.

Let Those Tears Fall

A time to weep and a time to laugh;
a time to mourn and a time to dance.

ECCLESIASTES 3:4 NASB

When I was a small child, we went out to a restaurant as a family. As the waitress set down hot serving platters, she warned me not to touch. But as children do, I completely forgot and moments later reached out and touched the scorching plate. The blister on my finger appeared immediately, but I was too embarrassed to say anything. At some point my parents noticed the glum look on my face and asked what was wrong. I knew if I said anything, I would burst into tears. In my efforts to hide my feelings, I had become completely motionless. Eventually I could hold it back no longer and the tears came flooding. As soon as my parents saw the blister, they ran me to the restroom and held my hand beneath the cold water. Finally knowing what had happened, they were able to help me.

REFLECTION

When you're hurt, trying to swallow that lump in your throat can render you motionless. It's okay to cry. It's okay to grieve when you lose something. It's okay to be disappointed when things don't turn out the way you had hoped. It's okay to admit you made a mistake and got burned. When you cry, the healing process can begin. So go on, let it out.

Today, I have very little to say, Lord. And that's okay. If I need to cry I will cry, for you have created a time for everything. Thank you for comforting me in my tears. In Jesus' name, amen.

Hold Out for Something Better

I consider that our present sufferings are not worth comparing
with the glory that will be revealed in us.

ROMANS 8:18

Things don't always work out as we would hope. There's every
chance you've been working on something for a long time that
didn't come together as you planned. I know the heartache of
putting my all into something that didn't seem to work. That
heartache can linger long after we think we've gotten over it too.
Despite all our good intentions, we can harbor hidden feelings of
resentment toward others and even toward God.

But God sincerely promises us that he is working in and
through all things for our good. He is not cruel. He has a
wonderful redemptive strategy for all our circumstances, and if
we allow him to work in us, we become better too. You may be in
a waiting phase right now, but today just quiet yourself in trust.
There will be a day when the mist will clear and you have your
"something better" moment.

REFLECTION

If you've had a setback that perhaps you're not "over" yet, take a
moment today to write and pray about it. Someday you will look
back and see that there was something better waiting for you.

Lord, it hurts when things don't work out. But I know that
you're still at work. I know that you have a beautiful outcome
planned for this situation so please, give me your grace and
patience while I wait. You are still good and I still love you. In
Jesus' name, amen.

Count Your Blessings

Bless the LORD, O my soul, and forget none of His benefits.
PSALM 103:2 NASB

It's so easy to become blind to the beauty in our lives. When my husband and I bought our first home, I was in love with it. I cherished every room. I was so grateful for the breakthrough of securing a mortgage, that to me our humble abode was practically a palace. But as I became used to my surroundings, I started to see only the imperfections and the jobs that needed doing. I became quite blind to the blessing of our home and instead became critical of it and dissatisfied.

We have to be careful not to fall into an "upgrade mentality." In our quest to constantly better our own lives, we can become oblivious to the blessings we have. We even become quite complacent and careless about them. Think long and hard before you give up on a good thing. When it's there every day, it's easy to take it for granted. Chances are if we could really see the blessings in our lives as if for the first time, we wouldn't want to let them go.

REFLECTION

Today, why not ask God to show you your blessings as if for the first time. Ask to see a sunset as though you've never seen those colors before. Ask to look at the ones you love and see them for the blessings they truly are.

Lord, you have blessed me greatly. If I can sit here and hold this book, then you have already given me countless good things in my life. Today, I pray you will truly open the eyes of my heart to see everything afresh. Let me be fully aware of the beauty in my world. Let me appreciate every wonderful gift because they all come from you. In Jesus' name, amen.

Climb for the View

On this mountain the LORD All-Powerful
will prepare for all nations a feast the finest foods.
Choice wines and the best meats will be served.

ISAIAH 25:6 CEV

My friend Rosie Hardy is a wonderful photographer. She does stunning conceptual work and finds the most incredible natural locations to shoot. I often look at her work and simply long to create something just as beautiful. But it's not as easy as it looks.

One day Joel and I took our own camera and hopped in the car to go location spotting. We found a perfect spot, the jagged crest of a hill that overlooked the stunning Peak District. We got out of the car, camera and hairspray in hand, and started for the hill. The winds were high and cold, and we battled every step of the way. By the time we got to the top, we were freezing, exhausted, and ready to give up on shooting. But the view was stunning.

It's easy to look at other people's pictures and feel location envy. But for every step toward the top there is a price to pay and a battle to fight. If you *really* want the beautiful view, you can have it. But you'll have to climb.

REFLECTION

What are you prepared to climb for? Have you taken time to consider the effort that your dream will take? Or are you just enjoying someone else's pictures? Remember the view will be every bit worth the climb.

Lord, what wonders await at the top of a mountain! Create in me a willingness to work and make sacrifices for the life I crave. Help me be ready to make whatever climb I must in order to arrive at that beautiful summit. In Jesus' name, amen.

Your Efforts Aren't a Waste

Let us not become weary in doing good, for at the proper time
we will reap a harvest if we do not give up.

GALATIANS 6:9

Sometimes we get tired of serving. We get tired of creating
things that people don't get chance to see. We become fatigued
by pouring out everything we have and not hearing the words
"thank you." We invest time into people who don't seem to
appreciate it or even remember our input. We invest money into
projects that struggle to get off the ground. But we must continue
to spend ourselves in good deeds. Because God promises us that
we'll eventually see a harvest.

REFLECTION

When your kind words seem to fall on deaf ears, keep speaking
them. If you're persecuted, ridiculed, or ignored for your
kindness, keep loving people. If all your efforts to do good feel
like climbing the sheerest cliff face, keep climbing. Everything
good you do, do as though you're serving God, and those efforts
don't go unnoticed.

God, I thank you right now, ahead of time, for the harvest that is
coming. Although I get tired sometimes, let me not lose heart in
doing good things. I so want to see that wonderful day when my
efforts are fruitful and people are won for you! Until then I trust
in you to keep renewing my strength. In Jesus' name, amen.

Recommit Your Plans to God

Let the favor of the Lord our God be upon us, and establish the work of our hands upon us; yes, establish the work of our hands!

PSALM 90:17 ESV

It's been a couple of months since we made our New Year's resolutions, so it's not a bad idea to take stock at this point. How have things progressed since January 1? Are you beginning to get momentum? If so it might be worth checking that God is still in the driver's seat with your plans. As you become more productive and creative, the people around you become more vocal with their ideas. People have all sorts of plans for your life! Leaders, family, and friends may have strong opinions about how you should be spending your time. But it's important to make sure God himself is still steering the ship of your purpose.

REFLECTION

Take a moment today to recommit your plans to God. Ask him to close doors that are wrong for you, and to give you discernment about which plans and suggestions to pursue.

Lord, thank you that there are people who want to speak into my life. But it's so important that you stay in the driver's seat of my dreams. Today, help me to recommit and refocus my heart and my intentions on your purposes. In Jesus' name, amen.

Mining for Gems

Whatever your hand finds to do, do it with all your might.
ECCLESIASTES 9:10 NASB

When I was nine years old, I made a trip to Australia with my parents. I'll never forget the time we met a gem miner in the sleepy opal-mining town of Coober Pedy. His name was Nicolas, and every day he awoke at dawn to mine the opal fields. He and his assistant would use dangerous heavy equipment to bore deep holes into the earth, working all the way through daylight hours in the blistering heat. Bucket after bucket of worthless shale would come up from the deep shafts. He'd sift through the dusty spoils, spraying water here and there to try to catch a seam of glittering opal. Roughly once a year he'd see that sparkle.

It took months of fruitless work to find that seam and have a payday. When those paydays finally came, it would always be a huge blessing. But he could never predict when they would come.

REFLECTION

It's very much the same with all our creative pursuits. You could write a hundred songs and not get a hit. But if you keep writing, eventually something will connect. You could share your testimony a hundred times without seeing a response. But the hundred-first time could be the one that sees a life changed. We must keep on planting if we're ever to reach a harvest.

Lord, today I'm simply praying for the strength to keep on grabbing my tools and heading out to the field. You have taught me that consistency is key when it comes to sowing, but that I will reap what I sow in due course. Thank you so much for your faithfulness, Lord. In Jesus' name, amen.

Thank God for Closed Doors

And we know that in all things God works for the good of those
who love him, who have been called according to his purpose.

ROMANS 8:28

Joel and I went out for dinner with some friends one evening.
After dinner we were looking for a coffee shop to continue
the fun, but everywhere was closed. The only place open was
McDonald's, so we went in. I took a copy of my latest record
inside to give to our friends.

The smiley kid behind the counter noticed the CD in my
hand. "What album is that?" he asked. "Er, it's mine," I said
awkwardly, turning pink. (I don't always walk around with my
CD in hand.) He flipped it over. "No way! You're Philippa Hanna!
I love that song, 'Arrow'!" He began singing my song to me!

After our coffee I felt God nudge me to sign and give the CD
to this chirpy server. He'd given up on a music dream because he
was rejected at a talent show audition. I told him to keep singing,
and we chatted about his other dreams. He was overwhelmed by
the gift. I was overwhelmed that "Arrow" had reached this boy I'd
never met. So glad the coffee shop was closed.

REFLECTION

What doors do you feel God has closed in your life recently?
Write them down for a future time of reflection. You may find
that you can finally see what God had in mind.

Lord, today I'm thanking you for every closed door I have faced
and will face going forward. You always have my best interests at
heart, and although it sometimes hurts at the time, I'm choosing
to celebrate the things that don't work out. Everything shows
your incredible favor. In Jesus' name, amen.

Be Careful What You Call a Bad Day

Therefore we do not lose heart. Though outwardly we are wasting away, yet inwardly we are being renewed day by day.

2 Corinthians 4:16

I recently caught myself saying, "I'm having a bad day," and felt a sharp conviction to take the words back immediately. I'd had a few minor setbacks, that was all. My house was still standing and my heart was still beating. Just hours earlier I'd been watching news footage of devastating forest fires in California. I realized just how many of those Californians might trade my day's setbacks for theirs.

At any given time, there are countless people who would gladly trade their day for yours. They'd trade their life-limiting illness for the cold that cancelled your lunch date. They'd gladly take your leaky roof over losing everything in a forest fire. They'd take the worst blind date over sweeping up the pieces of a broken marriage. And they'd possibly take any of the above over the grief of losing a loved one.

Perspective is healthy. It can help us to realize that our bad day is possibly not that bad at all.

Reflection

Is something bothering you today? Do you feel you're not having the best day or week? Consider who out there might be super grateful to trade places with you.

Lord, help me to be more patient in suffering. Life can be painful sometimes. But I know that at any given time, there will be many who would be grateful for the many blessings I have in my life. Help me to have a healthy perspective when it comes to my struggles. In Jesus' name, amen.

All That Glitters Ain't Gold

A heart at peace gives life to the body, but envy rots the bones.
PROVERBS 14:30

When I first started taking label meetings in Nashville, I was dazzled by the bright lights. It was so exciting to imagine having a big team and lots of money going into my career. I loved the idea of having radio ads to promote my music and shiny merchandise to sell online. It looked like a massive career upgrade.

But after learning a little more about the industry, I found out that the grass is not always greener. Speaking to a signed artist in a dressing room last year, I was surprised to hear her say, "I envy your situation. You have so much more control over what you do." I began to realize that what looks like a promotion can mean trading one set of issues for another.

The same goes for most things in life. We often presume that others have it easier or better than we do. But we're only seeing the shop window of their lives. Their stockroom is probably no tidier than yours.

REFLECTION

God advises not to look at someone else's blessings and feel envy. In fact, God's instruction to not covet our neighbor's things is so important that he even put it in the Ten Commandments. He takes covetousness seriously because it is deceptive, divisive, and destructive. It can eat us up from the inside out.

Lord, help me to keep my eyes on you and remain thankful for all the good things you give. Help me not to be deceived by the perfect shop-window appearance of other people's lives. Lord, today I pray you will simply fill my heart with peace so my body and soul may have the life you promise. In Jesus' name, amen.

The Darkest Hour Is before the Dawn

Weeping may stay for the night, but rejoicing comes in the morning.
PSALM 30:5

If I look back on my life since finding faith, there's a definite pattern—a cascade of problems right before a significant breakthrough. I'll receive a discouraging email the morning of an important engagement or find that finances are extra stretched before an increase comes. I've learned to remember that things tend to get a little worse right before they turn a corner.

As we approach a new season or chapter in our lives, it's common for darkness to close in. If you find yourself putting out more fires than usual, faced with all manner of spiritual distractions, there is every chance that God is about to do something significant in and through your life. The important thing is to remain focused on him during that dark hour that precedes sunrise.

REFLECTION

If things are feeling dark right now, it's more important than ever to cling to Jesus, who is the Light of the World. We have to hold fast to his promises that light our pathway even through seasons of night. Reading God's Word is harder than ever during hours of darkness. But we must cling to his promise that dawn is fast approaching and with it much rejoicing.

Lord, things may seem dark right now. But I choose to trust that you will come through, knowing you will never leave my side. The sun will rise, and I will feel the light upon my face once more. Give me strength to endure these hours of darkness. In Jesus' name, amen.

Do Less, Be More

"Martha, Martha," the Lord answered,
"you are worried and upset about many things,
but few things are needed—or indeed only one."
LUKE 10:41–42

Martha knew all too well what it was like to be the "doer" of the bunch. When entertaining Jesus in her home, she concerned herself entirely with doing a great job for him. She became frustrated when those around her didn't appear to be doing much to help. But Jesus saw that Martha had become so concerned with doing she was missing out entirely on the joy and richness of what it was like to simply *be* near him. To be in his company. To be within the sound of his voice.

I have never considered myself to be a Martha. I'm not an overly natural hostess or a domestic goddess. But if I'm honest, I certainly am guilty of trying to *do* too much in life to please God and others. I want to do great things. I want to do a great job. If I'm not careful, I can become so preoccupied with doing that I neglect to simply *be*. To *be* a child of God. To *be* still and enjoy his presence.

REFLECTION

Take a moment to breathe. Be still. Know that your spiritual well-being relies as much on being still in God's presence as it does on serving him. Today, try not to focus on doing a perfect job and settle for earnestly doing the best job you can.

Dear Lord, I don't want to miss the awesome things you have for me because I'm too busy. Help me to know when to sit down and simply listen to what you have to say. Let me be satisfied simply to be in your presence today. In Jesus' name, amen.

Don't Pout

*You who are young, be happy while you are young,
and let your heart give you joy in the days of your youth.*

ECCLESIASTES 11:9

When I was thirteen I went to the arena tour after-party for the band Jamiroquai. My brother Stuart was their original bass player, and even at the age of thirteen, I knew a wrap party at Wembley Arena was a pretty big deal. But mostly I was excited to see my brother. When we got there, it was obvious he was going to be too tied up entertaining his friends to hang out with his teenage sister, so I wound up sitting in the corner with my dad. Lead singer Jay Kay came to dance by me, perhaps seeing my blue expression. But I was too blue even to look up from my Diet Coke. He danced away. Eventually, after some well-timed jokes from my dad, I managed to lighten up and enjoy myself a little … right before we had to leave.

I believe that life is like a party God has planned. He doesn't control what happens at the party; he just sets it up and invites you. It's up to you what you eat and drink, who you speak to and who you don't. You can choose to socialize or sit it in the corner and sulk. Don't find yourself looking back and wishing you'd danced.

REFLECTION

Are you sitting out of the dance of life? Take a moment to give that disappointment to God and to rejoin the party!

Lord, today I lay down all past hurts and offenses. I no longer want to sit on the sidelines in a state of gloom because my heart has been disappointed. I know you have prepared a party for me in this life. Help me to enjoy every moment while I can. In Jesus' precious name, amen.

Have Fun on the Journey

So I recommend having fun, because there is nothing better for people in this world than to eat, drink, and enjoy life. That way they will experience some happiness along with all the hard work God gives them under the sun.

ECCLESIASTES 8:15 NLT

Joel and I spend a good portion of our year on the road. It can become quite repetitive, so we've had to learn to amuse ourselves. Last year we started collecting inexpensive treasures at services stations. We then developed this into a game. What was the most random and amusing product we could find? It was a completely pointless exercise except for one small fact: we had fun.

All of life can be tiring and tedious. So do what you can to make it fun! Enjoy the moment. Enjoy the project, the job, the colleagues. Enjoy the relationship you're in, the car journey, the song that's on radio, the food in front of you. Enjoy the roof you're under even if it's driving you crazy. If you can, find a way to enjoy even your broken heart. It won't be broken forever. These things are God's gift to you right now. You might not have them long. He's working through them.

REFLECTION

How can you make something mundane more fun today? God wants you to enjoy the journey! Accept the challenge today to play your way through the more boring tasks and create a little joy in the tedious moments.

Lord, thanks for the little things that bring me joy. Help me to be resourceful when it comes to fun! You have given me full permission to enjoy every aspect of life. Thank you for this great gift. In Jesus' name, amen.

Keep a Prayer Journal

Praise the LORD, my soul, and forget not all his benefits.
PSALM 103:2

It's so easy to jump from prayer to prayer, from want to want. But in doing so, we often forget the many prayers in our life that have been answered. A few years ago, I began keeping a list of my "little miracles," the instances in my life where I've seen God's hand. During a rough time, I decided to get out that list and review it. I was so inspired. I wound up turning the list into a book! Seeing that picture of God's faithfulness increased my expectation of what was to come and gave me renewed faith to start something fresh in my career.

Why not begin keeping a list of all the good things happening in your life? It doesn't have to be fancy, just a little reminder of those everyday answers to prayer. Seeing the amazing things that God has done for you will inspire your faith and increase your expectations. It might be just what you need to keep going.

REFLECTION

What are you praying for right now? Write your prayers down today in a journal or notebook, and don't forget to check back on them! It's easy to forget what God has done when our prayers are answered and our needs change. Prepare for future times of need by remembering the many times he has already come though.

Lord, you have been so good to me. You've done so much! You've seen me through countless tough seasons and blessed me beyond measure. Let me not forget all those wonderful works just because my needs and my focus have changed. Thank you for the wonderful things you're about to do. In Jesus' name, amen.

Better, Not Bitter

Let all bitterness and wrath and anger and clamor
and slander be put away from you, along with all malice.
Be kind to one another, tender-hearted, forgiving each other,
just as God in Christ also has forgiven you.

EPHESIANS 4:31–32 NASB

Bitterness threatens to affect us all at some time or other. We risk becoming bitter when we face injustice, when someone who is less hardworking or able gets promoted ahead of us, when an ex-partner who mistreated us finds love with someone new, when someone takes credit for our work or forgets to thank us.

These things can cause bitterness to take root. But the only person who tastes the bitterness in your own life is you. You'll face a crossroads at some point. One sign will say Bitter and the other sign, Better. The road to Bitter is broad. Better is a hard path, but the destination speaks for itself. It's a great gift to yourself and to others not to choose Bitter. You may have good reason. You may even have the right. But where would you rather live?

REFLECTION

Have you been a victim of injustice? Take a moment today to write that incident down. Call God into the center of it. Ask him to cultivate forgiveness in your heart where bitterness is threatening to put down its roots.

Lord, you have seen the injustices against me. You've seen it all, and you know how I feel. But I don't want to become bitter in my heart. I want my heart to be fully available to you instead of tangled with the weeds of bitterness. Today I forgive those who've hurt me. I choose for you to make me a better person. In Jesus' name, amen.

Choose Good Heroes

He who walks with wise men will be wise.
PROVERBS 13:20 NASB

Right in the beginning of my faith walk, I was introduced to Graham Kendrick. I had no clue at the time, but Graham is one of the founding fathers of modern worship music. He was close in age to my father and quickly became a mentor to me. He taught me the importance of walking the walk as well as sharing the message. He taught me to take care of my family and home before reaching out to others. Having a hero like Graham has been invaluable to me in times of confusion.

The world likes to market "heroes" to us on a daily basis, people such as movie stars, models, and all manner of public figures. But it's important to be mindful of who we look up to. Their behavior affects us. Russell Brand said it like this: "If you don't choose heroes, heroes will be chosen for you, and they will not represent values that empower you but powers that enslave you."

REFLECTION

Do you have someone in your life that you truly look up to? There's a difference between a mentor/role model and an idol. Idols pull our focus away from what's important while heroes in faith help us to serve God better and become all that we're meant to be. If you don't have good heroes, perhaps it's time to start choosing some.

Father, help me to know which of the figures in my life I look up to are helpful for my journey with you and which are just a distraction. Help me not to be enslaved by the role models that social media and pop culture choose for me and instead choose heroes of noble character. In Jesus' name, amen.

Everybody Hurts

A passerby named Simon, who was from Cyrene,
was coming in from the countryside just then,
and the soldiers forced him to carry Jesus' cross.

MARK 15:21 NLT

Most of us like to display our strength. We prefer to be the one reaching down to rescue others rather than to be that fallen friend. But even Jesus needed help. On that long and grueling journey to the place where he was crucified, Jesus was unable to carry the cross alone anymore. The one who went on to bear the weight of all sin and death on his shoulders had to receive help from a stranger in order to make the rest of that journey.

I believe that God allowed us to know this part of the story to remind us that even the King of kings couldn't make his journey alone. Even the strongest sometimes have to be carried. To be the one who carries a friend in need is a blessing all of its own. Oh, to be the man who assisted Jesus to the place where death was forever defeated!

REFLECTION

If you're in a season where you're not feeling all that strong, embrace this truth today: sometimes sickness, weakness, or circumstances mean that we must be carried. Guess what? That's okay. Just let go and allow yourself to be held. There's no shame in that.

Lord, thank you that I don't always have to be strong. Thank you that it's okay to be held or to reach out and ask for help. Please give me the courage today to ask for help carrying my burdens if I need it. Thank you that I can always cast my burdens on you. In Jesus' name, amen.

Keep Sowing

Those who sow in tears shall reap with joyful shouting.

PSALM 126:5 NASB

While visiting Haiti with children's charity Compassion International, we got to know our hosts quite well. Our hearts broke for them one afternoon. Haiti is the poorest country in the Western Hemisphere, with 80 percent of the population living below the poverty line. The missions team had been building a house for some of the children and, against all odds, had finally sourced doors, toilets, and sinks for the building. These precious commodities had only been acquired through prayer and relentless hard work. We did a trip one afternoon to see the progress of the building project. But on arrival we found to our great disappointment that all the materials had been stolen, the toilets even ripped out of the ground. I could see the grief in our guide's eyes. "What will you do now?" I asked. "Start again," he said.

REFLECTION

The hardest thing to do when you're grieving is to keep sowing, to keep investing in others when you've been rejected, to pray for others when your prayers remain unanswered, to build when your hard work has been razed to rubble. But God promises that joy will come as a reward for that great act of spiritual courage.

Lord, it's not easy to keep sowing when my heart is heavy or broken. But today I'm pledging to keep serving you. I pledge to continue sowing into my dreams, into others, and into your kingdom. I trust that you will give me a reward of pure joy when the time comes! In Jesus' name, amen.

Seasons of Failure

So Pharaoh said to Joseph, "I hereby put you in charge of the whole land of Egypt." Then Pharaoh took his signet ring from his finger and put it on Joseph's finger. He dressed him in robes of fine linen and put a gold chain around his neck.

GENESIS 41:41–42

There are many characters in the Bible who went on to be successful after a season of failure, but Joseph is one of my favorites. I can relate to failure. At age thirteen I was a complete failure on paper. I was underachieving in every subject, even my favorite, music. "Reluctant to perform for the class," said my supportive but very disappointed music teacher in her end-of-term report. I'd be lying if I said I was totally blameless in this. I had stopped trying in many ways after my anxiety had kept me away from school for so long. I was finding it difficult to catch up, and that was often mistaken for a lack of ability or effort.

I never could have imagined there'd be a place for me and my gifts in this world. But here I am. Not a hopeless case, but a person with a reason to get up and work each day doing something I enjoy.

REFLECTION

If you feel you're missing the mark at the moment, don't lose heart. Like Joseph, sometimes we must go through seasons of difficulty before we come into the role we're destined to fill.

Lord, I trust that you've put dreasm in my heart for a reason. I trust that this vision I have is not foolishness but rather a plan you have for my future. Help me to be patient and faithful in those seasons where my dreams are in jail and my plans seem to be on hold. You've promised me great things. In Jesus' name, amen.

Fail Well

The LORD is trustworthy in all he promises and faithful
in all he does. The LORD upholds all who fall
and lifts up all who are bowed down.

PSALM 145:13–14

Being discovered by a major record label and flown halfway
across the world was the best feeling I'd ever had. After decades
of work, I was mapping out in my mind inspirational posts about
believing and never giving up. My bright ball of inspirational zeal
was quickly zapped when I got the brush-off from the label.

For a few weeks I had nothing inspiring to say. I realized
that my favorite thing to talk about is victory, but that I had very
little to give at a time like that. Then one night some months
later, I felt brave enough to tell the story. I was doing a local show
and halfway through talking about this, I broke down. It was
unexpected and completely embarrassing. Afterward I got an
email thanking me for my honesty and vulnerability. Someone
had been very encouraged to hear that the journey was not
always plain sailing for me.

REFLECTION

People love to hear all about your happy endings. But being open
about what you're going through in the here and now can be
even more life-giving to others. People really need to see how you
found the strength to pick yourself up and try again—it just may
give you the best story you've ever had to tell.

Lord, thank you that you promise to hold me up when I fall and
lift me when I'm bowing to you. But in the meantime, thank
you that you're even able to use my failures as an inspiration to
others who may be struggling. In Jesus' name, amen.

Failure Is Discovery

The righteous may fall seven times but still get up.
PROVERBS 24:16 CEB

We praise artists for their hit songs. We remember inventors for the way they changed the world. But what we don't see is the stack of rejected demos that the songwriter submitted to the publisher. We don't see the mountain of failed experiments that led to the eureka moment.

Rumor has it that Thomas Edison's many failed experiments created a pile of junk higher than the house he lived in. We don't talk about those things. We prefer to talk about the great things he invented. Imagine if he'd given up halfway? Perhaps the world we live in would be quite different now. No record stores. No charts. No Grammys. No radio. Thank goodness he was able to see each failed attempt as part of his progress.

So has your last attempt at business, friendship, or invention failed? Great. You've identified one more way *not* to do things.

REFLECTION

Today, instead of feeling discouraged by your failures, congratulate yourself on the progress that they represent. Think of yourself as a scientist on a path of discovery and don't take those failed experiments personally.

Lord, thank you for all that you are teaching me. Thanks to my latest shortfall, I'm one step closer to the person you want me to be. Please give me the strength and the spiritual resources to stay on this path of discovery. In Jesus' name, amen.

Failure Is a Full Backpack

Brothers and sisters, I do not consider myself to have attained this. Instead I am single-minded: Forgetting the things that are behind and reaching out for the things that are ahead.

PHILIPPIANS 3:13 NET

It's not the worst thing in the world to make a mistake. But it *is* pretty bad not to learn anything from it. A mistake can be one of the greatest gifts to your ministry, career, or relationship—if you're prepared to learn from it.

I like to view my failures as a backpack of possibility. I open that backpack, face the contents, put them away in the drawer marked "experience," and move on. Facing those contents with an open heart can honestly make you a better person. It can cause you to face your humanity and help you empathize with others. Failure can be just the spiritual detox you need from ignorance or arrogance. Or it can simply teach you how to do things better next time. Thank God for the things you get wrong! Embrace your mistakes. But whatever you do, don't carry that backpack around with you.

REFLECTION

Did you fail recently? Today take a moment to ask what you can take from a recent failure. Ask God to help you extract every last bit of treasure from this experience.

Lord, thank you that you are able to bless me through this experience. Please don't let me walk away from it without becoming wiser. Help me to squeeze every last drop of value from my errors and finally to let any residual heaviness go. Help me be free to set down anything about this that burdens me. In Jesus' name, amen.

Failure Is Out of Our Control

I planted the seed, Apollos watered it, but God has been making it grow. So neither the one who plants nor the one who waters is anything, but only God, who makes things grow.

1 Corinthians 3:6–7

You can plant two plants in the same soil in the same season using the same tools, yet both might not thrive. You could have two students with the same work ethic and scores who interview just as well as one another, yet only one may be successful in landing the job. You could have two young women both in great health doing all they can to get pregnant, and one may not. I've been involved in many ventures that didn't succeed, and there was no obvious explanation.

When you're a person of faith, the natural response is to ask why certain things happen. If there seems to be no earthly reason, we look to God for his explanation. We wonder what he is doing. What is he trying to teach us? But this can leave us in a very unsatisfying loop. We can begin to feel we're to blame for our own suffering, and this can be a great foothold for doubt and resentment toward God.

REFLECTION

Sometimes in life we have to let go of the need to know why in order to have peace. Today if you're suffering, instead of asking God what he's trying to teach you, simply know that he won't leave you.

Lord, there are days when I don't understand why certain things happen and other things don't. But I'm choosing today to let go of that need to know why and hand it over to you. Thank you that you will never leave me. In Jesus' name, amen.

Failure Gives Us Space

He makes me lie down in green pastures; He leads me beside quiet waters. He restores my soul; He guides me in the paths of righteousness for His name's sake.

PSALM 23:2–3 NASB

Life is very busy for most of us. It begins to feel like a circus-worthy balancing act at times. We're spinning plates—the plates of marriage, family, friendship, work, fun, fitness, future. The trouble with having so many plates to spin is that we only have so many hands. If we spin one plate too many, we're likely to be faced with a couple of smashed ones. Don't worry. Those smashed plates are often just the reminder you need that you're doing a little too much. Some days we must stop spinning so many plates and rest.

REFLECTION

Do you need a break today? Does something need to go? Perhaps you don't really need to go to that party or extra gym session … or to see an extra client. Perhaps you just need a break. Take a moment to invite God into your schedule and let him help you strip it back a little.

Lord, thank you for the gift of space. Thank you that you allow me to see my own limitation and fragility so I am forced to slow down and rest in you. Today I will rest in you and await the restoration you faithfully promise. In Jesus' name, amen.

Failure Isn't Final

Trust in the LORD with all your heart and lean not on your own understanding; in all your ways submit to him, and he will make your paths straight.

PROVERBS 3:5–6

When something we've done or attempted has been what we see as a failure, it's very easy to remain in the shadow of that failure. But failure yesterday does not make *you* a failure today. As God's mercies are new every day you have permission to leave that failure behind and move on to success in your efforts today. When Thomas Edison's experiments failed he didn't take the pieces with him every day. He tossed them aside and tried again. Holding onto the weight of failed experiments is exhausting and unnecessary. You may as well be trying to bottle moonbeams! Let yesterday's failures—*and* successes—die along with yesterday. Make room for today to be today.

REFLECTION

As this month draws to a close, let's take a moment to bury the pieces of our failed experiments. As we begin a new chapter tomorrow, let's begin as new creations, cushioned by God's new mercies.

Lord, today I am laying down everything before you that hasn't worked. I lay all my mistakes and shortcomings at the foot of the cross and thank you that I don't have to carry them. I thank you that tomorrow is a new day and we can begin again. In Jesus' name, amen.

Say Thank You

Oh give thanks to the LORD, for he is good,
for his steadfast love endures forever!

PSALM 107:1 ESV

Thankfulness gives us life. When we take time to truly see and appreciate what we have, we become less stressed, more optimistic, and more joyful. Whenever I'm feeling low, I make a mental list of everything I'm thankful for—and nothing is off-limits! I express my gratitude for music, second chances, ice cream, even my dog's soft fur. I say thank you for all the things that make my life more enjoyable because I know they are all gifts to me.

Why not come up with a little list of things you're grateful for? Sometimes it's hard to get started, but once you get in the flow, you heart expands with gratitude and you can't stop. Here's a little example:

- Lord, I'm grateful for my husband and for my parents, who are all well.
- I'm grateful for my home, my health, and my guitar.
- I'm grateful for the many opportunities you've given me.
- Thank you for my gifts and talents.
- Thank you for sunsets and breakfasts.
- I'm so very, very blessed.

REFLECTION

Write down a messy list of all the things you're thankful for. You're bound to find it uplifting.

Lord, there is so much that I can thank you for today, too many things even to count. But I pray that as I begin to list these things, my heart will overflow with joy in you. In Jesus' name, amen.

Most of What You Need Is Right There

*I know what it is to be in need, and I know what it is
to have plenty. I have learned the secret of being content
in any and every situation, whether well fed or hungry,
whether living in plenty or in want.*

PHILIPPIANS 4:12

I spent quite a lot of time in Nashville, Tennessee when I was writing my fifth studio album. We began to pin all our hopes on moving there, but it didn't immediately pan out that way.

When we came home to England, I had a tough time. My heart was still overseas, and my disappointment had cast a gray shadow over everything I could see. But after a little time and a lot of prayer, a miracle began in my spirit. I began to realize how blessed my life here in the UK really is. I started to count my friends, my family members, and the many blessings that I've had as a musician here. I realized that most of what I hoped to gain by moving was already in my life, and then some. Most of what gives life its beauty and meaning can be found in our own backyard.

REFLECTION

To you, what makes home *home*? What is in your own backyard that you could never find elsewhere? It's tempting to keep searching over the rainbow for your joy, so take time today to consider all the things you have on your doorstep.

Lord, there really is no place like home. You've given me everything I need in order to be content. Teach me to be happy with my lot in life and not to constantly be looking over the fence, where the grass appears greener. In Jesus' name, amen.

Do What You Love

Do not neglect the gift you have, which was given you by prophecy when the council of elders laid their hands on you. Practice these things, immerse yourself in them, so that all may see you progress.

1 TIMOTHY 4:14–15 ESV

I've never felt more suffocated than I did when I had a job that truly didn't suit me. Don't get me wrong, we must be responsible. But doing something that doesn't make use of your gifts or requires going against your nature can cause mental and physical health problems. It's tough if you're a square peg being forced into a round hole.

When I first moved to Sheffield in Yorkshire, I had a telemarketing job. I liked the office and the staff, but quite honestly I was no good at convincing people to buy things they didn't need. I missed all my targets and cried most days. Eventually they "let me go" and I went on to work as a waitress for three years. Although that wasn't my dream job either, I became quite good at it and even had fun. Best of all, waitressing gave me the flexibility to invest time in my true passion and develop my gifts.

If you truly dread going to your workplace, don't feel bad looking for something new. Work makes up so much of your life; you don't want to feel trapped and misused day after day.

REFLECTION

What do you enjoy? Which skills do you like to use? Make a list of those things. You may find it useful later on.

Lord, it's so important that I find fulfillment in what I do. Please help me to identify what my strengths are and help me find opportunities in that area. In Jesus' name, amen.

Keep It Real

Therefore each of you must put off falsehood and speak truthfully to your neighbor, for we are all members of one body.

EPHESIANS 4:25

A visiting speaker at our church once said, "Social media is the anti-confession. It is more concerned with looking happy than being happy. The only thing that matters is you being real with others and before God. Anything else will drive your heart into the ground."

I admit that as an entertainer I live in an awkward social media tension between wanting to connect and seeking mass approval. It's not that I want to maintain a facade; I genuinely have intentions to be positive and to bless others. I want to be a witness of God's goodness. But I've learned that God's goodness is best seen through someone's true journey. People have an instinct for fakery. They know when someone is glossing over the truth. In reality, people need to see the full picture of our hard times in order to see the full picture of God's grace.

If you're feeling that your life looks less than perfect, don't worry about being a bad witness. The world needs to see his goodness, not yours.

REFLECTION

Why not share something super real today? If you are asked how you're doing, why not tell the whole truth?

Lord, I long to be my authentic self. I don't want to live a lie or mislead others. Please help me to be transparent in a healthy way with those who mean the most to me. Also, Lord, give me wisdom about what to share and how best to share it. In Jesus' name, amen.

Seek Joy

Finally, brothers and sisters, whatever is true, whatever is noble, whatever is right, whatever is pure, whatever is lovely, whatever is admirable—if anything is excellent or praiseworthy—think about such things.

PHILIPPIANS 4:8

"Despair is one of the most demotivating and deactivating things," says Eli Pariser, founder of the website Upworthy.

Joy isn't some trivial bonus emotion. Joy is power! It gives us strength and therefore life itself. It refuels a weary traveler and helps repair a broken heart. Never underestimate the uplifting value of simple pleasures. Whether you love dogs, musicals, crafts, or superhero movies, don't feel guilty for spending time on things that bring joy to your heart. In this world of many sorrows, don't apologize for enjoying what's beautiful. Keeping your joy tank full will activate you for good deeds.

REFLECTION

What makes you smile? Why not try and put more of those things into your day? Have you been deactivated by anything negative recently? Do you feel bad after watching news or reading certain things? It might be time to filter them out.

Lord, help me to focus on the things that help me to be fully alive in you. I don't want to be deactivated by despair. If there is anything in my life that needs to be removed because it's too negative, please show me. In Jesus' name, amen.

There's No Such Thing as an Easy Life

"In this world you will have trouble. But take heart!
I have overcome the world."

JOHN 16:33

God never promised us an easy life. This is a tough world with any number of hardships to face daily. Whatever makes up your life, whether you're a high or low earner, single or married, young or old, you face challenges right now.

Being single is hard. Being married is hard. Having kids is hard. Having no kids when you want kids is hard. Being unemployed is hard. Working full-time is hard. *Life* is hard. Whenever I get weary of any aspect of my life, I imagine the opposite and realize that I could easily get weary of that too. If we think that leaving our job, partner, or church will make things perfect, we're deceived. God never said there was an easy option. But he did promise us victory and eternal life in him.

REFLECTION

Wherever you are and whatever your life looks like, you're facing some kind of challenge right now. Today, thank God for his presence in your situation. Whatever you're facing, know that he is faithful and he is always with you.

Lord, thank you that you are with me in my struggles. Help me to realize that there really is no such thing as an easy life. We all have struggles, and we must have compassion for each other. Help me to practice humility and compassion today in my dealings with others. In Jesus' name, amen.

Editing, Part 1

Search me, God, and know my heart;
test me and know my anxious thoughts.

PSALM 130:23

We often focus on what we'd like to add to our lives. We pray for opportunities, relationships, and even possessions. God knows we need these things at times. But what we so often forget to do is *remove* things from our lives.

Sometimes when I'm writing a song, I have to delete a decent, perfectly acceptable lyric to find a *good* lyric. That's a bit like real life. It's hard to let decent things go. But we have to be brave enough to really edit our lives if we want them to be *good*.

REFLECTION

Does your life need to breathe a little better? Would it be good to remove certain responsibilities, commitments, or even relationships from the equation? Take a moment to pray about this today.

Lord, I want to live my best life in and for you. I'm sure there are many things I could remove from my life to make it simpler and more streamlined. Please help me to discern what I should hold on to and what I must let go of. In Jesus' name, amen.

Capture Beauty

He has filled them with skill to do all kinds of work as engravers,
designers, embroiderers in blue, purple and scarlet yarn and fine
linen, and weavers—all of them skilled workers and designers.

EXODUS 35:35

The world God created is beautiful. In England, my husband
and I live quite close to the Peak District, and although we pass
it almost weekly, its beauty *always* takes my breath away. All
year round—come rain, sun, or snow—it reflects the exciting
creativity of God, inspiring me to create in response.

Responding to nature with creativity is both healthy and
inspiring. That's why I began writing songs in the first place. In
a song you can catch something pretty in the net of time, like a
little truth butterfly, which would otherwise quickly slip through
your mind like sand through fingers. Using creativity as a means
of expressing ourselves and capturing beauty is something we
can all do.

REFLECTION

If you have a pen and paper or if you have a camera on your
phone, you can capture something. Why not try? One of the
traits that identifies us as children of God is our creativity. So let's
create!

Lord, thank you for the gift of creativity. It's who you are, and
you've placed that instinct within me too. Today please awaken
this in me afresh so I can take joy in creative things. If I am
not an artist, then help me to apply creativity in my work, my
relationships, and even my recreation. In Jesus' name, amen.

Beware Negativity

Rejoice in hope, be patient in tribulation, be constant in prayer.
ROMANS 12:12 ESV

It's easy to confuse being discerning with being negative. As a twentysomething Christian setting out in music ministry, I was extremely ambitious and filled with faith. I wish I had a dollar for every wise and learned Christian who tried to talk me out of my mission! I'm not afraid to admit I've found myself doing the same thing to others at times. My intentions have been to impart wisdom, but the outcome has been a little negative at times.

Please don't try to convince someone their glass is half empty. In this troubled world we need more optimists. Let other people count their blessings and embark upon their impossible dreams!

REFLECTION

Has someone cast negativity over something you're attempting? Or have you found yourself discouraging someone else in their rose-tinted view of the world? It's a common human error. But today let's take a moment to lay down all things negative and exchange them for faith-filled prayer.

Lord, help me to know the difference between discernment and negativity. Help me to remain optimistic and filled with faith, even when things don't work out as I first imagine or hope. Help me to share that faith and optimism with others always. In Jesus' name, amen.

One Day at a Time

"Therefore do not worry about tomorrow, for tomorrow will worry about itself. Each day has enough trouble of its own."

MATTHEW 6:34

Trying to live our whole lives in one day can become very stressful indeed. It's not uncommon for me to make a mental list of everything I'd like to fix in life while I'm still taking my morning shower! I take my itinerary and my shopping list to God, firing off everything I need in a frenzied prayer. Then I make a checklist of everything in the house that needs fixing. *Then* I make a mental list of everything I'd like to achieve in my life before I turn forty. This is all before I've left the house or even fed the dog! It can be overwhelming and exhausting to think this way.

REFLECTION

There are many things you need to tackle over the rest of the year. You have a lot of giving and a lot of living to do, but you don't have to do it all today! Instead of being overambitious, simply resign yourself to getting a handful of things done. Don't forget to include breathing space in the next twelve hours.

Lord, give me the strength for today. Just for today. Help me to achieve all that I'm meant to achieve in you and to let go of things I don't have capacity for. Have your way in me today. In Jesus' name, amen.

Don't Let Sadness Sink the Ship

May the God of hope fill you with all joy and peace as you trust in him, so that you may overflow with hope by the power of the Holy Spirit.

ROMANS 15:13

There are times in life when an ocean of sadness overwhelms us. In those times, it's important to keep the ship of our hearts watertight so that sadness doesn't get in and cause us to sink. One sad moment is easy to cope with. A marriage or relationship breakdown, a bereavement or financial crisis might mean that sadness leaks in. In these times we have to focus on sorrow-proofing our hearts so that sadness doesn't swamp the vessel. How do we do that?

By filling our sails with God's buoyant truth. Breathing in the life-giving Word of God enables us to stay afloat in spite of circumstances.

REFLECTION

Sometimes an incident or bereavement can cause sadness. If that's the case with you right now, seek help from a friend who is outside of the situation. Ask that person to pray and speak encouragement over you. Ask God to bless your heart with joy and faith.

Lord, I cannot control the sadness that sweeps across my life. There's no way to avoid sorrowful situations. But with your help, my heart can remain above the waters. Lord, I pray right now that you would surround my family with joy and peace in the Holy Spirit so darkness can't penetrate. Help us to fill our sails with your truth so we can journey forward through troubled waters. In Jesus' name, amen.

Deal with Anxiety

For God has not given us a spirit of fear,
but of power and of love and of a sound mind.

2 TIMOTHY 1:7 NKJV

It's now estimated that 80 percent of us will experience symptoms of anxiety and depression at some point in our lives. Creative people are especially prone to such issues. Add to a creative imagination the stress of pursuing a career attached to your gifting, and you have the perfect conditions for breakdown. We have to be aware that while we have the capacity to be immensely productive and strong, too much stress can cause cracks to appear. Start by knowing that it isn't a sin to experience these symptoms. It doesn't make you a bad or incapable Christian. But it's important to face and deal with these issues before they become less manageable. We believe in a God that can heal and deliver us from all things health related, but it's sensible to take a body, mind, *and* soul approach to mental health issues.

REFLECTION

Have you been struggling with anxiety or low mood? Take time today to assess how well you're feeling body, mind, and soul. Make sure you're taking care of your physical self. If you're battling persistent anxious or dark thoughts, seek help from a counselor. Don't forget to seek prayer covering from trusted friends.

Lord, thank you for your promise of a sound mind. Help me do all I can to take care of myself—body, mind, and soul. Please help me to reach out and seek help in any way I may need to. In Jesus' name, amen.

The Wonderful Counselor

And he will be called Wonderful Counselor, Mighty God, Everlasting Father, Prince of Peace.

ISAIAH 9:6

Just as the body needs to be nurtured and taken care of, so does the mind. Neglect to care for your mind, and everyday stress can become illness. As with a bodily injury, ignoring a problem with your mental well-being and continuing at full pace without treatment or recovery time can put you out of action.

If you've had a recent trauma or heartbreak but haven't taken time to address or work through it, you could become vulnerable to a longer-term problem. Has anything happened in your life that you have not yet truly worked through? Does something keep coming back to you and creating upset? Never forget that Jesus is the Wonderful Counselor, and you can bring *any* issue, memory, or thought to him.

REFLECTION

Very often we don't realize we've been carrying around a trauma or painful memory until we really sit down and search ourselves. Today let's ask God to take us on a journey into anything historical that might still be burdening us.

Lord, you truly know me better than I know myself. You have my every memory and experience on file. If there is anything in my heart or mind that I still need to deal with, help me to be mindful of that today and bring it to you. Thank you that you're the most wonderful counselor, more than able to reach into my innermost parts and begin my healing. Thank you that whatever you uncover within me will be guarded by your peace. In Jesus' name, amen.

Being Refined, Part 1

Behold, I have refined you, but not as silver;
I have tested you in the furnace of affliction.

ISAIAH 48:10 NASB

If you've experienced a season of hardship, it's not uncommon to feel as though you've lost something of your identity. You can look in the mirror and see a person whose viewpoint and character have been shaped by pain. But the great news is that God is able to work through these dark seasons to refine who you are *for the better*.

Remain his child.

God can find you in the billows of dark smoke and do a wonderful transforming work in you. He promises that if you have faith in him, he will not let you perish. In fact, he will make sure that you become a far better person than you used to be. Imagine that!

REFLECTION

Today take a moment to rest in God's presence, knowing although the fire or trouble burns fiercely around you, he won't let you go. He is refining you like silver and will ensure you emerge from this season reflecting his glory as never before.

Lord, I come to you today looking for your peace. This season is truly testing me, and the fire around me seems to be burning up the person that I was. But I'm choosing to trust you in this process. I know you're with me in the fire, and although I'm stretched, you won't let me break. You are shaping me and refining me for your glory. In Jesus' name, amen.

Being Refined, Part 2

For You have tried us, O God;
you have refined us as silver is refined.

PSALM 66:10 NASB

When life puts us through the fire, we might not always like what
emerges in us. Although we'd like to be ever-patient in times of
trouble and always to glorify God through our hardships, we may
find that a trial brings out the worst in us. We can find ourselves
feeling impatient, ungrateful, and even lacking in faith. Feelings
of condemnation and failure can then naturally follow. But don't
despair—it's all part of God's refining process. God *uses* the tests
of life to highlight and deal with the parts of our character that
need work. Before his glory can be fully evident in us we must
face the weaknesses and impurities in our character that can only
be brought out by the heat of the fire. This is what the process of
refinement is all about.

REFLECTION

Have you struggled to be patient in suffering? Has your faith felt
pushed to its limits? Great! These are all good signs of our growth
in God if we humbly commit to the process. Today, perhaps use
your journal to work through some of these thoughts. It's okay to
be in the middle of the process.

Lord, thank you for your faithfulness through this season of
refinement. But as my heart has been put through the flames,
I have not liked everything that has emerged in me. There are
clearly parts of my character that need work. But I'm thankful
that this is part of the process and that I don't need to feel any
shame. I trust that you'll see this process through to completion.
In Jesus' name, amen.

Describe Yourself on a Good Day

"But I will restore you to health and heal your wounds,"
declares the LORD.

JEREMIAH 30:17

If depression is something you genuinely struggle with, you'll be all too familiar with feeling out of sorts, that sensation of losing yourself when the shadows fall over your mood. You can also become very self-critical.

I have found it very helpful to write a positive paragraph about myself while enjoying a good mental health day. It's good to create that little reminder for yourself so that next time you're feeling a little lost you can remind yourself what makes you happy. Next time you're bouncing around feeling good, write up a little praise review of your best self, knowing that God will restore you every time you fall down.

REFLECTION

On a good day, are you playful? Funny? Do you listen when others speak and add great things to the conversation? Do you have a knack of making strangers feel comfortable? Write these things down so on days when you feel lost, you can be reminded of who you are in God and know that he will restore you fully in time.

Lord, thank you for the person that you've made me to be. On those days where I simply don't feel like myself, help me to know that I'm safe with you. God, as I consider who I am when I'm in full health, I ask that you would restore me to my best self soon. In Jesus' precious name. Amen.

Don't Compare Fires

"When you pass through the waters, I will be with you;
and through the rivers, they will not overflow you.
When you walk through the fire, you will not be scorched,
nor will the flame burn you."

ISAIAH 43:2 NASB

When life gets hard, it's too easy to feel that you're the only one going through such a thing. It's tempting to presume that your neighbor is coping far better than you are. But the truth is, regardless of the details, every one of us faces all manner of daily challenges. Don't make the mistake of comparing your woes to someone else's. Just as your gifts and calling are completely unique, so too is your journey through darkness. You're doing the best that you can, and that's all that matters. Never forget that God is with you in the fire.

REFLECTION

Today, let's simply thank God that he sustains us in these difficult times.

Lord, thank you that you are my ever-present help in times of trouble. I know you love me and you're not causing me this pain. Help me to be patient and compassionate when other people are hurting. Though they may appear to be coping very well, I have no idea what things are really like for them. Help me not to compare woes or my coping threshold to anyone else's. In Jesus' name, amen.

Ask for Help

For the body is not one member, but many.

1 Corinthians 12:14 NASB

We all have days where that one extra problem seems to tip the balance and make our situation unmanageable. We can ask God to be our supernatural strength. But God has provided us with hands and feet so we can minister to and assist one another.

When I first got married, the hardest adjustment for me was learning to share the load of life with my husband. I was used to doing shopping, cleaning, and business errands all by myself. But I quickly learned that not only was Joel able to help; he was also very willing. In fact, he *expected* to help, and I was denying him the joy by continuing to do my own thing. Though it can be difficult at first, we must regularly practice the art of asking for help. Not only may it be necessary for us complete the task at hand, but God may have a greater purpose in the teamwork.

REFLECTION

Do you need to engage the help of a friend? Can a member of your family pick up a chore or two? Don't feel bad for sharing the load.

Lord, thank you for the people in my life. Help me to trust others in the sharing of responsibilities. If I don't have those people in my life right now, please help me to find them. Help me to find a community where I am loved and embraced, and where others will take delight in coming to my rescue as I would for them. In Jesus' name, amen.

Ask for Prayer

In the same way, prayer is essential in this ongoing warfare.
Pray hard and long. Pray for your brothers and sisters.
Keep your eyes open. Keep each other's spirits up so that
no one falls behind or drops out.

ECCLESIASTES 6:18 MSG

I recently faced an awful situation online. Someone managed to hack my social media accounts and lock me out of them. While struggling to resolve the situation, I really had only one thing I could do—pray.

Immediately I thought of my online prayer group. I'd been in the group for a few months and had enjoyed praying for various situations for others. But somehow, I felt reluctant to ask for prayer, to make it about *me* this time. On some level I felt that by asking for prayer I was taking up time and space that someone might need more. I felt that if I asked for help, there'd be less prayer to go around. But quite desperate, I went ahead and asked. I was so blessed by the support; I felt immediately surrounded by an army! It wasn't long before I felt stronger and unafraid—and began to see circumstances turn around.

REFLECTION

Do you have someone who can pray for you? Don't be afraid to ask! It's good to nominate several people and reach out to them with issues, however small.

Lord, thank you that you promise that where two or more are gathered, you are there and you answer our prayers. Help me to know with whom I should team up. Give me the courage to step out and ask for that support where it is needed and to be ready to offer that help. In Jesus' name, amen.

Keep an Eye on the Dashboard

Therefore let him who thinks he stands take heed that he does not fall.

1 CORINTHIANS 10:12 NASB

The other day I got into my friend's car. The first thing I noticed was the pretty little light show on the dashboard—several alerts to check fluid levels and even a little "stoplight."

"Andy, your car is trying to tell you things!"

"Oh yeah," he said, "they've been on a while, and I guess I just don't notice them anymore."

The revelation hit me like a flash. *Begin to ignore the little stoplights that tell you your heart needs a tune-up, and you could find yourself broken down.* If you're finding it difficult to keep on driving, there could be good reason. Perhaps you need a rest or a time of refreshment. Perhaps you need to take time to deal with a fraught relationship or to see a doctor about some aches and pains. Whatever you do, don't ignore the warning signs, or you could find yourself stranded on the highway.

REFLECTION

Are there some red flags going up in your world right now? Do you have a relationship that may need some maintenance? Do you feel a little run down but tell yourself to keep going? Take today's reading as an extra signal to stop and deal with the problem.

Lord, thank you for speaking to me. If I've become ignorant to a warning you're trying to give me, please make it clear to me again. If there is something in my life that needs attention, help me to see it. I want this life of mine to run well and be taken care of in a way that pleases you. In Jesus' name, amen.

Grief

God my heart is steady. I will sing and praise you
with all my being.

PSALM 108:1 NCV

If you've lost someone you love, then you know what grief is. It can also extend beyond the loss of a loved one to the death of a dream. Grief can even come as a result of a relationship failure. Just as with the loss of a loved one, grief can reappear years down the line and show its face at an unexpected time. All it takes is to be reminded of someone or something that connects to that grief and you can be overcome.

Because grief can resurface in this way it's important to be ready for it. Prepare some positive reflections for moments of grief. If you've lost someone dear to you be ready to recall joyful memories. If that person doesn't evoke positive memories, perhaps reflect on how far you've come since the time of that initial loss. If you're feeling grief about a missed opportunity or broken dream, focus on the dreams that *have* come true and direct your thoughts toward what you're actively believing for today.

REFLECTION

Today let's ask God to steady and prepare our hearts for when grief comes knocking. Let's ask him to make us ready, to prepare us with positive thoughts in response.

Lord, today I ask that you would ready and steady my heart. You know that there are certain losses we don't recover from all at once. You know that memories can come alive to us at any time and cause that pain to remerge. Prepare me, God, and fill my soul with praise so I may sing through the hard times and be encouraged. In Jesus' name, amen.

Stress Fractures

The LORD is close to the brokenhearted
and saves those who are crushed in spirit.

PSALM 34:18

Hearts don't just get broken when a relationship ends.
Sometimes your heart has a hairline fracture that grows with
stress. Sometimes it's an old injury that causes new problems.
It can come from a broken dream, a difficult family time, or a
missed opportunity. It can happen during a change of season,
such as when a child leaves home or a job ends. Sometimes
it's just the weight of the world that causes the crack. If you're
nursing a broken heart today, take time to grieve a little and
receive comfort right now from the Spirit. Be kind to yourself.
Your heart is fragile and precious and takes time to heal. But with
God's help it will.

REFLECTION

God is a healing God. Spend a moment bringing that stress
fracture to God right now. Is it something new? Something old
that has been triggered again? It doesn't matter. He can deal with
it. So place it in his hands this moment and allow him to minister
to you.

Lord, thank you that you are near to me right now. Thank you
that in this moment you can minister to my pain and bring me
healing in the name of Jesus. Thank you that you promise to
save me even when I feel utterly crushed by pain and circumstance. Amen.

It's Okay to Be Weak

But he said to me, "My grace is sufficient for you, for my power is made perfect in weakness." Therefore I will boast all the more gladly about my weaknesses, so that Christ's power may rest on me.

2 CORINTHIANS 12:9

There are days when we feel ready to take on the world. But there are other days when sickness, sadness, and circumstance have the power to render us weaker than we'd like to be. There have been times when I'd give just about anything to be tucked up in bed rather than having to sing to a roomful of strangers. I think of times when a simple virus has left me with 30 percent of the power I would usually have in my voice or difficult family circumstances have interrupted my preparations for a public performance. In those times I have learned just how much God can work through my weakness. In fact, some of my best and most memorable testimonies have come from when I was at my weakest. I've come to anticipate great things from God when I feel anything but great. How amazing it is that even our weakness is a resource to God.

REFLECTION

Our weakness allows God to move in power. So rejoice in weakness today, knowing that God can have space to do even more in and through our lives.

Lord, thank you for the great design of your grace. You've organized life so that when I am weak, I am strong. This takes all the pressure off me to be awesome and to get everything done in my own strength. Thank you for the power that rests on me now, even though I don't feel powerful. In Jesus' name, amen.

You Can Still Impact the World

Jesus answered, "The work of God is this:
to believe in the one he has sent."

JOHN 6:29

Sometimes in life we find ourselves feeling redundant. In those seasons of life, you might look at yourself and ask, *What can God really do with me?*

I certainly found myself asking this during the darkest times of my depression. I'll be honest: being redundant was my greatest fear for a time. I was afraid that struggling with my mental well-being would rob me of what God had in store.

But today's verse—words directly from Jesus—has always encouraged me greatly. It's a mistake to think that your occupation or even your calling is God's work. God's true work is simply to have faith in every situation and to believe in Jesus. So whatever your situation, however incapable you may feel right now, know that simply having faith is the work God wants you to do.

REFLECTION

Your health, struggles, or challenges will not hold you back. If you're believing for a healing today, this is your work. If you're recovering from a sickness or injury, that is today's work. If you're embarking on a project or adventure for God's glory, this is your work today.

Lord, I commit myself fully to the work of believing. Let me apply myself to it as if it were a career. Let me have faith as though my salary were coming directly from every hour of believing. Help me not see the job I get paid for as my true work or as representative of my true worth. My work is to believe in you in every season of my life. In Jesus' name, amen.

Encourage Sadness to Move On

But I will sing of your strength, in the morning I will sing of your love, for you are my fortress, my refuge in times of trouble.

PSALM 59:16

Sadness swoops by every so often. There is no stopping it. There is no harm and certainly no shame in feeling sadness, and it's not healthy to resist it completely. But what we *must* do is encourage it to move on in due course. If we spend too much time exploring the sensation of misery, it can become too comfortable and familiar. Don't invite misery to live with you. It often outstays its welcome. Send it packing while you're still in control.

REFLECTION

It might seem impossible if you're going through something difficult, but make every effort to do something that invites joy to take misery's place. Don't feel guilty for laughing. Don't feel insensitive for taking pleasure in your favorite music, places, and people. Misery must only ever be a brief visitor. Joy can take up permanent residence.

Lord, help me to banish sadness now if it has outstayed its welcome. I am ready to feel good again! I'm ready to be restored to full function and health in you, Lord. Today I will speak to sadness in Jesus' name and say, "Thank you for all you've taught me, but your time is up. Joy is ready to move in again." In Jesus' name, amen.

The Season Will Always Change

"As surely as the sun rises, he will appear; he will come to us like
the winter rains, like the spring rains that water the earth."

HOSEA 6:3

In the UK we very much feel the seasons. When winter comes,
we switch out everything in our closets to deal with the bitter
cold. We prepare ourselves for a season of long dreary nights,
and in spite of holiday festivities, many of us feel heaviness. The
national mood improves when those first buds of spring appear.
Then it goes around again.

It's worth remembering that the seasons of our souls shift
as dramatically as the seasons of the year. When we're in dark
seasons of the soul it's tough to see beyond them. But the seasons
will change. It's inevitable. However cold and long this winter of
life may have been, the air is changing.

REFLECTION

God created the seasons to allow perfect harmony within nature.
He also put unique and beautiful things in each one so we'd
be constantly stimulated and inspired. He created seasons for
growth and seasons for harvest. He created seasons of less and
seasons of much. But although some seasons are hard, they
always change. Today may your hope come out of its winter
hibernation and into spring!

Lord, thank you for each of the amazing seasons we're blessed
with. You give us light, life, and renewal. You strip things away
to make room for new buds to appear. Thank you for the season
I'm in right now and for the change that will surely come! In
Jesus' precious name. Amen.

Declutter

Then he said to them, "Watch out! Be on your guard against all kinds of greed; life does not consist in an abundance of possessions."
LUKE 12:15

I'm quite sentimental about the things in my life. But I've come to realize that holding on to too much stuff clutters my space, makes things harder to find, and increases my stress levels. There's nothing like a good spring clean! I love to clear out the deadwood in my life, from old clothes to makeup and even mementos.

Much of what we own is clutter and burdens rather than serves us. Go through your clothing and ask yourself, *Do I wear this anymore?* Go through your ornaments and ask yourself, *Is this making me smile every day? Would it make someone else smile more?* I genuinely find that after a good clear-out yard sale, putting some stuff on a sellers' website, and giving a bunch of stuff to charity, my world is filled suddenly with fresh air and energy.

REFLECTION

Today, why not give decluttering a try? It's likely that you have clothes that no longer fit or inspire you. It's likely you have collected mementos from times in your life you don't even want to remember. You'd be surprised at how much space a good clear-out will give you both physically and emotionally.

Lord, give me the courage to let go of some of these things. There really isn't any need to become so emotionally attached to material possessions. Of course, it's nice to keep hold of certain things that have sentimental value or serve me well. But unless the things in my life are functional or truly beautiful, there's no need for them to add noise to my life! Help me declutter. In Jesus' name, amen.

You're Not Alone

Therefore confess your sins to each other … so that you may be healed. The prayer of a righteous person is powerful and effective.

JAMES 5:16

Odds tell me that if you're reading this, you could be suffering from addiction, grief, financial issues, marriage or relationship problems, identity challenges, shame, depression, or spiritual attack. Odds are, you're not the only one; you're certainly not alone. You'd be utterly amazed at how many of your peers are going through the same things. Most of us will be connected to at least one of the above issues at any given time whether in our own lives or in the life of a loved one.

If you're a part of a church community, you might have become used to keeping these issues out of conversation. But that isn't what God intended for us as the body. Part of the purpose for church family is to form a safe zone for sharing our burdens.

REFLECTION

These are things we must work on together and though it's not easy, it's worth fighting for. Start by knowing you're not strange and you're certainly not alone. Chances are that as you choose to confide in a select few, you'll find that others are walking a similar walk.

Lord, help me be courageous enough to confide in others. Help me to wisely choose my confidants and to be truly open with those trustworthy people. I know this is important for my walk with you, Lord, so please have your way in this area of my life. In Jesus' name, amen.

Mental Well-Being Checklist

Beloved, I pray that all may go well with you and that you may be in good health, as it goes well with your soul.

3 JOHN 2 ESV

There are some basic things in our lives that we need for mental well-being. If you're not feeling great, it might be helpful to take a look through this simple checklist:

- Are you well-rested?
- Are you clean and fed?
- Do you have people you can call upon for simple company?
- Are you on top of basic household jobs and self-care?
- Do you have some pleasant plans for the future?

If you are struggling, maybe take time to consider this list. Do you need some time to rest? Have you taken on too much? Do you feel lonely? Do you have gifts you need to be using?

REFLECTION

If you see some unchecked boxes above, take a moment to pray about these things. How can some practical balance be restored? What do you need? God knows and cares about these needs.

Lord, I know you see these unchecked boxes in my well-being checklist. You know far better than I do how I should take care of myself. I pray that you'll help me to take time for these things and get them in order. In Jesus' name, amen.

Gifts Have a Flip Side

And we know that in all things God works for the good of those
who love him, who have been called according to his purpose.

ROMANS 8:28

As someone who has suffered with mental health issues, I can
testify that they are the flip side of my gift. My creativity and
imagination are what God has given me to serve in this world.
But when I'm at a low point, these wonderful things turn on me.
My creativity and imagination become instruments of anxiety.
I've known it to be similar for others. I've met highly emotionally
intelligent and sensitive people who find themselves self-harming
when they're down. I've met many young people who grapple
with a sense of perfectionism that serves them well academically,
but the flip side can be control-centered illnesses such as OCD
and eating disorders. Try to remember that on the other side of
your issue may be an incredible strength.

REFLECTION

It's important to change the way we view mental health issues
and those who suffer from them, because these individuals may
in fact be giants in the kingdom of God—once they allow God to
move through their lives. We must remember that God promises
to work in and through *all* things, even the negative flip side of
serious, chronic problems.

Lord, help me to have wisdom in this area. Help me to see that
what slows me down mentally might be another facet of my
talents and strengths. Help me to keep renewing my mind and
my strength in you so I can continue to be creative and useful in
your kingdom. In Jesus' name, amen.

Create a Peaceful Space

"But when you pray, go into your room, close the door and pray to your Father who is unseen."

MATTHEW 6:6

Humans struggle when they feel out of control. Life can present all kinds of uncertainties, so it's surprising how effective a few simple habits can be for restoring calm. During a really hectic time when I was around fifteen, I discovered an incredible trick for resetting my peace button—tidying my room! I gutted the space, organized my clothes and music, cleaned all the surfaces, and bought a few new candles to add light. Lying in bed that night, I felt clearheaded for the first time in months.

Creating a safe, calming space where you can retreat in solitude can help when things get intense. By keeping that space clean and tidy, you give a gift to yourself. You might also like to fill the space with candles, soft lighting ("fairy lights" are cheap and cheerful), and a bunch of soft cushions to flop on.

You might not have the luxury of an entire room, but even a corner can do nicely. Let it be your corner for prayer reflection and simple peace.

REFLECTION

Today, why not put a little time into creating a nice space for yourself? Take a pen and paper and jot down some ideas. You'll be amazed what you can do if you get a little creative!

Lord, whatever the physical space in my life, let me always make space for you. I pray you'll help me to find even the smallest corner where I can just be still and have peace in you. In Jesus' name, amen.

Distract Yourself

Set your minds on things above, not on earthly things.
COLOSSIANS 3:2

Have you ever received an insulting email or comment and felt so mad you just wanted to drive straight over to the sender's house and confront the person … only to find the next morning that you've cooled off and you're really glad you didn't? This is the power of distraction.

You've probably used distraction with the children in your life. They fall, panic, and cry. We pick up a soft toy or a piece of candy and lo—the crying ceases! We love to think we're a whole lot more sophisticated than a two-year-old, but essentially we're the same. In the wake of a disappointment, a shove from a friend, or the confiscation of something we're attached to, we're prone to emotional outbursts. Distraction works to our advantage too.

REFLECTION

Instead of trying to solve a problem on the spot, why not take a few hours out? Go see a movie. Take a walk in the park. See a friend. You might find that when you return to the issue, the tension has settled a little and things look less catastrophic.

Lord, please help me to know when I should take a break from things. Help me to get safely lost in something pleasant in order to regain perspective. In Jesus' name, amen.

The Garden of Your Mind

The mind governed by the Spirit is life and peace.
ROMANS 8:6

Thoughts pass through our minds quickly, and quite often we don't pay much attention to them. But thoughts, when repeated, become *thought patterns*. As the term would suggest, repeated thoughts create neural pathways (patterns) in your brain. Think of it like this: if your mind is like earth, then thoughts are like water running through and over it. Each repeated thought carves a pathway. So whatever you spend a lot of time thinking about shapes the landscape in your mind.

What that means is that if you spend a lot of time focusing on worries, fears, and problems, the landscape of your mind will likely begin to look very dismal. But if you choose to channel good thoughts, the pathways in your mind will become healthy and the landscape will flourish. If you can teach yourself to focus on God's promises when a worried thought comes, the pathway will become positive and peace filled.

REFLECTION

Do you have repeated, worried thoughts or a negative thinking habit? Are you fed up with feeling that your mind is a dreary place? Today, find a verse of Scripture that might turn this around in the future.

Lord, help my mind to be like a picturesque garden where beautiful things can grow. Let your Holy Spirit flow through and bring things to life. Let me be intentional about planting good thoughts and allowing positive thoughts to shape the landscape of my mind. In Jesus' name, amen.

Learn Your Triggers

Since, then, you have been raised with Christ, set your hearts on
things above, where Christ is, seated at the right hand of God.

COLOSSIANS 3:1

When it comes to our mental well-being, sometimes we don't do
ourselves any favors. We actually go toward things that we *know*
won't make us feel any better.

Our curiosity about our health may cause us to spend hours
on Google, researching illnesses. In our bid to understand mental
health, we might find ourselves watching documentaries. If
we're afraid of being cheated on in a relationship, we may find
ourselves reading articles about infidelity. Some of these things
may be helpful, but most are sensationalist and gloomy, and do
little to help.

If you know that watching a documentary about eating
disorders will cause you to think about your battle with food
even more, switch it off. If you feel more vulnerable at night,
stay away from things like social media then. Avoid anything that
might cause you to fall into a tailspin of insecurity.

REFLECTION

What brings you down? They could be quite harmless things like
shopping websites or fashion blogs. But if they're making you feel
bad, they're not worth it. Take a moment to write down a couple
of things that trigger your anxiety or low mood.

Lord, thank you that you want to protect my thoughts and keep
me in good spirits. Help me to be more disciplined about setting
my heart on things above and avoiding that which holds me
back. In Jesus' name, amen.

Laugh

A joyful heart is good medicine,
but a broken spirit dries up the bones.
PROVERBS 17:22 NASB

They say, "Laughter is the best medicine," and time and again I've found that to be true. There's a reason we feel the need to laugh during testing times. That's why comedians write material about dark subjects. Laughter is a defense that helps us cope.

It isn't just an old wives' tale; great things happen chemically in our bodies when we laugh. It has been proven to lower our stress levels and boost our immune responses. Laughter also bonds us with others, as most of us will have experienced when everything goes a little pear shaped for the day!

So make jokes! They don't have to be great jokes—they just have to be kind. I once worked with an assistant who made about fifteen jokes a minute and believe me, a lot of them were ridiculous. But I used to find myself laughing more and more, because his attempts at humor lightened everyone's mood. It gave people permission to relax and enjoy themselves. So make jokes even if you're not a comedy genius. At least people will know you're trying to be fun and have a nice time.

REFLECTION

It's important not to always take life too seriously. Do you need to lighten up a little? It's not a sin to laugh!

God thank you so much for the gift of laughter. Let me never take it for granted. In fact, give me more laughter, Lord! Let me overflow with the giggles. In Jesus' name, amen.

Take Care of Your Body

For you were bought with a price. So glorify God in your body.
1 CORINTHIANS 6:20 ESV

If I could sit down with my fifteen-year-old self, I'd say this: "I know you think that partying and pushing your body and mind to their limits is grabbing life with both hands. You're going to learn the hard way that grabbing life with both hands is about being kind to yourself, being good to your body, and building a future. Protect your heart so goodness can flow from it to others. Protect your body so that you have the health and stamina you need to impact the world. Do everything you can to stay alive and well."

Most of us "burn the candle at both ends" during our youth, playing and working as hard as we can. Many of us have food habits that aren't ideal or we neglect to make enough time for good sleep. But abusing your body to make the most of now can mean robbing from your future. It's true, our bodies are just packaging. But a long, happy, and fruitful life is much easier to achieve when we're taking care of that packaging.

REFLECTION

Why not set some achievable health goals? Can you add some exercise into your week? Perhaps cut out something unhealthy from your diet? Can you aim to get an extra hour of sleep per night? Do it for yourself and your great future.

Lord, thank you so much for my body! I'm so grateful for all to the amazing things it does and allows me to do. Please help me to take good care of it. If I have habits or addictions that won't do me good in the long run, please help me to deal with them and beat them in the name of Jesus. Amen.

Be Aware of the Seasons

And after you have suffered a little while, the God of all grace,
who has called you to his eternal glory in Christ, will himself
restore, confirm, strengthen, and establish you.

1 PETER 5:10 ESV

During the spring we often find that the clouds are clearing in
more ways than one. We find the blue sky makes us feel a whole
lot brighter and more ready to take on the world. If you've been
feeling especially low throughout the winter, you may have been
suffering from seasonal affective disorder (SAD). It's worth
taking time to speak to a doctor about this and to research the
many ways you can tackle it. Sunlight is a basic human need and
without enough, we can start to feel low and irritable.

If this sounds like you, I want to remind you that the sun
will come out again and these feelings will change. But in the
meantime, please look into the practical and simple techniques
that can offset the symptoms of SAD. Now and again we all need
someone to remind us we're going to be okay. So here goes: *You're
going to be okay.*

REFLECTION

Try to get out in the sunlight a little more or buy a special lamp.
It also helps to enjoy whatever special things the season holds. A
walk in the falling leaves can brighten an autumn day, and warm
spiced drinks can lift the spirits on a dark winter night.

Lord, help me overcome the gloominess that comes with a
darker season. Help me to find whatever joys lie within the
current months and make the most of them until the season
shifts. In Jesus' name, amen.

By His Spirit

"Not by might nor by power, but by my Spirit,"
says the LORD Almighty.

ZECHARIAH 4:6

Sometimes the task or battle that faces us *is* impossible. There is too much work for one person, or we don't have the resources. We usually don't have the power or the authority to make the changes we want to see in the world, and this can lead us to feeling defeated. But if you're attempting the impossible, you're a fool. Yes, that's right—a fool!

No, I'm not trying to discourage you from attempting the impossible. This is just a gentle reminder that human beings can't do the impossible! Only God can do the impossible. So the pressure to feed five thousand with five loaves and two fish is not on you. The pressure to part the Red Sea is not on you. God, by his Spirit, accomplishes these things *through* you.

REFLECTION

I no longer worry that I'm not strong enough to accomplish my dreams. We don't need to be strong in order to do the impossible. The impossible cannot be done in our own strength. So today, let's allow ourselves the peace that comes by knowing God is the one who does the heavy lifting.

Thank you, Lord, that all things are possible in you. Thank you even more that my lack of strength or worldly power is irrelevant, because your Holy Spirit is the one who makes the impossible possible. I'm trusting that you'll do the impossible in my life. In Jesus' name, amen.

Encourage Others

Whoever brings blessing will be enriched,
and the one who waters will himself be watered.

PROVERBS 11:25 ESV

The first young adults' conference I went to was very powerful, and I loved watching thousands of young people sing and engage in worship together. But I wasn't doing so great myself. I'd been struggling to get my head around a few faith-related things and not "feeling" God's presence very much. I was beginning to wonder if I believed at all.

Then one evening the pastor encouraged us to pray for one another. I walked over to a friend and placed my hand on her back. As I began to pray, I felt the Holy Spirit surging through me. I was sure this was God's response to my friend. But another friend came over and placed a hand on me and said, "I think God's really doing something in you, Philippa." I felt the tremendous power of God's presence in me and the dreary feeling began to clear out. The next day I felt that a totally new season had begun.

When we make ourselves a channel for God's Holy Spirit to reach someone else, his moving through us brings new life. We feel his presence and become renewed.

REFLECTION

Take time today to refresh someone else. Take out your phone and send someone a lovely text. Thank someone for something. Even offer to pray with someone. You might feel wonderfully refreshed.

Lord, today I'm taking time to pray for someone else. I believe that by fully focusing on that person, you will refresh me too! So bless this person abundantly now. In Jesus' name, amen.

God Knows Your Mountain

The mountains quake before him and the hills melt away.

NAHUM 1:5

You may have a mountain in your life right now—a large, overwhelming, and seemingly impossible obstacle. It could be an illness, a relationship, or a work crisis. Perhaps you're stuck between a rock and a hard place and just don't know which way to turn. Perhaps you have a dream but lack the resource to see that dream come to fruition. Perhaps you've received a diagnosis and the odds for your recovery have left you in shock. Whatever your mountain, it's likely to cause anxiety because you can't see beyond it or move around it, and you have no idea what the journey might cost you.

REFLECTION

Here's a comforting thought: When I'm facing a mountain, it helps me to know that God in his infinite wisdom knows *everything* there is to know about that mountain. Nothing about it surprises him. It isn't intimidating to him, and he doesn't need you to describe it. To God your impossible barrier is but a grain of sand. Here's a prayer I've been praying that might help you too:

Lord, you know my mountain. You know its dimensions and scale. You know what it weighs. As I call this mountain to mind, I pray in Jesus' name that you would move it. Thank you, Lord. In Jesus' name, amen.

Don't Wait for a Crisis to Access Your Strength

"Have I not commanded you? Be strong and courageous!
Do not tremble or be dismayed, for the LORD your God
is with you wherever you go."

JOSHUA 1:9 NASB

If there's one thing I've learned, it's that a crisis brings out the best in me. It brings out my fighting spirit and even my compassion. I'm amazed at what I can get done when the pressure is on and it's do or die! But we don't have to wait for a crisis to access those great qualities. All that passion, tenacity, and inner strength is within you right now. Those amazing, superhuman resources are already there.

Imagine what we might be able to achieve if we applied a crisis action spirit to the things we care about right now. Let's not wait for a do-or-die moment to give our best. Let's resolve today to fight for what we believe in as though today is all we have.

REFLECTION

If today was all you really had, what would you prioritize? What impossible goal would you reach for? Don't wait! Write down what you're desperate to achieve and go for it today.

Lord, help me to reach out and access the incredible strength your Spirit provides. Help me to use all my battle instincts to fight the good fight and not just defend myself. Thank you, Lord, that you are with me every time I go on the offensive for your good. In Jesus' name, amen.

Pray

You know when I sit down and when I rise up; You understand
my thought from afar. You scrutinize my path and my lying down,
and are intimately acquainted with all my ways. Even before there
is a word is on my tongue, behold, O LORD, You know it all.

PSALM 139:2–4 NASB

There is no job too small for God. When I first moved to
Sheffield, I was totally new to all things "faith." I had a job I
wasn't very good at, and every day felt like a real battle. I moved
in with a couple of students who were strong believers, and we
began a daily tradition of praying together at breakfast. A first
this tradition was a bit of a chore to me. Along with the stress of
facing work, I didn't feel I could make time for a prayer meeting.
But I decided to try—and it changed my life!

Taking a few minutes with friends to speak out my thoughts
and fears changed my entire outlook on the day. The key was not
overlooking a small worry. I learned that small thoughts had the
power to mount up and create bigger issues. Bringing them to
God helped calm the chatter of an anxious mind with his peace.

REFLECTION

Is something bothering you right now? Today I encourage you to
hand it *all* over to God. It doesn't matter how small the issue may
be, because he has the capacity to deal with *everything* you bring
to him. I pray you'll feel peace and the protection of a loving
Father with you in every part of today.

Lord, I bring each and every thing that bothers me before you
right now, from the very smallest to the greatest concern. You
care about everything I'm going through; if it bothers me, it
bothers you. So I lay it all before you now. In Jesus' name, amen.

Celebrate All Your Achievements

The Lord is my strength and my shield; my heart trusts in him,
and he helps me.

PSALM 28:7

I felt a great sense of accomplishment when I completed my
first album. But rewind a few years, and it was an achievement
for me even to get out of the house. If you're a new parent,
victory for you might be having your new baby's clothes clean
and organized. If you're a chronic illness warrior, you might
congratulate yourself for a successful trip to the mall. To this day
I consider it an achievement when the house is clean, everyone's
fed, and the bills are paid because these boxes can be hard to keep
checked in a busy life. The achievements one person may take for
granted could be a huge accomplishment for you, so it won't do
you any good to compare.

Don't look at the person who just climbed Mount Everest
and feel like a failure. For you, completing your basic self-care
might be like climbing Everest. So go ahead and celebrate all your
achievements.

REFLECTION

Why not make a little list of the things you managed to
accomplish today? They may not be huge things, but everything
counts. You're doing great.

Lord, thank you for what I've been able to accomplish today.
What I have achieved may not look great next what others have
managed. But for me it was a journey and I'm pleased with what
you've been able to do through me. Help me to keep moving
forward, one small accomplishment at a time. In Jesus' name,
amen.

Face the Storm

As the Philistine moved closer to attack him, David ran quickly
toward the battle line to meet him.

1 Samuel 17:48

Some storms in life we must flee; others need to be faced.
When times get hard, running away can seem like the most
appealing option. If we truly believe that another city, church,
or workplace will be full of perfect friends and easygoing
people, we're deceiving ourselves. If we think a new partner will
eliminate every unhappiness, we're likewise deceived. No city or
relationship has 24/7 sunshine.

We were made to take light and sun with us wherever we
tread. But if we don't deal with that bad weather in our own
lives, we can travel far and wide and the clouds will follow. Face
the storm and it just might relent. When David was faced with a
giant, he didn't run. Although his adversary was far greater in size
and strength, he knew that in order to beat him he had to face
him. So today, face the giant. Face the storm.

REFLECTION

What in your life do you need to face up to? What do you feel
tempted to run away from? If all is well for you in this area, take a
moment to pray for someone in your life who seems to be under
the weather and needs to see a break in the clouds.

Lord, help me to have courage and face down the storms
in my life. When I feel I want to run to avoid the inevitable
consequences of my own choices, give me the strength to stand
firm and face my giants. I know that through me you can beat
them all. In Jesus' name, amen.

Be Creative!

And whatever you do, in word or deed, do everything in the name of the Lord Jesus, giving thanks to God the Father through him.

COLOSSIANS 3:17 ESV

Our creative capacities can be incredibly uplifting and bring healing. We all have creativity in our DNA; after all we are made in the image of the Creator!

Creativity takes many forms. I love to write, make music, and occasionally draw. But at this very moment, my husband is taking a piece of wood that he found in the loft and turning it into some shelves for our kitchen. From engineering to homemaking, creativity is an integral part of what makes us tick.

If you're feeling a little blue, it might be because your creative muscles need flexing. Perhaps you've been neglecting your creative side—or perhaps you need to discover it for the first time. Why not find some way of expressing yourself creatively? It could be just the pick-me-up you need.

REFLECTION

What's your favorite creative outlet? Is there something you could spend a little more time on? Is there something creative you'd like to try? Take a little time to pray about this today.

Lord, thank you for being such an incredible, creative God. Thank you that you've placed in me a desire to make something new out of nothing. Help me to identify ways to be creative and flex those creative "muscles." In Jesus' name, amen.

Worship in an Original Way

Sing to the LORD a new song; sing to the LORD, all the earth.
PSALM 96:1

When it comes to glorifying the Master of this universe, don't let history or culture put your worship in a box. A person of faith should never feel creatively restricted. We represent the Author of creation, the one who thought of stars, rainbow fish, and snowflakes. A God so creatively free surely doesn't have rules about how worship should look and sound.

Take just a moment to think about the hilarity, the obscenity, and the boundless innovation in nature. See how he has given us permission to forget the lines and boxes and do something original? You were not chosen despite being different; you were chosen *because* you are different. Feel free to do something new.

REFLECTION
Do you have an idea for how God could use you creatively in worship? Write out some thoughts. Remember, there are no right answers and no limitations to what can be done.

Lord, I'm so in awe of the innovative artist that you are. There is simply no end to what you can invent! So help me never to be bound by what other people do as their expressions of worship to you. Put a new song in my mouth today, Lord! Help me to bless everyone I meet with fresh expressions of who you are. In Jesus' name, amen.

Learn to Play

"Blessed are the pure in heart, for they shall see God."
MATTHEW 5:8 NASB

We love the idea of being forever young. Most of us enjoy getting lost in a favorite childhood story or movie. If we're honest, there's probably a touch of Peter Pan in all of us; we never *really* want to grow up. How awesome, then, that God actually *requires* us to be childlike in order to enter the kingdom of heaven? He loves for us to cast off the cares of adult life and simply be as children.

If we look at the children in our lives, what can they teach us? What is it that lights them up? Here are some observations:

- They know how to love without judgment.
- They usually make friends easily and love indiscriminately.
- They love to be outdoors, exploring the wonders of their natural surroundings and finding joy in simple pleasures like making daisy chains and eating ice cream.
- They view each day as a new chance to play, have fun, and make thrilling discoveries about life.

REFLECTION

If God requires us to be childlike, then it stands to reason that he encourages these qualities. How can you nurture the child within today? Do something that awakens the little you.

Lord, help me to grow down today! I want to see the world as I used to see it—as a place of discovery and adventure. Today, help blow off the layers of dust that the years have brought and bring youth back into my perspective. In Jesus' name, amen.

God as Father

"And I will be a father to you, and you shall be sons and daughters to Me," says the Lord Almighty.

2 CORINTHIANS 6:18 NASB

If we are required to come to God as a child, guess what that makes him? Yes, a Father. This imagery can be unappealing for those who haven't enjoyed great relationships with their earthly parents. But grasping this is so integral to a fulfilled and joyful life as a believer. What does that dad/kid relationship look like? As someone who has been blessed with a treasured relationship with a good dad, here are some parallels I've drawn that might help.

I used to run to my dad at the school gates. I looked forward to seeing him and missed spending time with him. He was my friend. I loved to share my stories and experiences with him after school. I wanted to be close to him and I trusted him. My dad used to cover for me if I made a mistake. I once spilled tea in a hotel bed and he took the blame when the maid came. I was accepted. I knew I could rely on my dad to be proud of who I was and my accomplishments. I was dear to him and he'd do anything for me. He was kind to me. He always bought what he could for me and loved to see me smile.

REFLECTION

God's love is all these things and more. He feels a deep, rich affection for you. You are free to approach him with all the familiarity that you would a best friend, a good dad.

Lord, help me to truly know you as Father. I want to have that closeness and affection with you. I want to feel as protected by you as a child should feel protected by a dad. It will be a process, Lord, but guide me through this. In Jesus' name, amen.

Childlike Faith

"Truly I tell you, anyone who will not receive the kingdom of God like a little child will never enter it." And he took the children in his arms, placed his hands on them and blessed them.

MARK 10:15–16

A child's belief that anything is possible is sometimes viewed as naïveté. But the Bible tells us that such faith is spiritual clarity, a gift straight from heaven. It's a purity that only time spent in the world can rob us of. The world teaches us to be unbelieving and cynical. We're taught to treat people with suspicion, to shake off the wide-eyed beliefs of childhood and become more "realistic" about what's possible.

There's certainly a maturing process that needs to happen, and wisdom should come alongside our childlike faith in time. Of course, we must use our discernment to guard our hearts in relationships. But it's a mistake to confuse those things with being cynical. Living with a cynical view of everything is a sure way to become unhappy.

REFLECTION

Prayerfully ask God to give you wisdom while allowing you to retain your faith that all things are possible! Today, cast off the dust you've gathered in life and be restored to childlike faith.

Lord, I want to run to you like a child. I want to truly believe that you are capable of anything. I have picked up some doubts and even become cynical at times. So today I'm praying for you to restore the clarity that others may deem naïveté. It's never naïve to believe you, Lord. In Jesus' name, amen.

Progress is Messy

I am confident of this, that the one who began a good work among you will bring it to completion by the day of Jesus Christ.

PHILIPPIANS 1:6 NRSV

I have some friends who work for a fabulous Christian debt management agency, Christians Against Poverty (CAP). They often enter people's lives at the toughest time and save the day. People may be quite desperate, struggling to make ends meet, or even afford food to eat. It's always a great relief when CAP comes in to deal with creditors and bring things back under control. But before they can begin the rescue mission, all of the details have to emerge. It often means facing some tough numbers, hard truths, and accepting some real responsibility. It's a tough process, but every bit worth the hassle for the peace on the other side.

If you've begun a restoration work in your life, don't be discouraged when things appear worse for a time. Think about it. The bed looks messy while you're making it. A house can look like a disaster zone while you're redecorating. Life can look like its deteriorating while you're working on your circumstances. But just because it's not pretty yet doesn't mean you've failed.

REFLECTION

If life looks a little messy today, say a prayer for patience. Know that while things might look like chaos, you're working on it with God's help, and the dust will settle soon.

Lord, things sure are upside down right now. There are many areas of my life that need work. But I'm thankful that you're faithful to complete what you have begun in me. Eventually things will make more sense, and I will be able to sit in the tidy surroundings of a well-tended life with you. In Jesus' name, amen.

Count the Answers

Every good gift and every perfect gift is from above, coming down from the Father of lights, with whom there is no variation or shadow due to change.

JAMES 1:17 ESV

As we're discussing happy habits this month, it's worth reminding ourselves yet again to count our blessings. All too often we swiftly move from prayer to prayer, want to want. It's very easy to lose sight of how far we've come and to forget the many times we've had breakthroughs and answers to prayer! We don't like to reminisce too often about the horrible things we've been through. But doing so can remind us of this wonderful fact: we made it through! What harrowed you in January is quite likely far from your mind at this point. That in itself is a reason to celebrate and to be grateful. After all, a life filled with gratitude cannot fail to be filled with joy.

REFLECTION

Take a moment today to look back at the year so far and take stock of some of the incredible blessings you have received.

Lord, thank you that everything good in my life has come from you. My loved ones, my home, and everything that brings me joy. Thank you that you're always good, always showering me with blessings. You are good in your very nature, God. Today all I want to say is thank you. In Jesus' name, amen.

People Are the Only Real Treasure

"Do not store up for yourselves treasures on earth, where moths and vermin destroy, and where thieves break in and steal. But store up for yourselves treasures in heaven, where moths and vermin do not destroy, and where thieves do not break in and steal. For where your treasure is, there your heart will be also."

MATTHEW 6:19–21

Many of our woes connect to material things. No question, it's irritating when the washer breaks. It can be a huge inconvenience when the car breaks down. But it's always good to remember this: Our cars, houses, gadgets, and other treasures will become obsolete in time. The things we worked and saved for only a couple of years ago are already losing value. It's probably only a matter of time before the four walls you prayed so hard to earn begin to lose their charm or their suitability for your lifestyle.

The only thing in this world that never loses value is a human being. So no matter how hard we might work to maintain our lifestyles, it must never eclipse the time investment we make into the people we love. After all, they're the only things we can take with us to heaven.

REFLECTION

Is there someone you need to set time aside for? Have you been allowing a relationship to slide? Why not put down what you're doing and invite someone you love for coffee. It could be life-giving for that person in ways you'll never know.

Lord, help me to remember that the people I reach for you are all I can take with me beyond this life. Help me not to so much focus on the things that will burn up. Please, Lord, steer me toward each person you want me to reach. In Jesus' name, amen.

No Day Is Wasted

"For as the rain and the snow come down from heaven, and do not return there without watering the earth and making it bear and sprout, and furnishing seed to the sower and bread to the eater; so will My word be which goes forth from My mouth; it will not return to Me empty, without accomplishing what I desire, and without succeeding in the matter for which I sent it."

ISAIAH 55:10–11 NASB

I've had many a day that didn't turn out the way I planned. Chasing a dream or goal means constantly "showing up," whatever the weather. We send thousands of email messages and attend countless meetings. We do writing sessions that lead nowhere and go to networking events that come up empty. We put on outreach events that are poorly attended and bake cakes that don't get eaten. Things usually pick up eventually, but truthfully we may never see the fruit we'd like to see from our efforts.

But, you know, *nothing* is wasted. God promises that his word never returns to him empty (Isaiah 55:11). So every time we move forward to achieve something positive in his name, *he is working*—even if we can't see the results with our eyes.

REFLECTION

God can use even a no-show moment to bless you. So let go of what didn't happen today and know that God was working, even in the empty spaces.

Lord, even though parts of today felt like a waste of time, I know you were working in everything. You don't waste a thing. Thank you for the amazing things you are always doing behind the scenes and that whenever I step out in your name, you accomplish something. In Jesus' name, amen.

The Beauty in Suffering

Praise be to the God and Father of our Lord Jesus Christ, the
Father of compassion and the God of all comfort, who comforts
us in all our troubles, so that we can comfort those in any trouble
with the comfort we ourselves receive from God.

2 CORINTHIANS 1:3–4

The news can be a distressing overview of humanity. The amount
of suffering and evil in the world can be overwhelming.

Surfing the channels, I stumbled upon an emotional tribute
concert to our armed servicemen. The love expressed for these
men and women who laid down their lives during a time of
war was one of the most beautiful things I'd ever seen. Later I
stumbled upon two reports about people making a personal
sacrifice to care for others. I realized that all these moving
displays of humanity had been born out of suffering.

In these testing times, when evil so often seems to triumph,
God's goodness overflows in the hearts of kind people. There is a
wealth of generosity, compassion, and charity that matches evil,
step for step. In the end, the light of good always outshines the
darkness. Everywhere there are glimpses of heaven on earth.

REFLECTION

Don't be discouraged by what you see in the news. When we care
for one another, grieving and celebrating as brothers and sisters,
the kingdom of heaven shines in the darkness.

Lord, thank you for the incredible compassion that can be found
among your people. Thank you that even in darkness, your light
always shines brightly through the love and kindness of your
children. Help me always to see and to celebrate this. In Jesus'
name, amen.

Chipping Away at Freedom

"So if the Son sets you free, you will be free indeed."
JOHN 8:36

One of my favorite movies is *The Shawshank Redemption*. The plot is about an innocent man, wrongly accused and convicted of murder. He has no choice but to resign himself to life behind bars. But after decades within prison walls, the guards enter his room one morning to find him gone. They can't see how this could possibly have happened. Until they pull back a poster to find a makeshift tunnel.

It turns out that years earlier he acquired a tiny craft hammer, only big enough to remove the tiniest chips of the stone. But the moment the small tool hits the palm of his hand, you see the light of freedom in his eyes. He begins a nightly ritual of chipping away, inch by inch at the wall of his lonely cell. It takes years, but every day that passes becomes that much easier because he knows he is free. Inside the prison grounds—doing chores, suffering abuse from prison guards—he is free. Because he's been given the right tool and he's begun the journey.

When it comes to our struggles and addictions, we tend to think of ourselves as either "free" or "enslaved." This can be confusing for those who as Christians feel they should be experiencing complete freedom, yet they still feel bound.

The distinction is this: As believers we receive *spiritual* freedom instantly, but complete freedom from our circumstances doesn't come right away. Freedom is more of a journey. It's something that begins in our spirit and takes a little time to work its way into our lives. Freedom may *begin* when we invite God into our hearts. But freedom from financial problems, bad habits, addictions, or difficult situations can be a slow process.

REFLECTION

Perhaps something in your life still enslaves you. Perhaps you have an addiction or an abusive relationship you feel imprisoned by. Perhaps you suffer from something as ordinary as low self-esteem. Why not ask God to minister to you in this area of your life? It may take a little time. But once you are free in his Spirit, you will be free indeed.

Lord, thank you that you have set me free in Jesus. Today help me to take the tools you've given me and faithfully continue to work on freedom from old habits and behaviors. Help my mind and body to quickly catch up with the freedom you've given me within. In Jesus' name, amen.

Unhelpful Phrases

Be completely humble and gentle; be patient, baring with one another in love.

EPHESIANS 4:2

Telling someone who is struggling with something like depression to "snap out of it" is like telling someone to solve a math problem on a broken calculator. You can't do it because the hardware has failed. It doesn't matter how well the numbers should add up; the calculator won't work.

There is a real difference between the low moods and thoughts that accompany tough times, and the dark, nonsensical fog that is mental illness. I know because I've experienced both. Being "down" is horrible but normal. Being depressed is a system failure. We have to remember that those who have taken their own lives haven't necessarily been making a rational choice based on their assessment of life; more often they are unwell people who are experiencing unbearable symptoms.

REFLECTION

The *truth* is, there is always *hope*. Your mind and body can be well again. Your life has great value and purpose. If anything is telling you otherwise, please recognize that this might not be just a "low" period—seek help.

Father, for all those out there who are experiencing the agony of depression, I reach out to you and pray right now. I pray that you would heal and deliver them. I pray you would lead them to the best possible professional and spiritual help. Please, Lord, allow them to feel and experience renewed hope in you. In Jesus' name, amen.

Ditch Old Coping Mechanisms

Therefore, if anyone is in Christ, the new creation has come: The old has gone, the new is here!

2 Corinthians 5:17

Our old TV remote was broken. Only the Down and Up buttons worked, so naturally I stopped trying to use the number buttons all together. One day I made an amusing discovery about myself. Nearly six months after getting a new TV and remote, I was still doing the same thing on the brand-new remote. The new device worked just fine, yet I remained stuck in that old coping habit.

Coping methods die hard. Even though as believers we are new creations in Jesus, it's easy to revert to our broken behavior purely out of habit. Our default coping measures in themselves create extra work and potentially new problems. Remind yourself that you've been restored. You don't need to act like the broken remote you once were!

REFLECTION

If there's a habit you've been resorting to out of your former brokenness, today is the day to let it go. Ask God to show you what you've been using as a coping mechanism but no longer need. Now ask him to replace it with habits of wholeness! Today is a new day.

Lord, I am so thankful to be a new creation in you. You have done incredible miracles in my life already. So now I pray that you would help me kick my own coping habits. I want to live as the whole and free person you've called me to be. Help me to let go of the old way of doing things to make way for something far better. In Jesus' name, amen.

Get That Filter On

Do not conform to the pattern of this world, but be transformed by the renewing of your mind. Then you will be able to test and approve what God's will is—his good, pleasing and perfect will.

ROMANS 12:2

A few years ago, I had a morning revelation. Not ten minutes out of bed, and I realized that every single one of my thoughts had been negative. It went something like this:

I'm tired. I can't face work today. I'm going to get something wrong and get into trouble with the boss. If I lose this job, I might have to move. What if I never achieve my dreams and have to work there forever?

It was about this time that I realized I was bringing myself down. Instead of fighting my wall of negative thoughts, I was inviting them. That's when I developed my "filter on" trick. I pictured a switch in my brain that could turn on a negative thought filter. Whenever I'm spiraling into negativity, I picture it, then I say it aloud. It's amazingly effective.

REFLECTION

Try it for yourself today! Make an effort to notice those negative thoughts and kick that filter into gear. Let "filter on" be your mantra for the day!

Lord, you know how important it is for my mind to be filled with good thoughts. I pray that you would renew my mind today. Transform me as I fix my thoughts on you. Be my filter, Lord, and help me see what is good so I can figure out what your will is for my day. In Jesus' name, amen.

Love Yourself

Love is patient and kind; love does not envy or boast;
it is not arrogant or rude.

1 CORINTHIANS 13:4 ESV

What do you say when you look in the mirror? Do you say kind things? Or are you critical? Motivational speakers are popular for a reason—they help people. They change a person's outlook for the better. Be careful, dear reader, not to be your own worst enemy, your own worst critic. If you're constantly criticizing your own character and appearance, those thoughts can really demotivate you. Before you know it, you will slow down and even grind to a halt.

When God talks about love, he doesn't intend for us to only offer it to others. Each one of us is a child of God; therefore, we're also required to love ourselves.

REFLECTION

God describes all of the aspects of love in the first letter to the Corinthians. Today, try to apply these principles to the way you view and treat yourself. Are you patient with yourself when you make mistakes? Are you kind to yourself at all times? Do you allow yourself to move on from mistakes, or are you keeping a record of your own wrongs? God means for you to be as gracious toward the person in the mirror as you are toward everyone else.

Lord, thank you that you love me so much. Help me to love myself as you do. I do not want to ignore what you teach about love when it comes to myself. In Jesus' name, amen.

Your Weakness Can Bring Someone Else Strength

That is why, for Christ's sake, I delight in weaknesses,
in insults, in hardships, in persecutions, in difficulties.
For when I am weak, then I am strong.

2 Corinthians 12:10

At thirteen years of age, I had such a hard time in school that my daily project was getting out of it. Going through those gates made me panic. I cried when my alarm went off. I hid in the school bathroom when the bell rang for lessons to begin. At the time I was afraid, angry, and worried that I didn't have a future. But years later I find myself answering questions and giving advice on a regular basis to teenagers just like the one I used to be. Somehow, God has been able to use my weakness to bring strength to others. If you're struggling in any area right now, be it relational, spiritual, emotional, or financial, take heart. What you're going through can become golden guidance for someone like you in years to come.

REFLECTION

Why not begin to journal your experiences? Even the bad ones could be vital for someone else down the line. Turn your trash into treasure right now by mining out the gold from your trial.

Lord, it's not always easy to believe my weakness could be useful to you. But I so want to set others free from what has bound me. Help me to see the value in what I'm learning and to store up these experiences for the right moment. In Jesus' name, amen.

Miracles Happen

Then He who sat on the throne said, "Behold, I make all things new."
REVELATION 21:5 NKJV

When it comes to mental health and well-being, miracles truly happen. If a girl like me, who used to feel panic in the supermarket and spent most of my hours hiding away, can tour the world and entertain people as a job, God can do *anything.*

I never thought I would lead a regular life, let alone a life that might encourage others. What has taken place in my mind, body, and spirit is nothing short of miraculous. I believe that on top of all the practical measures we can put in place for our mental good, we should never underestimate the power of the Holy Spirit. God can heal our broken circuits. He can dig down into the most malfunctioning parts of us. If you feel you've tried everything and nothing seems to work, that is the perfect place for God's glory to shine.

REFLECTION

Right now, I'm joining with you in prayer for our freedom and renewed mental well-being. I'm coming alongside you to say yes and amen to a joy-filled life overflowing with adventure and wholeness. Today I am believing with you for the miracle you need, as well as a miracle someone you love might need.

God, you're more than able to fully restore us, mind, body, and soul. Today we invite your healing touch into our innermost parts—the parts where bad habits live and where memories of hurtful words and actions have left scars. We invite you in to do what you do best, Lord—make all things new! In Jesus' name, amen.

Happy Is Beautiful

Strength and dignity are her clothing, and she smiles at the future.

PROVERBS 31:25 NASB

Apparently you can avoid wrinkles by not smiling. But then you also avoid wearing the most beautiful thing of all! A smile lights up the face like nothing else. It's the quickest way to connect and share a little love in everyday life. Sure, we may avoid a few laughter lines by choosing the pout over the grin, but who wants to live in a world that values looks over laughter? Who wants to be miserably flawless?

When we're surrounded by celebrities who put such a high premium on flawlessness, it's easy to become influenced. But don't ever forget the people who've impacted your life the most. Did they always have a straight face? Or did they laugh and enjoy laughter?

REFLECTION

So many social media posts share a message of physical perfection. We can begin to adopt the standard that we must look doll-like and immaculate. How does that mesh with God's plan for us to love life?

Thank you, Lord, for my face. But thank you more for the things in life that make me smile. Thank you for the laughter that creates laughter lines. I'd rather have a heart filled with joy than perfect skin and a heavy heart. Amen.

Beautiful Is as Beautiful Does

How beautiful on the mountains are the feet
of those who bring good news.
ISAIAH 52:7

My Nanna had a saying: "Handsome is as handsome does." It's true. Outward appearances are empty without kindness, integrity, and love.

Maya Angelou said, "I've learned that people will forget what you said, people will forget what you did, but people will never forget how you made them feel." The same can be said regarding appearances. In the end it isn't our clothes, physique, or symmetry that will be remembered; it's how we made people feel. If we gossip or mistreat others, those around us will not like what they see. If we can be kind and make people feel safe, beauty will always shine from within. So go on—do beautiful and be beautiful!

REFLECTION

Have quarrels or disagreements with others brought out the worst in you? You're not alone; we all have done it. But you don't have to be the person who gossips or slings insults anymore. You can begin today to be the person who brings only good news.

Lord, I know I haven't always treated people exactly how I'd like to be treated myself. I've engaged in gossip, and I've said things about others that weren't very favorable. I'm sorry. Help me to be a beacon of positivity today. Help my words carry light and life so my days may be filled with beauty. In Jesus' name, amen.

Kindness Is Beautiful

She opens her mouth in wisdom,
and the teaching of kindness is on her tongue.

PROVERBS 31:26 NASB

After spending a lot of my life in the entertainment industry, I thought I'd seen a lot of beautiful faces. But I was truly blown away by the beauty I witnessed in 2016 when I took a trip to Africa with the Leprosy Mission. I didn't know much about this horrible disease, other than that it was both disabling and disfiguring.

On my trip it was sobering to spend time among those afflicted with the disease. I learned that the disease is very treatable and highly unlikely to affect anyone with a healthy immune system like me. Still, it's severely disfiguring, attacking the nerves and causing numbness, which leads to accidents and injuries for the sufferer, particularly in the hands and feet. By meeting the people who spend their days caring for these unfortunate people—dressing their wounds in the blistering heat, giving them care and advice, and literally washing their feet as Jesus might—I saw true beauty as never before.

REFLECTION

When you reach out to others, your internal critic begins to quiet down. Consider a mission trip. Or do something to help another person to shift your focus. There is nothing more beautiful than kindness. Always be kind and you'll always be beautiful.

Lord, help me to be kind as you are kind. Help me to have the light of love burning so strongly in me that people see it first. Let them see your Spirit, your gentleness, and your all-encompassing love. Provide an opportunity and the resources for me to go show kindness—here and abroad. In Jesus' name, amen.

You're Flawesome!

You are altogether beautiful, my darling; there is no flaw in you.
SONG OF SOLOMON 4:7

Grab a mirror. Now, take a long look at the details you consider to be flaws. If you have wrinkles, pay attention to them. If you have scars, take a moment to run your finger gently along each one. If you have time, even count them.

Now think of each one as a medal. A passed driving test, a finished project. A child raised, a marriage saved, a breakdown survived. Laughter, tears, blemishes, life. This is you. Your face tells a story like no one else's.

We live in an age where imperfections can be erased with fillers and chemicals, but only time, experience, and survival can add them! Perhaps it's time to unlearn the idea that your face is flawed and begin to see it more as a work of art that God began and you are finishing.

REFLECTION

Take a moment to appreciate the flaws that make you unique. Try to view them as something beautiful instead of something to hide. You're flawesome!

Lord, thank you for the story my face tells. Thank you for everything I've experienced and survived. Please help me not to be so critical of my so-called flaws but instead to embrace them as a part of me and a totally unique work of art. It won't be easy, but please help me start today. In Jesus' name, amen.

Your Power Isn't in Your Looks

Your beauty should not come from outward adornment,
such as elaborate hairstyles and the wearing of gold jewelry
or fine clothes. Rather, it should be that of your inner self,
the unfading beauty of a gentle and quiet spirit,
which is of great worth in God's sight.

1 PETER 3:3–4

There's a popular notion in twenty-first-century society that showing flesh makes a girl more powerful. Young women are encouraged to assert their identity by showing more skin. This comes from the evolution of our culture across the centuries. As the role and perception of women has changed in society, so too has fashion. As society has rightfully recognized the equal rights of womankind, fashion has become more liberal. I agree that all people should feel free to dress however they feel comfortable. But to limit a woman's power to her clothing choices is to objectify and devalue her all over again.

REFLECTION

There certainly is power in the way a woman presents herself. But a woman's true power is found in her intellect, kindness, creativity, and passion. Don't let anyone make you feel shame for the way you choose to dress. Instead, always remember that you can conquer the world in your jeans and T-shirt.

Lord, help me focus on the things that truly give me power—my personality, gentleness, intellect, and your Holy Spirit. Thank you for the freedom to wear whatever makes me feel most comfortable instead of trying to achieve a certain dominant appearance ("power dressing"). In Jesus' name, amen.

Beauty Is Cultural

How beautiful you are my darling! Oh, how beautiful!
Your eyes are like doves.

SONG OF SOLOMON 1:15

What the world considers to be physically beautiful is changing every moment. Everything from eyebrow shape to body type falls in and out of fashion year upon year. Not only that, but from continent to continent different things are considered appealing. Where one culture will favor a lean physique, another will admire the fuller figure. Where one culture likes a tanned skin, another will stay out of the sun.

What does this tell us? It tells us two things: First, whatever your look, you're likely to be the archetype of beauty somewhere in the world! But more importantly, beauty is totally subjective; it lies in the eye of the beholder. We all see it and appreciate it differently. Therefore, it's a huge mistake to put it in a box and try to aim for it. It's a waste of energy and attention.

REFLECTION

Take a moment today to think outside the beauty box. Realize that your beauty is unique and interesting—ultimately, it's not what matters most at all. The One who created you made you beautiful and anyone who matters will see that beauty as clear as day.

Lord, help me to embrace my unique beauty. My mind may be full of ideas as to what true beauty is, but you designed me and I'm beautiful in your eyes. Help me to know that this is all that matters. In Jesus' name, amen.

Beware Memes

But test everything that is said. Hold on to what is good.

1 Thessalonians 5:21 NLT

In this digital age, we often see captioned pics ("memes") that go viral, and for some reason they carry a type of authority. If a meme goes viral, we presume that it represents the truth. But many of these phrases are far from truthful. Phrases like, "Real woman have curves" are particularly toxic, because they reinforce the lie that a woman's worth is in her body shape, her biology.

But the truth is that women come in every shape, and what makes a woman real is not her measurements but her ability to be herself. Her kindness, character, intellect, tenacity, and individuality are what make her fabulous. Real women are encouragers, daughters, mothers, friends, doctors, teachers, thinkers, pioneers, artists, and so much more. Dress size doesn't come into it.

Next time you see a meme like this, pull out your filter. You don't need these kinds of unhelpful lies in your mind.

REFLECTION

Social media can be truly awesome! We can share so much life and so much life-giving truth on platforms such as Facebook. But it's good to prepare yourself for the confusion that comes along with it. Remind yourself not to take memes as gospel truth! They're just slides thrown together by ordinary people who may have very different agendas and views from yours.

Lord, prepare my mind for the images that I'm bound to encounter online. Help me be ready to challenge their truth and their relevance, rooting myself not in what memes say about me but in what you say. In Jesus' name, amen.

"Transformation" Pictures

For physical training is of some value, but godliness has value for all things, holding promise for both the present life and the life to come.

1 TIMOTHY 4:8

Be a little wary of the many "transformation" photos on social media. If you browse suggested profiles and posts, you're likely to see lots of people in fitness gear sporting perfect gym bodies and those all-powerful "Before" and "After" pics side by side. Don't fall for it or click on it. Remember that as you fall down that rabbit hole, most social media platforms are gathering basic information about your age, gender, and interests. They then target you with these posts in order to sell you things.

It's wonderful when people take the time to work on their physical health. It certainly is worth celebrating when someone makes a huge lifestyle change that brings about better health. But most of those "Before" pics are not people whose health was in jeopardy. It's okay if you don't look like the person selling the protein shakes. It's okay if having the perfect physique is not your goal in life. Don't allow social media to decide your priorities.

REFLECTION

The Word tells us that godliness is more important than having the perfect physique. God does instruct us to take care of ourselves, but it's very easy to take this too far and become obsessed. Fitness has some value, but good character is far more valuable.

Lord, thank you for the great resources available for training and taking care of my body. But help me not to focus too hard on physical perfection. I want to be healthy and strong, yet I know you don't want me to focus all my attention there. Give me clarity and self-control in this matter. In Jesus' name, amen.

Scales Can Be a Killjoy

For the kingdom of God is not eating and drinking, but righteousness and peace and joy in the Holy Spirit.

ROMANS 14:17 NASB

A scale can be a useful tool for monitoring your health. If weight is something you're struggling with, then by all means keep using one. I decided a few years ago to ditch mine. I had spent a month in Norway touring and was feeling truly happy in my skin. The cold air made my cheeks rosy, and I love wrapping up in cozy sweaters. Norwegians aren't into wearing makeup very much, so I'd been enjoying wearing less too.

When I hopped on the scale after getting home, I was horrified to find I'd gained five pounds. The way this made me feel was kind of ridiculous. *I've been loving life. Why should that little number affect my mood so much?* I realized at that moment that I'd rather take my sense of beauty from feeling comfortable with myself than from that little needle on the scale! I suggest you do the same.

REFLECTION

As with fitness, self-control with food is a good thing. But obsessively measuring yourself based on a number is not at all healthy. If it robs you of joy, it isn't worth it.

Lord, help me to balance good health and self-control with everything else in life that matters. Help me to have a balanced approach to my weight. It may be a struggle, but I know that with you all things are possible. In Jesus' name, amen.

Beauty Is Ageless

Gray hair is a crown of glory;
it is obtained by following a righteous path.
PROVERBS 16:31 ISV

One day a little before Christmas, I'd gone to our local mall to finish my shopping. Heavy-laden with bags and boxes, I stopped at a small coffee shop for a festive brew and cake. Being alone with my thoughts led me to people watching, and my gaze fell upon an elderly couple seated close by. They both had silvery-white hair and sipped tea side by side, fingers intertwined. I'm guessing that they were in their mid eighties. I was captivated by how handsome and elegant they were. Their appreciation of one another and the sparkle in their eyes was truly beautiful. And in that moment, I realized that love is timeless. And that makes beauty ageless!

REFLECTION

Western society is quite ageist. Many cultures honor their aged better than we do. It's time we restored a healthy admiration for growing old. It doesn't have to mean less fun, less love, or less beauty. Aged beauty is simply a new kind of beauty. So many of us fear getting older, but why not decide to look forward to it instead? To live long while keeping love in your heart would be a wonderful outcome.

Lord, I pray that I would always know love in my heart. If I can live to a ripe old age and still have someone to love, I'll be so very blessed. Help me to embrace aging as a precious gift from you. Old age means more time to enjoy life and more time to love! In Jesus' name, amen.

Beauty Is Unique

But now, O LORD, You are our Father, we are the clay, and you our potter; and all of us are the work of your hand.

ISAIAH 64:8 NASB

In a world of Instagram pictures and plastic surgery, we're beginning to view a certain face as the archetype of beauty. But put the majority of these pictures side by side, and you'll see they're alarmingly similar! All of this can lead us to see our differences as flaws when being unique is exactly what makes us appealing. Variety enhances what appeals to our senses. Scientists have proven that we eat up to 75 percent more food when there is variety in front of us. The changes keep our taste buds engaged and our senses stimulated. Gardeners plant a rich variety of flowers because they complement one another. If we had only yellow tulips in our gardens, we'd soon stop paying attention to them!

Don't ever think that you're ugly because you're different. You might feel like the odd one out on Instagram, but that doesn't make you unattractive. Your unique beauty makes the world a more colorful place and even enhances the beauty of others.

REFLECTION

Take a moment today to thank God for your unique beauty. Thank him for creating such a varied universe that keeps our senses stimulated. You are an integral part of his great design.

Lord, thank you that you only made one of me. Out of seven billion human beings, I am the only one that looks exactly like me. Thank you for your endless creativity. Help me to celebrate and embrace the diversity in and around me. In Jesus' name, amen.

Beauty Is within All of Us

So God created mankind in his own image, in the image of God
he created them; male and female he created them.

GENESIS 1:27

No one is perfect. For some of us, life has deposited all kinds of
rubbish in our hearts. But deep within all of us is a heart that
was created by the Father. He created that heart full of his love
to reflect his beauty. Sometimes, the fullness of that beauty is
obscured by layers of hurt, protective armor, and even shame.
When we allow God's love to polish us up, the beauty of what lies
within is breathtaking. When the layers added by the world are
chipped away by the unfailing hand of grace, the magnificence
underneath is revealed. Your heart is a mirror that shows the
glory of God—revealing his love, kindness, and beauty.

REFLECTION

We're very used to hearing that we were made in God's image.
But think about this for a moment. That we're image-bearers
is taught in God's Word! God is the most glorious, powerful,
beautiful, good, and powerful King. Chances are you're vastly
underestimating your own appeal.

Lord, thank you that you created me in your image. I know
I vastly underestimate myself and that I often criticize the
creation that I am. Help me to view myself as a little piece of
you that deserves to be honored and cherished. In Jesus' name,
amen.

Like Jewels

You shall be a crown of beauty in the hand of the Lord.
ISAIAH 62:3 ESV

When I was a teenager, I wanted nothing more than to look like my friends. I dyed my hair dark to look more like them, and we all wore the same clothes. Because my friends were very beautiful to me, I presumed I had to be like them to be attractive. But looking at us now, grown up and comfortable in our skin, we're more like jewels in a crown—all different shapes, sizes, and colors! Together we represent so much diversity that we're altogether more interesting to look at than we were when we were sixteen.

Our unique beauty serves a valuable purpose in this world. I like to think that we all represent a unique facet of God—that a different part of him is revealed in each of us. Together we are his crown, reflecting his glory.

REFLECTION

Today, remember that your differences are glorious. Remember that your body, mind, and soul are all a reflection of God's character, grace, and incredible creativity.

Lord, help me to see myself for the precious jewel that I am. In your hands I am part of a remarkable crown of beauty. I reflect your glory and splendor. Help me to truly know this about myself today. In Jesus' name, amen.

You're Fine without the Paint

And we all, who with unveiled faces contemplate the Lord's glory,
are being transformed into his image with ever-increasing glory,
which comes from the Lord, who is the Spirit.

2 Corinthians 3:18

Makeup can be a lot of fun. I've enjoyed it since the days of
raiding my teenage sister's makeup bag—smearing her lipstick all
over my four-year-old face. There are those who are quite ready
to shame a woman for wearing makeup, but it's no different
from buying a nice pair of shoes or a great new shirt. It's about
expression and presentation.

However, it's super important to embrace the face you were
born with and not hide behind paint. Makeup, when used as a
mask, might make us feel confident for the day. Before long, it
will achieve the opposite, causing us to feel incomplete without
it. There is nothing wrong with using makeup and clothing as an
extension of your personality and a means of enjoying yourself.
But it's also good to look in the mirror, knowing God only made
one of you and his design is just fine without the paint.

Reflection

Are you used to wearing a lot of makeup? Why not try to cut
back this week? Dare to let your skin breathe and just be. It can
be hard, especially for those with skin conditions. But don't
forget that God loves you with or without the paint and we must
all learn to love ourselves too.

God, being barefaced and unveiled can make me feel vulnerable,
but you want me to be empowered. Please help me to be bold
and accept who I am in you. Give me the courage to be happy in
my skin and not always to cover it up. In Jesus' name, amen.

Diet Yourself Beautiful

But they delight in the law of the LORD,
meditating on it day and night.

PSALM 1:2 NLT

There are so many quick-fix diet ideas online. But so far, the only
one that's *really* made me feel beautiful is the social media diet!
Crazy as it sounds, the consumption of so much social media
can leave us swollen with self-loathing. Lots of people try cutting
out social media altogether, which is an option. It *is* possible,
however, to simply clean up what you're consuming and have
a much better time. Why not give yourself a single week on the
social media diet? It's very simple to follow.

Restrict your Instagram consumption to healthy stuff like
sunsets, real-life friends, and cute animals. Instead of cutting out
carbs, cut out beauty bloggers and fashion accounts! They love
to feed you the lie that you're not good enough. All they really
want you to do is consume the products. Instead, feed on truth.
Consume the verses that tell you you're worth dying for. See how
it goes for a week! You'll probably find you look in the mirror
and see someone pretty special.

REFLECTION

Suggestion: Collect the past few Scripture verses from this book
and simply meditate on them. You could write them out (be
creative!) and leave them where you will see them. Whatever you
do, make sure they're easier to find than the pictures and posts
that drag you down.

God, help me to meditate on your truth rather than on lies.
Thank you for giving me so much great truth to focus on. In
Jesus' name, amen.

The Ultimate Detox

A wise person is hungry for knowledge,
while the fool feeds on trash.
PROVERBS 15:14 NLT

Our goals and aspirations are shaped by what we see daily. When we're constantly sold an ideal of what's attractive and valuable, we can't help but begin to aspire to that ideal. If we want our self-image to be healthy and our goals to be righteous, it's important we take a long hard look at what we consider to be "normal." Chances are our idea of "normal" is based more on advertising than on truth.

This was highlighted for me during a holiday in Cuba. In Cuba there is no advertising. Ten days in Cuba meant seeing far less advertising than I usually would. A couple of days after getting back, I felt quite bombarded by the sheer volume of advertisements.

There is no question that it's a sort of brainwashing, and we need to be fully aware of this to maintain a healthy self-image. Maybe it's not another diet we all need—maybe it's our minds that need the detox.

REFLECTION

As you move throughout the day, pay attention to the power of advertising. Make a few notes about what you observe.

Lord, help me to detox my mind. If I need to remove myself from certain types of social media, please help me. Help me to be aware of the constant advertising I'm exposed to that doesn't aim to build me up, but rather is meant to sell things to me. In Jesus' name, amen.

Go as You

The King's daughter is all glorious within;
her clothing is interwoven with gold.
PSALM 45:13 ESV

As a performer, I've had countless auditions, and as each
opportunity came up, the first thing I would think would be,
What should I wear for this? I would agonize over the right way to
present myself for maximum impact—how to *look* like an artist
so they'd listen to my music and take it seriously. Imagining what
they wanted to see, I would compare myself to other performers
and long to have more of a glamorous image. But after years of
getting it wrong, I finally realized I was trying way too hard.

It's kind of like dating—when it comes to romance, if
someone doesn't love you at your most casual, then they will
probably never truly love you.

REFLECTION

Life can feel a little like a costume party sometimes. If that's what
it is, why not go as yourself? Some people will love your approach
and some people won't. Choose to be the real you, and the right
people will love what they see.

Lord, thank you for this liberation! I don't have to dress up as
someone else to impress others. Help me to identify my own
tastes when it comes to clothing and style so I can be myself.
Teach me to focus on who I am more than whose label I'm
wearing! In Jesus' name, amen.

You Are Enough

But you belong to God, my dear children.
1 JOHN 4:4 NLT

Feeling you're not enough often comes from trying to *be* enough. Everywhere we turn in life, there are expectations and standards to live up to. It's hard work always trying to win at life and stay on top of things, and the pressure can be immense. We find ourselves bending over backward to keep everyone happy, fearing that if we don't, we won't measure up. But we're not "enough" because of what we do or achieve—we're enough because of *whose* we are. Before we even lift a finger to please someone else, we're already enough.

REFLECTION

Have you been overdoing things recently? Perhaps it's time to remind yourself that you're enough as you are—you don't have to try so hard. It's okay if you can't check everyone's boxes—you already have the full seal of approval from God, the one who matters.

Lord, thank you that I am yours—you left heaven and laid down your life for me. Please help me to stop trying harder to be enough and embrace that I already belong to you, just as I am. In Jesus' name, amen.

Advice for My Seventeen-Year-Old Self

Remember your Creator in the days of your youth.

ECCLESIASTES 12:1

Enjoy your life. No one else is going to enjoy it for you. What has happened so far doesn't have to reflect what comes next. The years to come will be infinitely better. You're not old, trust me. The people whose opinion of you means *so* much right now will likely be a distant memory in five years' time, so don't waste too much longer trying to impress them. Keep hold of that Bible. You'll read it one day and it'll … change things. Love and respect yourself and others. Do this and the right people will show up and stay around. Stop telling yourself you're less than others—it's not true. You were born beautiful, so embrace what makes you different. Don't shut out your mother—she'll be your best friend when you're thirty-three. Pursue your dreams but don't always listen to your heart. Check your heart with your head. And check your head with people who'll tell you the truth. You're more loved than you will ever know.

REFLECTION

What advice would you give your younger self? It might be helpful to write this down and reflect on it. It could also be helpful for someone in your life who is going through what you once did.

Lord, help me to learn from my past mistakes. Help me to distill these lessons into wisdom for others and even for myself. In Jesus' name, amen.

You're a Genius

Children born to a young man are like arrows in a warrior's hands. How joyful is the man whose quiver is full of them!
PSALM 127:4–5 NLT

Einstein famously said, "Everybody is a genius. But if you judge a fish by its ability to climb a tree, it will live its whole life believing that it is stupid."

Being in the wrong job, position, relationship, or partnership can be damaging to your self-esteem. Here's the bottom line: You are precious. You are beautiful. You are here for a purpose. If the people around you can't see that, then you *may* be around the wrong people. I've seen it time and again—a person in the wrong role or relationship will experience feelings of continual failure. But surrounded by love, encouragement, and the chance to explore who they are, they open like a flower.

I'll never forget the first time I saw my husband behind a drum set. This shy, low-key guy suddenly was on fire and became an absolute show-off! I felt as if I was seeing him for the first time. The same can happen for all of us when we are free to explore what we were created for.

REFLECTION

In God's hands we truly find our lane in life. He can propel us into our given destinies. In our element, we can excel. It's not always easy to change lanes. But start by knowing that you are a genius—a precious gift who deserves to be valued and encouraged.

Lord, help me to be as sharp and as sure as an arrow. When you pull me back, let me be propelled into your purpose. Make my direction sure and my target certain. In Jesus' name, amen.

You Have a Purpose

"I have raised you up for this very purpose, that I might show you my power and that my name might be proclaimed in all the earth."

EXODUS 9:16

I felt like a fish out of water at school. After I graduated, I sought work to support myself as I pursued a career in music. I usually found that I struggled to keep up where others sailed past in the workplace. After I found faith and began to pursue my music as a full-time ministry, I discovered a gift for encouraging people! For the first time, I felt strong, competent, and alive. I even felt beautiful. When I tell people they're amazing, I feel as if I'm flying—firing on all cylinders instead of struggling along with a broken engine.

REFLECTION

Seek and pursue the function that makes you feel alive. Life is too short, and you are far too precious to walk around feeling inadequate. This world needs the real you—it needs your unique brand of genius. You were made to fly! And when you fly, everyone around you begins to find their wings too. Everyone— *everyone*—has a purpose.

Lord, thank you for the incredible purposes you have for me. Thank you that you've raised me up for a specific reason and that through me your name can be glorified. Help me to seek out, identify, and remain true to my purpose. In Jesus' name, amen.

You Are Amazing

God created mankind in his own image, in the image of God he created them; male and female he created them.

GENESIS 1:27

I didn't have a great deal of confidence as a teenager, so having a dream to reach others with my music was a little inconvenient. I quickly realized that to have my songs heard, I was going to have to sing them. I began auditioning for everything I could find— bands, shows, and TV talent competitions—and door after door closed. I couldn't seem to impress the right people, and I began to feel a looming sense of mediocrity.

This feeling was compounded one day by the comments of a hotshot music producer who told me I was too ordinary looking for the music industry. I was crushed! I took those words with me, wearing them around my neck like a heavy stone. It affected my self-esteem, my career, and even my relationship choices.

Believing I was ordinary caused me to treat myself with zero respect. Until one November evening in 2004. I walked into a church and found myself caught up in the worship. Heartbroken, I dragged myself to Jesus, asking him to reveal himself to me if he was even real. From that moment, a powerful sense of peace and awesome presence entered my heart. That powerful Spirit taught me to view myself not as ordinary, but as *amazing*. I learned that I was created and chosen by God to do good things. When I began walking in that awesome truth, wonderful things began to take place in my life.

You Are God's Masterpiece

For we are God's masterpiece. He has created us anew in Christ Jesus, so we can do the good things he planned for us long ago.

EPHESIANS 2:10 NLT

At the beginning of last year, I had a flu that lasted a little under a month. One morning, I was feeling a little better and got excited about going shopping. I went to the mirror and found that I looked tired and a little pale. For the briefest of moments, I thought about staying inside because putting on makeup seemed like too much effort. But I caught myself in this foolishness and left the house before I could change my mind.

In the age of social media, we too hastily diminish ourselves to that small square window through which the world looks in. We're in danger of forgetting that we've been given our senses, these faces, and these bodies to look outward. As Renee Engeln said in her wonderful TED Talk, "Stop looking at your body as a collection of parts for other people to look at. Think of it as unified whole—your tool for exploring the world."

REFLECTION

Our bodies were never meant to limit or imprison us; they were never meant to be a collection of parts to be observed and evaluated by the eyes of the world. Our bodies are vehicles for adventure, so don't let anyone stop you from embracing life today, not even you!

Lord, please help me remember that my body is just packaging. You've created me to do great things and have wonderful adventures. Help me not to limit my own enjoyment of life because I don't feel good enough. In Jesus' name, amen.

Be Body Grateful

For You formed my inward parts; You wove me in
my mother's womb. I will give thanks to You, for I am
fearfully and wonderfully made.

PSALM 139:13–14 NASB

Your body may not be perfect, but it's yours and it's the only one
you have. Society puts a lot of pressure on us to have bodies that
are desirable to others. Far more importantly, however, we learn
to appreciate what our bodies do to serve us—they are a gift to us.

I began following a YouTuber a few years ago—a beautiful,
brave young woman whose body fights a daily battle with cystic
fibrosis. Despite hours of daily treatments to keep her airways
clear, she said in one blog, "I'm just happy that I'm able to
breathe freely today. I'm happy for the function that I have in my
lungs because I know there are others out there today who can't
breathe quite so easily."

REFLECTION

Today, if you're not feeling so attractive, perhaps be grateful that
you're enjoying deep, clear breaths. If you have health issues, why
not focus on what you can still do? Can you enjoy a sunrise? Can
you encourage someone via a card or text? Chances are you can
do much more than you realize. Regardless of your limitations, if
you're here, God still has work for you to do.

Lord, thank you for my good health. Even if my health isn't
perfect, I know there will be others who have it far worse in life.
You've given me so much, let me not take it for granted. In Jesus'
name, amen.

A Little Poem to Brighten Your Day!

"He will take great delight in you; in his love he will no longer rebuke you, but will rejoice over you with singing."

ZEPHANIAH 3:17

If God could write you a poem today it might go something like this:

You. The genius. The breath of fresh air. / The blessing. / You. The beauty. The brave. The survivor. / You. The one reading this. I'm overwhelmed by your brilliance, your luminance. / You're breathtaking, outstanding. By your very existence you teach the world something new because you're the only one I ever made; that makes you a doctor of a science no one else can fathom. / When the world sees you, it's like they see a brand-new color. / You're splendid, elegant. / You're fierce and your heart beats with a rhythm no one else can create. Child, if only you could see. / The stars have nothing on your beauty, even when you're broken, torn, bruised, and grazed. / YOU amaze me.

REFLECTION

Isn't it amazing? God so delights in you that it makes him want to sing. He is in love with you! His whole Word is one long love letter to you. Today try to focus on the *affection* God feels for you—it's endless.

Lord, thank you that you love me so much. Thank you that you're delighting in me right now—celebrating and making music because you adore me. Help me to know and feel that love in every fiber of my being today. In Jesus' name, amen.

Custom-Built for a Purpose

For we are God's handiwork, created in Christ Jesus to do good
works, which God prepared in advance for us to do.

EPHESIANS 2:10

What if the way you look is no accident? What if you were
custom-made for the life you're leading? What if your face and
body were prepared in advance so you can reach a generation? It's
a fact that we respond best to people we identify with, so it stands
to reason that God would design you according to your mission.
I've always had a baby face. It used to annoy me incredibly when
people in public wouldn't recognize me as a full-grown adult.
But when I found myself on tour with a mainstream girl band at
age thirty-two, looking young was quite useful as thousands of
teenage girls listened to what I had to say.

I have a friend whose hobby is motorcycles. His friends are
all bearded, leather-wearing bikers covered in tattoos. Because my
friend has a similar look, he has no problem spending time with
them, sharing stories with them, and doing life alongside them.
It's no accident he is the perfectly crafted missionary for that
field. The way you look may well serve an important purpose.

REFLECTION

Today, resolve to embrace your natural self. There may well be
an important cog in God's well-oiled machine that turns just
because of who you are and how you naturally present yourself.

Lord, thank you that I'm different. Thank you that you've
constructed me for a purpose and you've given me certain
people in life to reach. Help me to embrace all that makes me
unique, knowing that I'm custom designed to reach others. In
Jesus' name, amen.

Embrace Your Face!

"Before I formed you in the womb I knew you,
before you were born I set you apart."

JEREMIAH 1:5

Thousands upon thousands of people go under the knife each year—not for medical reasons, but in quest of the perfect nose. I didn't used to like my nose very much as a girl. It wasn't perfect like the ones on my dolls. But I've come to really appreciate my face as a unique mixture of both my mother and my father's DNA. Looking at pictures of my parents' families, I feel a connection with them.

At a recent funeral, we all joked about the echoes of each other, even though many of us had never met. It was fascinating and quite magical. There's a hint of the Irish look about my face too, and being a musician, I'm quite proud of my Irish heritage. All these observations have made me appreciate the story that my face tells. If I were to surgically change or "perfect" those features, something of my identity would be hidden or lost.

Our faces can be the most instant and outward celebration of the cultures we represent.

REFLECTION

Today, rather than just thinking of your face as a project to be perfected, why not think of it as a celebration and story of your heritage?

Lord, thank you for my heritage. Thank you that you love all body types, skin tones, and faces. Help me to be excited about the diversity in this world. You made us all different because you're a creative, storytelling God. Thank you for the story you're telling through me. In Jesus' name, amen.

Speak Kind Words about Yourself

The tongue has the power of life and death,
and those who love it will eat its fruit.

PROVERBS 18:21

There is nothing worse than a bully. Imagine you just walked into a public bathroom to find two people standing by the mirror. One is staring at their reflection, the other standing over their shoulder, listing the first person's flaws. Would you be horrified? Offended? Probably. You might even step in and say something. So why do we think it so much more acceptable to do this to ourselves?

Hopefully, when you look at your reflection, you pay yourself compliments and celebrate the glorious creation that you are. Experience tells me, however, that this is not usually the case. We often use a trip to the mirror as an opportunity to be critical, even cruel, to the person looking back. We make comments about our skin, weight, or age that we would never *dream* of uttering to another person. We must never forget that words hold the power of life and death, even those we silently whisper to ourselves.

REFLECTION

Take a moment today to speak some kind words to your reflection. Remind the person in the mirror, *You are a unique, custom-made one-in-seven-billion miracle!* If you've been giving air time to your inner bully, it's time to silence that bully with God's truth.

Lord, I never want to be a bully, even toward myself. It's not who I am, and it's not your plan for me. May I always express only life-giving words. In Jesus' name, amen.

Vessels

But we have this treasure in jars of clay to show that this all-sur-passing power is from God and not from us.

2 CORINTHIANS 4:7

Most of us take great interest in our appearance. We agonize over the way we look, especially as our bodies age, change, and are affected by sickness. On those days when social media fills our consciousness, we must remind ourselves that our bodies are simple vessels that hold the treasure of our souls.

Our bodies are gifts that the Father entrusts to us, and we are free to do with them as we choose. The polite and respectful way to view those bodies are as fragile containers on loan to us. When we give our lives to Jesus, we admit that he purchased each one of by his blood. To hate ourselves—to constantly view that body as a project—is to take it back from him and presume that we know better. To say that we are worthless is to say that Jesus paid too much.

REFLECTION

Never forget to thank God for making the ultimate sacrifice. He paid the ultimate price for your body, imperfect as it is. The least you can do is take care of that fragile vessel and be grateful for what it can do.

Lord, I am sorry that I give myself such a hard time. I'm sorry that I compare this simple vessel to others'. I want to be grateful for what I have. Help me to use my body to the best of my ability to serve and glorify you while I'm alive. In Jesus' name, amen.

Feeling Different

God has given each of you a gift from his great variety of spiritual gifts. Use them well to serve one another.

1 PETER 4:10 NLT

I never found it easy to fit it in—growing up in show business, having a wacky imagination and a passion to use my music to reach others made me stand out from the crowd. When I found faith, I was super excited to be fully embraced by this club called "church." But even at church, I found that I was unusual. I loved to write songs that might connect with everyday folk—those who'd never heard about Jesus. I was fired up to take life-giving art out of the church walls so it might find others like me.

I quickly found that most Christian musicians were composing worship music to be performed within and to the church. It made me feel lonely at times—even judged. A few even accused me of compromising my faith and selling out to a worldly agenda. All I wanted to do was share my faith! I was tempted to change who I was so people would understand me and I could finally fit in. But ten years later, I am *so* glad I stuck with my passion. I regularly hear stories about how my music has been able to reach those who would perhaps never step inside the walls of a church. I've even had folks say, "Thank you for doing something different. Thank you for being who God has asked you to be." There is no greater sense of accomplishment!

REFLECTION

Resist the idea that you need to walk, talk, and act a certain way to belong in God's family. God has big ideas for your unique appeal. You never know who you might bless or even set free just by being who you are.

God, help me to hold on to the unique point of view you've given me. It's okay that my tastes are outside the box. It's okay that what I do is not like other worship leaders or speakers. You have a design for my identity. Make my paths straight in all I do and help me to faithfully steward the gifts you've given me. In Jesus' name, amen.

Resisting the Box

For those God foreknew he also predestined to be conformed to
the image of his Son, that he might be the firstborn among many
brothers and sisters.

ROMANS 8:29

You don't become depressed because people try to put you into
a box. You become depressed when you let them. After a stint
in Nashville "dating" record labels and trying to secure a record
deal, I began to feel extremely down. It had been a long few weeks
of difficult discussions, mostly about what the gatekeepers of
Christian radio were looking for in a song. I spent days agonizing
over how I could be what they wanted me to be.

As I felt the looming shadows of depression press in on me, I
realized I'd been allowing the process to chip away at my sense of
self. I felt a little angry at the people who'd been trying to create
this new identity for me. In a moment of clarity, I realized I was
the one allowing that to take place.

REFLECTION

God never said we had to be transformed into someone else's
ideal or gradually morph into the likeness of another person.
He only ever said we should become more like him—the
original pioneer. When you try to transform into a false version
of yourself in order to gain popularity, you are attempting to
become an idol. And that's no good at all.

Lord, help me today to resist being squeezed into the boxes that
others may try to put me into. Liberate me to always be myself.
I want to reflect your glory, not the glory of an idol. Thank you
that you broke the mold when you created me, Lord. In Jesus'
name, amen.

People Won't Always See the Big Picture

Jesus turned and said to Peter, "Get behind me, Satan! You are a stumbling block to me; you do not have in mind the concerns of God, but merely human concerns."

MATTHEW 16:23

When we begin to fully embrace who we are in God, we must prepare to face criticism. Even those closest to Jesus—those who knew his character and saw him do miracles—had doubts about his destiny. They tried to dissuade him from completing what the Father had asked him to do. Jesus' response to Peter may seem harsh. Notice he didn't say, "Get behind me, Peter." He simply recognized that Peter was entertaining the voice of doubt that tries to influence each of us.

When people began to criticize me for singing songs in mainstream settings, it gave me some comfort to know that Jesus faced a similar scrutiny. Jesus' approach to ministry was extremely controversial. You can imagine the scorn of his religious peers when they saw Jesus socializing with former prostitutes and criminals. It must have looked scandalous! But there was a story— he was building with those people. It was as if he were a doctor to the sick, just as he'd been commanded by the Father.

REFLECTION

If you're living out a God-given vision, don't be surprised when people don't fully understand. Walk in obedience and people will experience the love of Jesus through what you're doing.

Lord, help me to be strong in the conviction of my calling. When the voice of doubt or scrutiny comes, help me say, "Get behind me, satan." Let nothing stand in the way of my fulfilling the tasks for which you have sent me. In Jesus' name, amen.

Seek Guidance

Where there is no guidance the people fall,
but in abundance of counselors there is victory.

PROVERBS 11:14 NASB

I fully encourage you to be yourself in Jesus. Do something unique. Don't be put off by idle criticism and religious chatter. It isn't wise, however, to do all this completely alone.

My father-in-law shared powerful words of wisdom with me years before I even knew my husband, Joel. Whilst praying for me in a youth meeting, he encouraged me to set out into the world and share songs of hope. He encouraged me to appoint a handful of trusted advisors to help me make good choices and to have several trustworthy, prayed-up believers to seek counsel from. So I did, and to this day I have never made a pivotal decision without asking for their prayer and advice.

When you have trusted confidants, you create for yourself an army of advocates and a wall of protection. You don't have to shoulder the burden of your choices alone and you can be shielded from distraction. Ultimately, if I'm ever targeted by a cruel naysayer, I can rest in the knowledge that I'm not in the fight alone and I'm not being reckless or impulsive—I'm using wisdom.

REFLECTION

Do you need to appoint some advisors or mentors? Whatever you long to do, getting advice from someone you trust is like gold dust! Take it with both hands and treasure it.

Lord, help me to identify some trustworthy counselors. Help me to know who will best guide me in your truth. Thank you for the abundance of life you promise through this approach. In Jesus' name, amen.

You Are an Influencer!

Be wise in the way you act toward outsiders;
make the most of every opportunity.

COLOSSIANS 4:5

You may not think you're having a huge impact on those around you, but you truly are! Studies show that people are up to 30 percent more likely to do something because they saw another do it or talk about it. Your beliefs, choices, and actions are changing things around you. This is obviously a message of caution. If you make poor choices or pursue bad habits, family and friends could be negatively impacted. On the flip side, if you're working hard to be a *positive* influence, even just by your example you are changing things. The way you live is making a difference—never forget that!

REFLECTION

Today, say a prayer for those around you who are being influenced by your choices. Pray that the good things you do and say will have a deep and lasting effect on their point of view. They could be closer than you think to a huge faith breakthrough.

Lord, help me to be a good influence. I know I'm not perfect, but help me to be mindful of the fact that my choices affect people. I want my presence and my influence to be as life-giving as possible. In Jesus' name, amen.

The Power of Integrity

The integrity of the upright guides them,
but the unfaithful are destroyed by their duplicity.

PROVERBS 11:3

Over the years I've come to understand the importance of living in agreement with your own beliefs. What does this mean? If you value honesty, but you're not being honest with people, it can lead to self-esteem issues. If you truly value bravery, but you're avoiding something important out of fear, you can begin to lack self-respect. If you value fidelity, but you're not being faithful, you're not likely to feel too fond of the person in the mirror.

When we disappoint ourselves, it can lead to all kinds of confidence issues. Often, we don't even make the connection. Take some time to examine your life. Ask yourself, *Am I living in agreement with own beliefs? Am I doing what I believe is the right thing?* If you've let things slip and the answer is no, don't despair and don't allow condemnation to settle on you. But it might be a great opportunity to invite gentle conviction by the Holy Spirit.

REFLECTION

Does something about your life need to change? Today is the day to begin. If you're not sure where to begin, tell someone you trust about the battle you're fighting and ask them to hold you accountable. You will be utterly amazed at the transformation you begin to see and the peace you begin to feel.

Lord, thank you for your grace. Thank you that even though I make mistakes, you forgive me and help me to start over. If there is anything in my life that needs to change, please draw my eye to it. I want my life to match my ideals and to reflect my heart—and yours. In Jesus' name, amen.

It's Okay Not to Appeal to Everyone

"If the world hates you, know that it has hated me
before it hated you."

JOHN 15:18 ESV

You won't appeal to everyone, and that's okay. Even the people you consider to be geniuses, role models, and the ones "getting it right" have *armies* of haters. Only yesterday, I saw a famous and very popular pastor tweet a great passage. I couldn't help but notice the stampede of critics calling him every name under the sun in response, as well as the many supporters applauding him.

Sadly, once we put our heads above the parapet, we can't avoid being attacked, so it's important that we make peace with this as soon as possible. You won't succeed in being loved by all. Does that mean you should give up or hide away? Of course not! Even chocolate doesn't appeal to everyone, but it would be a huge mistake to stop making it. Focus on those who appreciate you, even when they're not the majority. And don't forget that you always have the Father's love and approval.

REFLECTION

Jesus had an army of haters who stood against him. He encountered every type of criticism and discrimination, but he didn't retaliate. Instead, he focused on delivering the good news to those who would listen. Today, resolve to do the same in love.

Lord, it's not easy for me to cope with being disliked. I want to be appreciated, and I thank you for all the times that I am. But when I'm not, help me to remember that this is not a terrible thing. It's simply a natural part of living for you. Help me always to respond to hate with patience and love. In Jesus' name, amen.

Dance, Sing, Try

Let them praise his name with dancing and make music to him
with timbrel and harp. For the LORD takes delight in his people;
he crowns the humble with victory.

PSALM 149:3–4

A few years ago, I was asked to play bass guitar at a women's conference. Just one small problem—I don't play bass. But there was no one else available, so I spent all week learning the *very* basic baselines to four songs. After arriving and plugging in, the worship leader arrived with laryngitis! The pastor sheepishly came over and asked me to lead from the bass guitar. I was horrified!

"I don't think I can do that," I said. "This is my first time playing bass!" The pastor looked me sadly in the eye. "But if you can't, there'll be no one to lead." That sealed it—I was leading.

I played bass that week because there was no one else to play. I led worship because there was no one else to lead. I wonder how many songs and sermons are out there that we'll never hear because we're leaving it to someone we feel is more capable? Who knows what wonderful things we could achieve if we stepped out even *before* we're the last resort?

REFLECTION

If there were no dancers left in the world, would you dance? If there was no one left to sing, would you get up and take the mic? Life's too short to hide in the shadows.

Lord, give me the courage to try. There is so much I want to do in life, and I know I won't always be amazing at everything. Help me not miss out on anything due to fear. Please give me the boldness and courage to step up and out today. In Jesus' name, amen.

A Valuable Cell

Now you are the body of Christ,
and each one of you is a part of it.
1 CORINTHIANS 12:27

The Bible teaches us that as Christians, we are all parts of a body.
We are individuals who serve unique purposes and together
fulfill a shared mission. Scripture encourages us not to view ourselves as separate but as parts that work together. It also encourages us not to view any part as superior to the others.

But we may still be limiting our understanding when it
comes to our personal value within the body. There is far more
to the inner workings of a physical body than just hands and feet.
The body has six main parts: body, head, neck, torso, arms, and
legs. There are also twelve biological systems that carry out vital
functions to make the human body work. Within those systems,
the body contains nearly 100 trillion cells. The brain alone contains around 100 billion nerve cells.

Cells are small, but they are what the vital organs and systems ae made of. However small you may feel, there is a specific
function you can help to fulfill! You might even be just like one of
those brain cells delivering a powerful idea to the entire body.

REFLECTION
Everything you are gifted to do has a place in the body of Christ.
Today, pray that the Lord will help you find and fulfill your
function.

Lord, thank you for my unique function in the body of Christ.
Help me to do all that I'm able to do and to work harmonious-
ly alongside others, helping them fulfill their functions too. In
Jesus' name, amen.

Stop Competing with Yourself

We do not dare to classify or compare ourselves with some who commend themselves. When they measure themselves by themselves and compare themselves with themselves, they are not wise.

2 Corinthians 10:12

We all want to better ourselves. But trying to always "do one better" can be exhausting and erosive for our self-esteem. The battle to keep from comparing ourselves with others is hard enough! Comparing yourself to the way you looked, what you weighed, and who you were five years ago can be just as painful and damaging. We are who we are today. The only way is forward!

REFLECTION

Have you been hanging onto the glory days of when you first got saved? Are you stuck in a memory of when you were more active for the kingdom or in your career? Resolve today to let go of your past glories and move to new ones.

Lord, help me to look at who and where I am right now and accept myself. Thank you for the journey I am on and the blessings you bring each day. Help me to be the best I can be for this moment. In Jesus' name, amen.

Feeling Out of Place

For this world is not our permanent home; we are looking forward to a home yet to come.

HEBREWS 13:14 NLT

Many of us struggle to figure out where we fit in the world and so often feel disconnected. It's especially hard to identify with a world so governed by evil and filled with hurt. When we switch on the TV to see bad news on one channel, people fighting on a reality TV show on the next, and all kinds of darkness in between, it can be distressing. But the Bible offers a refreshing release. We learn that it's natural to feel out of place in this world, because we are only visitors! We are temporary tenants on a short lease—our eternal home awaits.

We are citizens of a place called heaven, where love is endless and glory surrounds us every moment. Though this planet is beautiful, it's only a preview of the beauty that awaits. Isn't that a comforting thought?

REFLECTION

Realizing that we are merely visitors here can change our approach to life for the better. This world is just a mission field—we won't be here forever. Try to see yourself as someone who is here only for a short time, not stuck in a place you don't belong.

Lord, I thank you that there are many rooms in your house. Whenever I feel out of place, let me remember the place you've prepared for me. As much as possible, let me make the most of my short time here on earth. In Jesus' name, amen.

Struggling with Identity?

Christ's life showed me how, and enabled me to do it. I identified myself completely with him.

GALATIANS 2:20 MSG

There are lots of confusing identity conversations going on today. Deciding how to identify can be very confusing for a young person in the twenty-first century. But if we're to look at Scripture, it makes for some reassuring thoughts:

We were made for more than this world. It's understandable that we sometimes feel like the odd one out. No two people are the same! We are more than skin, shape, sexuality, class, politics, and opinions. We are more than faces, money, medical conditions, male or female, or marital status. We are a generation struggling to define ourselves because we're trying to define ourselves by things that don't define us. There'll never be a box on a form or a symbol on a door that fully represents us because we will never fit inside a box!

REFLECTION

Does knowing your identity trouble you? Right now, start with this truth: Your body is a temporary vessel, given to you so you can make an exciting journey on earth. Your identity is in Christ, and getting to know him better will help you feel peaceful in your own skin.

Lord, I trust you to make me comfortable in my identity. I thank you that I am not my body or my sexuality but so much more in you. Help me to embrace all of who I am in you. In Jesus' name, amen.

Learn to Hear His Voice the Loudest

"My sheep listen to my voice; I know them, and they follow me."

JOHN 10:27

Time spent with God helps us to recognize his voice more easily. This is important because there are so many other voices in our lives. Things can become noisy, overwhelming, and very confusing. It's so important to spend time wrapped up in his promises, leaning in to learn his character, and knowing without a doubt the tender, unmatchable tones of the Father's heart.

The voices in your life may be pulling you in many directions right now. Even the well-meaning voices of our friends and family can throw our spirit into chaos. God's gentle whisper says, *This is the way, walk in it.*

REFLECTION

There may be doubters, scoffers, and even abusers who seek to pull you down. God's voice tells you that you were created with a purpose. You are unique, powerful, and beautiful. He has put something spectacular in you. Let his guidance and approval speak louder than the voices of doubt and fear—that's when you will find your wings and learn to fly like an arrow from his hand.

Lord, let me learn to hear your voice. Help me to spend more time close to you so when I hear your gentle whisper in my heart, I will feel no hesitation in following. In Jesus' name, amen.

It's Okay Not to Be Cliché

I say to myself, "The Lord is my portion;
therefore I will wait for him."

LAMENTATIONS 3:24

The world has a well-mapped-out idea of where we should all be at different times in our lives. That map tells us when we should learn, when we should seek adventure, and when we should settle down. These traditions are tried, tested, and very popular for the most part, but they should never limit or bind you. The story of our lives doesn't have to follow any specific pattern. Where's the adventure in that?

It's okay if you're not married. It's okay if you don't have kids. It's okay if you married at twenty, your kids are your life, and you have no desire to conquer the world on your lunch hour. And it's okay if you're still figuring things out. God broke the mold when he made each of us, so feel free to go ahead and break the mold with life!

REFLECTION

Take a moment to shake off the clichés that have bound you. Have you been asked repeatedly when you're getting married? Are people still waiting for you to have a career breakthrough? Just remember: You're not on anyone else's timeframe. It's okay to let go and take things at your own pace.

Lord, help me to deal with the pain that can come from playing the waiting game. Always remind me I'm on your timeframe and your timing is perfect. I don't want to jump ahead before the time is right. Thank you, Lord. In Jesus' name, amen.

Remove the "You" Lens

I pray that the eyes of your heart may be enlightened in order that you may know the hope to which he has called you, the riches of his glorious inheritance in his holy people.

EPHESIANS 1:18

It's amazing the way we can look at ourselves and see weakness while others see strength.

You may look in the mirror and see a wreck while others see an overcomer.

You may look at your reflection and see a person struggling with negative thoughts while others see someone who is putting their best foot forward and doing all they can to succeed.

We know ourselves so well that we become our own worst critics, collecting a catalog of failures and flaws as evidence against our better nature. We forget that *everyone* is flawed, and we are all fighting the same battles.

REFLECTION

Today, give yourself a break. Try not to look at yourself through the lens of your own weaknesses. Instead, begin to see yourself doing everything you can to access spiritual strength and live your best life.

Lord, please help me to clean up the lens through which I view myself. Help me to see myself as you see me—full of potential and unique beauty. May I see all the things I am and could be rather than simply the things I am not. In Jesus' name, amen.

Remove the Failure Lens

As far as the east is from the west,
so far has He removed our transgressions from us.
PSALM 103:12 NASB

We all make mistakes and fail. But if we're not careful, we can begin to expect failure from ourselves, internalizing phrases like *I can't do anything right.*

Great news! Today is a brand-new day. Whatever happened yesterday is gone, and you have full permission to let it go. It's not always easy for us to treat each day as a new day, because we were there yesterday and saw our failures. God promises new mercies every day, so we must practice putting yesterday's failures to bed! If we begin this awesome new morning looking through the lens of yesterday's mistakes, even our successes will look cloudy. God has given you his grace, so receive it!

REFLECTION

Is something troubling you today? Are you still living in the cloud of a past failure? Remind yourself right now that God has dealt with it.

Lord, thank you that I'm free to start over today with a clean slate. Please take this lens through which I view myself and clean it up. Help me see myself as a winner and not a failure. In Jesus' name, amen.

Know Who You Are

And now that you belong to Christ, you are the
true children of Abraham. You are his heirs, and
God's promise to Abraham belongs to you.

GALATIANS 3:29 NLT

In lots of areas in our lives, we are required to show something
of who we are. We are expected to demonstrate our personalities
during school, work, or team exercises. We must attend
auditions, meetings, and even things like parents' evenings where
people will quietly make judgments on our character. Today you
might be heading to school, work, or some other opportunity,
hoping that people will see and embrace who you are. But
before we can expect or even hope for this from others, we have
to spend time embracing ourselves. It can be difficult to view
yourself as royalty if you started out poor. It can be difficult to
see yourself as a light in this world when you began in darkness.
But this is what God has done for us—he has called us out into
the light. It doesn't matter where you began your life, you now
belong inside the palace walls.

REFLECTION

Today, begin by proclaiming your status in God. As a believer,
you are a son or daughter of the Most High God. Together, we
are a royal priesthood, and we've been called out of darkness.
Whatever you're doing today, he looks upon you with his
kindness and his unfailing love.

Lord, help me to walk in this truth. No matter where I began in
life, I am now royalty in you! I've been adopted into your royal
family. Thank you, Lord. In Jesus' name, amen.

You Are Royalty

But you are a chosen people, a royal priesthood, a holy nation, God's special possession, that you may declare the praises of him who called you out of darkness into his wonderful light.

1 PETER 2:9

As I write this, the United Kingdom is dizzy with royal wedding fever. The esteemed event will light up billions of screens across the world this summer, and we're all doe-eyed with delight. There is something so special, so refined about the British royals. Their worldwide status, rich history, and decadent world steeped in tradition commands respect, pride, and affection.

Not everyone is a royalist. But most of us agree in theory that to be a king or queen would be rather divine. How easily we forget that, in fact, we are! We are sons and daughters of the King of kings. We have been adopted into a royal family, and his blood now flows through our veins. All of God's rich history now belongs to us, and we bear that coveted title—child of the King.

REFLECTION

Let that lovely thought be something that goes with you today—simply that you are a true royal. God gave Jesus the name above all monarchs and dignitaries, and you are alive in him.

Lord, thank you for the amazing favor you've blessed me with. I'm so honored that your blood now flows through my veins. What an incredible inheritance I have in you. Let me never forget how you've taken me out of poverty and placed me beside you, the King of kings. In Jesus' name, amen.

Your Value Never Decreases

But God demonstrates his own love for us in this:
While we were still sinners, Christ died for us.

ROMANS 5:8

I was shadowing a Christian girl band named BlushUK—an all-girl vocal harmony group who did workshops and concerts for teenagers.

One of the singers, Nichola, held up a twenty-pound note. "Who wants this?" Hands went up and a chorus of kids yelled, "Me! Me!" She threw it onto the floor and stomped on it. "Who wants it now?" she asked. The kids were even more hysterical, some reaching for the money. "I've had a bit of a cough and cold this week." She coughed on the note and then held it high again. "Who wants it now?" The kids looked at each other for a moment and once again dove toward the note. She explained, "I crumpled it, stomped on it, and coughed on it, but you still wanted it. Why?" One kid shouted, "Because it's still twenty pounds!"

It doesn't matter what you've been through—how used, crumpled, and contaminated you feel—nothing can decrease your value in the eyes of God. You will always be worth what he paid for you.

REFLECTION

Today, remind yourself that you are not worth any less because you've made mistakes. The Father still goes after you, even when you're lying crumpled on the floor.

Thank you, Lord, that I'm not valuable to you only because of what I do. You've proven my worth to you by dying for me, even while I was still living completely my own way. You're truly an amazing God. Never let me determine my own value based on how well I feel or how others treat me. In Jesus' name, amen.

Bear Your Title Well

I urge you to live a life worthy of the calling you have received.
EPHESIANS 4:1

Sometimes we believe that we've depreciated in value. We make mistakes and can't help feeling that they make us less valuable. But kings and queens are kings and queens despite their transgressions. "Once a king or queen in Narnia," Aslan tells the children in *The Lion the Witch and the Wardrobe*, "always a king or queen. Bear it well, Sons of Adam! Bear it well, Daughters of Eve!"

Does this mean we should continue failing on purpose? Should we take our status for granted and do as we please? We have that freedom, and some of us may. But when we look at our government rulers, do we want them to succeed or fail? Do we want them to be treacherous or righteous rulers?

REFLECTION

We all want to see royals wear their titles well. We want to see them representing their kingdom with honor. As a child of God, you're an heir of the King of kings, and if you fall away, you will still bear that title. Yet you and I have the chance to be righteous historymakers. Bear your title well, sons of Adam. Bear it well, daughters of Eve.

Lord, help me to live a life worthy of your calling. Help me to be all that I need to be to carry out your mission. I know I've made mistakes—help me to do better. In Jesus' name, amen.

You're Not What You Own

God paid a high price for you, so don't be enslaved by the world.

1 CORINTHIANS 7:23 NLT

When journalists talk about tycoons, movie stars, and heirs, they talk a lot about each person's net worth. Wikipedia states that Taylor Swift's net worth is around $280 million. They say Steve Jobs was worth $31.6 billion when he died. But if we're to believe what the Bible tells us, this estimate is way off. The truth is, Steve Jobs was priceless. He was priceless the day he was born and the day he died, because there was only one Steve Jobs, and God paid the ultimate price for him—his Son.

REFLECTION

The amazing news? Jesus paid the same price for you. Whatever your bank balance or the car you drive, you were worth dying for even before you cared about God. Your value never changes—you're priceless.

Lord, thank you for the amazing price you paid for me. I'm no longer my own; I've been purchased by your blood. Thank you that although I don't always feel worthy of your attention, you thought I was worth dying for. In Jesus' name, amen.

You Are Not What You Do

"Greater love has no one than this,
that one lay down his life for his friends."
JOHN 15:13 NASB

Regardless of the effort you put in for the kingdom, those works don't define you. This might seem like great news to you, for others it might seem like a disappointment. The moment we start to measure our worth as a child of God by what we *do* for him, we devalue what he did for us. Our salvation was bought by Jesus on the cross; it isn't bought by the events we put on or the songs we sing. It isn't even bought by the good we do or the people we share Jesus with. We do those things in service to God because of what he already did for us.

REFLECTION

There is nothing you can do to earn God's love. Your relationship with him was made possible purely by Jesus' sacrifice. Although you may live a life in service and gratitude, you are not what you do—you are what was done for you.

Lord, thank you for your unconditional love. I won't try to earn it today by what I do or say. Instead, I will simply thank you for it from the bottom of my heart. Thank you. In Jesus' name, amen.

Women Are Amazing

Honor her for all that her hands have done, and let her works
bring her praise at the city gate.

PROVERBS 31:31

Regardless if you are a woman yourself, most of us have been
deeply influenced by one or more, and all of us arrived here by
one! If you *are* a woman, the following words are especially for
you. If not, it's still important to celebrate womankind when we
talk about identity!

Woman is…A carrier of vision / A walking contradiction /
Of power and emotion / Beautiful and broken / And from the
well of life within her / Sacrificially she gives / So when you see
her in the mirror / Don't forget to tell her / Just how awesome /
She is.

REFLECTION

Growing up, you may not have always gotten along with other
girls or women. There were the "mean girls" at school who made
us struggle with female friendships. There are sometimes issues
with our own sisters or mothers. But God loves all women, so we
must too.

Lord, help me to honor the amazing women in my life. Where
would I be without them? In an age where women are still
battling for equality and justice, thank you that you honor
women. You chose Mary to carry your Son. You chose Mary
Magdalene to share the first news of the resurrection. You love
women, so I do too. In Jesus' name, amen.

Stop Looking for Approval

Am I now trying to win the approval of human beings, or of God? Or am I trying to please people?

GALATIANS 1:10

Approval addiction is on the rise thanks to social media. We now have several outlets for our approval seeking. We can post a nicely lit selfie and watch instant responses pour in—people showering us with compliments and emojis. But it can quickly become just like a drug fix. The high wears off quickly, and before we know it, we're chasing down our next high. Lecrae said, "If you live for people's acceptance, you'll die from their rejection." If we rely on the approval of others to fill our confidence tank, we'll spend our whole lives struggling to keep it filled. We must learn to love and accept ourselves.

REFLECTION

Why not take a break from social media, if only for a week or so? Instead of logging on, check in with God's Word. Remind yourself of the many great promises he makes over you. If you're not a social media user, there are other ways to seek the approval of others. Ask God to help you be more aware of ways you seek the approval of others over his approval of you.

Lord, give me some wisdom in this area. If I need to distance myself from approval-centered mediums of communication, please show me what to do and help me to be disciplined. Help me to understand that the only approval I truly need is yours— and I have it! In Jesus' name, amen.

People Can Change

Therefore, if anyone is in Christ, he is a new creation.

2 Corinthians 5:17 esv

They say, "A leopard never changes its spots," and in the natural this is true. But a leopard doesn't have the redeeming power of the Holy Spirit! God promises that when the Holy Spirit comes to live in us, we begin to transform from the inside out. It's true, old habits die hard and we can be very set in our ways. But God can undo the damage that has shaped our behavior and our mind-set.

I know that God can not only change a leopard's spots, but give it a whole new identity. My glass used to be half empty; now it's full. I used to spend my days sleeping, just praying to get through the day. Now I'm here, writing this book of encouragement for you. Anything can happen, so don't write anyone off just yet—especially not yourself! God *can* change a leopard's spots; he can turn a leopard into a tiger!

REFLECTION

Are you trying to start over but feeling the same as before? In Jesus you are an entirely new creation. Are you struggling to give someone a second chance? It's hard to believe that someone could experience a complete "character 180." But if the Bible tells us anything, it's that 180-degree change truly is possible.

Lord, help me to believe this. Help me to know I am truly transformed—I am not the person I was! I have a completely clean slate in you. Help me to be patient and gracious with others who have started anew in you; they also have access to this total transformation in Jesus. Thank you, Lord, for this promise. In Jesus' name, amen.

You're Forgiven

"Now have come the salvation and the power and the kingdom of our God, and the authority of his Messiah. For the accuser of our brothers and sisters, who accuses them before our God day and night, has been hurled down."

REVELATION 12:10

When I first became a Christian, there were a handful of people who couldn't believe it. There were those who knew me as a partying teenager and a rebellious young adult who simply couldn't believe that a person could change so much. They even tried to convince me I was faking my new beginning and was still the old Philippa deep down. My instinct was to defend myself!

But then I looked at my husband. My husband, a pastor's son, had never dated anyone before we met. Because I had a "past," I felt obliged to warn Joel on our first date and make him aware that I wasn't as "pure" as he was.

He put me in my place right away. "You're a new creation," he said. "You're a great girl of God." We've never had any secrets, and he has always displayed the grace of God to me.

REFLECTION

Anyone who has begun a new life in Christ no longer has to bear the shame of the past. The past is gone! Those who accuse us about our past are simply messengers of the enemy who has been defeated by Jesus' work on the cross.

Lord, thank you for the cross! Thank you that you've dealt with everything in my past. The old me is gone and my debts have been paid. Whenever the enemy accuses me, remind me to show him the cross. In Jesus' name, amen.

Cinderella Syndrome

How beautiful you are my darling! Oh, how beautiful! Your eyes
behind your veil are doves.

SONG OF SONGS 4:1

I'm a big fan of fairy tales. Like most little girls, I read all the
books, watched all the movies, and learned all the songs. I still
love them to this day. But there are some interesting and amusing
parallels between those famous fairy stories and the twenty-first
century dating fiasco. Cinderella was beautiful but poor—she
had to rely on the magic of a fairy godmother to transform
her look and make her fit for the dating scene. Only when
transformed into a lady could she have an audience with the
prince and have a chance at winning his heart.

We're a little like Cinderella in today's society—we do lots of
self-improvement in order to measure up to our peers and live in
fear of being seen as we really are. When we do take off the mask,
we can only pray that our suitors still like what they see.

REFLECTION

Be real. Don't hide behind a full-glam mask, because you will
live in fear of being found out and you risk being unhappy with
who is underneath. You don't want the kind of love that only
recognizes you when you're dressed for the ball. You want the one
who loves to see how beautiful you are behind the veil.

Lord, give me the courage and confidence to be the real me.
Help me to present others with an authentic image so those who
like what they see will be attracted to who I really am. In Jesus'
name, amen.

Use Positive Language

The one who acquires good sense loves himself; one who safe-guards understanding finds success.

PROVERBS 19:8 HCSB

I occasionally get messages from discouraged people who want me to pray for them to find love and friendship. But it alarms me when their messages contain phrases like, "I'm hopeless. People find me repulsive. No one wants me." Those phrases raise red flags to me, a stranger, so I'm sure they ring alarm bells with potential friends and partners.

The language we use about ourselves changes the way people see us. We can create a tragic identity for ourselves if we're persistently negative in the presence of others. Having a positive vocabulary lays the foundation for how we'll be treated and valued in relationships. If you're prone to pulling yourself down in the presence of others, this *must* change. Relationships, especially in the beginning, need lots of positivity. People are put off—even repelled—by constant confessions of self-loathing.

REFLECTION

If you've been unsuccessful with relationships recently, practice framing things positively. Say things such as, "I'm open to finding love, and I love to make friends," and, "I haven't found 'the one' yet, but I've learned a lot and I believe in God's timing."

Lord, help me to be mindful of the language I'm using about myself and my situation. Help me to have a positive outlook and to frame things in an optimistic way. I want to project good sense and understanding so others can feel positive in my presence. If I need to work on loving myself a little more, please help me with that, Lord. In Jesus' name, amen.

Wearing Masks

First of all, then, I urge that supplications, prayers, intercessions,
and thanksgivings be made for all people.

1 TIMOTHY 2:1 ESV

We often mask what we feel with what we *want* people to see. A little while ago, I was working with an artist. He was a talented guitarist and very charismatic. Although he oozed confidence and happiness, I had a feeling that things weren't as they appeared. I got up the courage and sent him a text telling him I was concerned. He replied immediately, overwhelmed that I could have known! Thankfully, the power of the Holy Spirit can see beneath the surface of our output and postings on social media to what is in our hearts.

The social media age has caused us more than ever to know each other by the avatars we show the world. We can be quite put off by someone's vain selfies when they are trying to fit themselves into the definition society holds of attractiveness and beauty. Always be prepared to see the true face beneath the facade.

REFLECTION

Do certain people you follow on social media seem to misrepresent themselves? Take a moment to consider what may be going on. What does your own social media avatar look like to others? Does it represent who you really are and what you're going through?

Lord, help me to see beyond the surface of people's social media lives. If there is someone who might need my help or guidance, please show me so I can extend some prayer. In Jesus' name, amen.

You're Worthy

This is how we know what love is:
Jesus Christ laid down his life for us.

1 JOHN 3:16

When you don't know your value, you'll take almost any offer. Part of the reason I stayed in a relationship after it became abusive was because I was unsure I would find anyone else to love me. I wasn't convinced anyone else *could* love me. Worse still, I wasn't sure I deserved it. It took meeting the Lord and understanding that he considered me worth dying for to realize I didn't need to stay in an abusive situation. If I never loved another man, it would be better than selling myself so short of my true worth.

Don't settle for a half-decent relationship when you deserve a deep and passionate one. If ever you doubt that you are worthy of true love, just remind yourself of the deep passion God has for you.

REFLECTION

If you're single now, take a moment to consider your past relationships. Have they gone well? What went wrong? Often, we accept the love we think we deserve. We may have entered into a relationship with someone who doesn't really cherish us—because we don't yet cherish ourselves.

Lord, help me to understand my value to you. You want only the best for me, and you want any relationship I'm in to bring me closer to you. Help me hold out for someone gentle whose eyes are fixed on you. In Jesus' name, amen.

You're Whole

In Him you have been made complete,
and He is the head over all rule and authority.

COLOSSIANS 2:10 NASB

"When you can't see the wood for the trees / You'll fall in love with any stranger that you meet / They may seem strong but who knows what's underneath / Just 'cause somebody shows you kindness when you're weak /Don't share your heart / 'Til it's complete." These are words from a song of mine named "Apples."

When we are living outside the wholeness that comes through Christ, we will often look for a missing part of ourselves in someone else. We often hear people refer to their partner as the "other half." But in truth, the only person who can make us whole is Jesus. When we look to another person to make us whole, we wind up in unhealthy relationships.

When we're broken, we fall in love with just about anybody who shows kindness; relationships formed out of brokenness become codependent and volatile. When you're so hungry to be loved, you'll bite into just about any poisoned apple that you're offered—just like poor, lost, and rejected Snow White.

REFLECTION

Don't go looking for the other half of your broken heart—focus instead on finding inner wholeness in Christ. When our hearts are made complete in Jesus, we begin to understand our worth and seek a partner or friend who sees it too.

Lord, you are enough for me. Your presence in my life has made me whole. Let me focus on completeness in you so I'm ready to love when the right relationship comes along. In Jesus' name, amen.

Insecurity Is Human

If you say, "The LORD is my refuge," and you make the Most High your dwelling, no harm will overtake you, no disaster will come near your tent. For he will command his angels concerning you to guard you in all your ways.

PSALM 91:9–11

We all want to live a life where we feel protected and safe. If you're feeling insecure today, there's every chance you have a valid reason and that it's coming from an instinct. You may feel that something or someone is threatening your happiness. Perhaps you may be worried that your housing or financial situations aren't stable. These are all areas of insecurity that come from an instinct. But the way we act when we feel insecure can be damaging and destructive to relationships, so it's crucial that we get a grip on these feelings.

REFLECTION

We have to learn to process insecurity objectively— understanding it's human, but God is bigger. While you can't help feeling concerned about your security in this world, you can react soberly. The last thing you want is to rob yourself of happiness because insecurity got the better of you. Today let's seek a kingdom perspective and find security in God.

God, as I unravel some of my insecurities this month, please guide me. Help me to see with clarity through the lens of your truth. Help me never to rob myself of blessings because of a natural instinct to protect my heart. In Jesus' name, amen.

Insecurity Comes from Experience

Rejoice with those who rejoice, weep with those who weep.
Live in harmony with one another.

ROMANS 12:15–16 ESV

A lot of our insecurities are learned. If you've had an awful experience being rejected by so-called friends, you're likely to feel very insecure among your peers. If you've missed opportunities because someone stabbed you in the back to get ahead, you might feel insecure at work. If you've had a cheating spouse, you're likely to have a lot of fear in your current relationship.

This kind of learned insecurity can be hard to shake. Ultimately, you're traumatized, and it's natural for you to default to a fight-or-flight mode. It's so important to remember that not all people are the same—not all spouses are unfaithful and not all friends are fickle. It would be a tragedy to let the ones who hurt you in the past rob you of your future relationships as well.

REFLECTION

Today, let's make a conscious effort to lay old hurts to rest. While we need to protect our hearts, we don't want to harden them. The people in your life don't deserve to be treated with suspicion, so it's time to ask God to remove our negative expectations and replace them with faith.

Lord, you know how I've been hurt in the past and that I am afraid to be hurt again. I know you see and understand why I'm protective over what I have because it was so hard to lose last time. Please help me to have an open heart and to leave those past hurts where they should be—in the past. Help me to have faith in the people around me. In Jesus' name, amen.

Insecurity Is a Thief

"The thief comes only to steal and kill and destroy;
I have come that they may have life, and have it to the full."

John 10:10

Feeling insecure is something that takes time to work on. In the meantime, we must be super careful not to *act* out of insecurity. If we let insecurity affect our behavior and make our decisions, it will have only one agenda—to steal. When insecurity makes your choices, it will take your joy, your opportunities, and even your relationships. Don't let it. Don't let insecurity sit in the driver's seat of your life. Grip it by the shoulder and tell it, *Not today, insecurity. You're not having my relationships, my joy, and my dreams. You've already had too much of me. Back off!*

Reflection

If you're feeling a little insecure, take a moment to breathe before you make a decision that could be damaging. Breathe before you speak a negative word about someone. Breathe before you refuse to help someone you feel threatened by. Breathe before you pick up your partner's phone and invade his or her privacy without due cause. Your actions could well be more damaging than anything another person is doing.

Lord, today I come against the thief of insecurity in the name of Jesus. I declare that it has no place in my life and no claim over my relationships. If ever I feel tempted to do something destructive out of insecurity, please give me the self-control to take hold of my impulses. If there is reason to believe that someone is deceiving me, please help me to confront and handle that situation maturely. In Jesus' name, amen.

Jealousy Is a Liar

Therefore, putting aside all malice and all deceit and
hypocrisy and envy and all slander, like newborn babies,
long for the pure milk of the word, so that by it you may
grow in respect to salvation.

1 PETER 2:1-2 NASB

Jealousy usually begins as a light whisper that tells you delicious
little lies. It tells you to look at someone else's blessings and view
them as a curse upon you. It taunts you with phrases like: *They
have it all, and you have nothing. They're getting ahead, and you're
being left behind. They're loved and favored, you're ignored and
neglected.*

When we allow these lies to take hold, we become paranoid
and destructive. Call out the lies for what they truly are.

REFLECTION

In the face of these kinds of lies, it's helpful to respond with
truth. The truth is that God has blessed you abundantly, he has
a plan for you and his timing is perfect. You are *loved* and *highly
favored.* Don't let jealousy deceive you and steal your joy today.

Lord, help me today to guard against the lies of the enemy
with these incredible truths. Let me drink the pure milk of the
Word and be strengthened against this deception. I trust you
and believe that you always have in mind what's best for me. In
Jesus' name, amen.

Impatience Can Cause Jealousy

But if we hope for what we do not yet have,
we wait for it patiently.

ROMANS 8:25

Quite often we become jealous when we don't receive our breakthrough fast enough. A little while ago, I was praying for a breakthrough in my career and became sensitive about the breaks other people seemed to be getting. I started to take it personally when someone got a record deal or an opportunity. I felt it was unfair and I was being overlooked. What was becoming clear in me was my lack of faith! I had stopped believing that God was going to take care of me. I had stopped looking at my blessings and begun looking over the fence at my neighbors'. I was preoccupied with other people's lives instead of giving thanks for my own.

REFLECTION

When this kind of jealousy occurs, it's important to begin giving thanks. God is doing all manner of things for us behind the scenes, and we have no way of knowing what God is doing in our neighbors' lives or what they've gone through to achieve their breakthrough. Looking over your neighbor's fence at *their* blooming flowers is no way to judge the seeds *you* just planted. Tend to your garden and rejoice that the soil is good in your neighborhood.

Lord, help me to keep my eyes on my own garden. Help me to understand that there is a process of cultivation in my life and I can't judge my progress by someone else's. Thank you for all that you're doing in my life and for the amazing favor you give me. In Jesus' name, amen.

Jealousy Is Often Misguided

Remember that your family of believers all over the world is
going through the same kind of suffering you are.

1 PETER 5:9 NLT

It's easy to envy other's successes. We regard them as having
arrived on some beautiful, exclusive island of their own. But
chances are, if we really knew what it took to get there, we
wouldn't be up for the voyage.

Lots of people think that life on the road is all lights,
laughter, and applause. But when people come out with us as
volunteers, they quickly learn that late nights, days in the car,
financial instability, diet changes, and unpredictable audiences
are more than they bargained for! Most are quite relieved to get
back to their own lives.

REFLECTION

What looks exciting from a distance is quite often a battle
up close. If you ever feel envy, try to remind yourself that
appearances are deceiving. No one has it quite as easy as you
imagine.

Lord, help me to have more sense when it comes to my view of
others. Please help me switch jealousy for compassion toward
others. In Jesus' name, amen.

There's Enough Favor to Go Around

Above all else, guard your heart,
for everything you do flows from it.
PROVERBS 4:23

A popular female pastor once spoke about her struggle to become pregnant. After praying regularly for others facing similar struggles, she found herself in a dark place when these women returned with gratitude that their prayers had been answered. She felt angry. She even felt jealous. But she fought those emotions and continued praying for whoever might need prayer. Eventually, she was blessed with beautiful children of her own.

When we find ourselves in this painful place, it's important not to let jealousy win. God is not cruel and hasn't passed you by. He didn't give your blessing to someone else and forget all about you. Was God being cruel, prompting young women to go to that pastor asking for prayer? No. I'm convinced he knew that this pastor's prayers came from somewhere deep and sincere because she truly understood the pain. Was he cruel giving those mothers their babies first? No. I'm convinced that he was showing his power, proving that a miracle was possible.

REFLECTION

Life is hard while you're in that waiting place. But in the meantime, guard your heart from becoming consumed by jealousy and remember that he has more than enough blessing to go around.

Lord, thank you that all the blessings in all of creation belong to you—you will never run out of money or opportunity to share with your children. Today, help me guard my heart so good things can flow from it. In Jesus' name, amen.

There Are No Inferior Keys

My frame was not hidden from you, when I was being made in
secret, intricately woven in the depths of the earth.

PSALM 139:15 ESV

My uncle Harold used to collect keys. He had dozens of them, all
shapes and sizes, and I loved them. As a child, I loved examining
and organizing them—there was so much variety in his collection and I loved imagining what each key was meant to unlock.

Let me ask you: Does it matter what the key to your home
looks like when you're scrambling around in the dark? Do you
care what the color or shape is? No. All you care about is that
it fits, turns, and opens the door. Its size and age don't matter.
It doesn't even matter if it's a plain or a pretty key when you're
standing in the dark struggling to open the door.

All that matters is that it opens the door it was made to
open. And guess what? It's the same with us! We were formed
with mathematical precision to fit into a small space in history
and open a door that no one else can open. You're perfectly
formed for your destiny. You are the key. Don't change shape.

REFLECTION

When we realize that our purposes are so specific, it helps us to
overcome insecurity. No one else can really do what you were
sent here to do. If you ever feel envious of how someone else was
made, remind yourself that God formed you intentionally for
your destiny.

Lord, thank you that you made me on purpose. Thank you that
you don't make inferior people. Today, let me love my shape
and focus on the door you've called me to open. In Jesus' name,
amen.

Others Are Not Your Problem

For though we live in the world, we do not wage war as the world does. The weapons we fight with are not the weapons of the world. On the contrary, they have divine power to demolish strongholds. We demolish arguments and every pretension that sets itself up against the knowledge of God, and we take captive every thought to make it obedient to Christ.

2 Corinthians 10:3–5

Women have an unhealthy habit of seeing other women as competition, a problem. This creates division and disharmony. But in just the same way we each are a cell in the body of Christ, each of us is also an *answer* to a problem.

Jealousy wants to compete with and diminish one another to elevate ourselves. What does this achieve? It limits the amount of problems we can find a solution for. There is a problem out there to which only you are the answer. And if you can lay jealousy aside and edify those around you, the problems we could solve are mind-blowing. Let's uphold and support one another in being medicine for this world!

Reflection

Is there someone in your life you've felt threatened by? Have you struggled to build up and promote that person? Today, call that person to mind and be mindful that God has created them as an answer to a problem.

Lord, help me to overcome jealousy. I want to be someone who uplifts others and releases them into their callings. Help me overcome the lie from the enemy that others are a threat to my position. Help me to take all those thoughts captive to you. In Jesus' name, amen.

The Blessing of Collaboration

Let the word of Christ dwell in you richly, teaching and admonishing one another in all wisdom, singing psalms and hymns and spiritual songs, with thankfulness in your hearts to God.

COLOSSIANS 3:16 ESV

Recently, I had the chance to write a song with someone I admire very much. I wanted to go for it, but my insecurity was holding me back. I was afraid that I would get in the room and be intimidated, that the outcome wouldn't be good enough for her. I was all kinds of afraid! But that day I bit the bullet and allowed common sense to prevail. I knew this was an opportunity to share my gift and create something beautiful with someone I respected.

In the writing room that day, we sat together and laughed, cried, sang, and shared our hearts, writing a song we both loved. As we reflected later, we agreed that the song was something extra special because it had both of our fingerprints on it—our hearts, experience, and gifting were sewn into its seams. Don't be afraid or let insecurity hold you back! Collaboration brings about things you could never do alone.

REFLECTION

Is there someone in your world you could collaborate with? Could your organization join with another to do an outreach event or ministry? Could you get together with some friends and create something amazing? There's nothing to fear in working together.

Lord, please show me how collaboration could enrich my life and help me to achieve more for you. I don't want to be held back by insecurity on this. Help me be a blessing to my brothers and sisters. In Jesus' name, amen.

The Blessing of Community

Each one should test their own actions. Then they can take pride in themselves alone, without comparing themselves to someone else.

GALATIANS 6:4

When I was sixteen, my community was nearly nonexistent. My family loved me, but they were spread out. I had a boyfriend but didn't see much of my other friends. When I found faith and joined a church, I experienced community for the first time. I knew what it was to be part of a team! I had people I could ask about finances and computers as well as singers and musicians I could call upon for back up. People of all backgrounds were available to me to confide in and seek guidance from.

When we guard our gifts and resources out of fear, we lose the blessings that come from sharing. If you want to do everything by yourself, take all the blame, and get a fraction of the work done, embrace jealousy! That will make sure you're isolated. You may get all the credit, but there may not be much to take credit for. You may be safe from heartbreak, but you may not have much to celebrate either.

REFLECTION

Take a moment today to ask God to keep working on this with you. Community is hard sometimes. We tend to get competitive and sometimes must deal with difficult individuals. Through it all, there is so much more blessing than burden in community!

Lord, if I need to be better knitted into a community today, please show me how. I will follow your lead. If I'm right where I should be already, help me to do a great job for my community today. Help my actions do good for others. In Jesus' name, amen.

The World Needs Your Light Too

Do everything without grumbling or arguing, so that you may
become blameless and pure, "children of God without fault in
a warped and crooked generation." Then you will shine among
them like stars in the sky.

PHILIPPIANS 2:14–15

As an artist, it's easy to become insecure about another emerging
artist. No matter your occupation, there's every chance you'll
be intimidated by the presence of someone new with a similar
passion and talent. I have a solution for this.

Switch on the TV and watch the news for a few moments.
There is no shortage of people striving to make this world a darker
place. If you're anything like me, you've prayed many times for a
peaceful, more loving world. You've prayed for a generation of great
servants and honorable leaders to rise up and create music and
film that would shine a light in this deprived generation. So how
petty and pointless to find yourself intimidated by the light you've
prayed for. Instead, do all you can to help that light shine brighter.

REFLECTION

There is more than enough darkness; an army of light bearers is
needed. There will never be a shortage of lives to save, hearts to
reach, and good news to share. Don't let these insecurities cause
you to fear someone else's light. Work together to help the light
shine even brighter.

Lord, thank you that you've made your children a light in this
world. Let there be even more light! Help me to share mine
and magnify others' lights. Help our light to multiply and be
contagious. Let us never fear being outshone but continue to
shine ever brighter for you. In Jesus' name, amen.

Don't Try to Be like Anyone Else

Not that I have already obtained all this, or have already arrived at my goal, but I press on to take hold of that for which Christ Jesus took hold of me.

PHILIPPIANS 3:12

God has taken hold of our lives for a reason. We must take hold of who we are and the things only we can bring. I learned something in my early years a singer—trying to sound like someone else only makes you easier to forget. Trying to look like someone else only makes you more invisible. You can never outshine someone with their own light! Try to be like someone you admire, and you'll only look like a knockoff copy—a marketplace counterfeit of something more expensive and special. Just like a hundred-dollar bill, each of us is marked with a unique number that can't be duplicated.

Every soul has a unique outline that can't be copied or matched. If you try to be the same shape as someone else, you'll only disappear into their shadow! Be yourself, and you'll always stand out.

REFLECTION

Have you been influenced heavily by another person, leader, or artist? It's great to have influences and mentors, but retaining your unique perspective is important. Is there more you could do to explore your God-given silhouette?

Lord, thank you that you made me like no other. If I've been tempted to become like someone else please, return me to the purpose you have for me. Help me to focus on being more like you and a better version of me. In Jesus' name, amen.

No One Can Be You

> "Do not fear, for I have redeemed you;
> I have called you by name; you are Mine!"
>
> ISAIAH 43:1 NASB

There's nothing more awkward than introducing your husband to a woman who looks just like you did ten years ago. No singer really likes to hear the words, "I thought I heard you on the radio yesterday—it sounded just like you!" We want to be unique. But let me remind you—*no one is exactly like you*. There is no one who possesses the same mix of everything that makes you wonderful.

Even if people *try* to be just like you, they'll never pull it off. If you're doing something unique and interesting, you may find people trying to emulate you. It can be a little strange to post something on social media and moments later see something eerily similar by a friend of yours. Even if someone has a similar gift, they'll never have your point of view. They may have similar eyes, but they won't have seen what you have seen. So relax, no one can rob you of who you are.

REFLECTION

Feeling like someone is copying you can be quite irritating and alarming. If you're a pioneer, you're bound to see people trying to emulate your style or approach. But take heart, it means you're inspiring people! No one else can ever truly be you, but it's a great encouragement that you're held in such high regard.

Lord, help me not to be anxious when people imitate my style. Help me not to be afraid when someone has a similar appeal. You've given me a completely unique set of experiences and abilities, and you've only made one me. Help me rest in that today, Father. In Jesus' name, amen.

Life Is Short

Yet you do not know what your life will be like tomorrow. You are just a vapor that appears for a little while and then vanishes away.

James 4:14 NASB

If I look back on life up to this point, there are two things I regret wasting time on—fear and insecurity. We'll get to the fear later. But let's deal with the insecurity now. Every time I've chosen to step out and do something despite my insecurities, I've been highly blessed. There have been many times, however, when I've stayed quiet or avoided doing something because it made me feel unsafe. I've come to a place where I'm determined not to waste another moment protecting my heart or my reputation. There have already been too many times where doing so meant I missed out on blessing others. Life is short. You have a job to do and a life to live—don't let insecurity hold you back.

Reflection

The enemy loves to waste our time. When he realizes we can't be stopped, he settles for slowing us down. Quarrelling, doubting yourself, and being distracted by other people's business are all hurdles designed to keep us doing less of our good work. Today, let's keep our eyes off the nonsense and on the prize.

Lord, thank you that your will is being done in my life. I've asked for you to be King in my heart, and every day you're leading me forward. Help me to trust in that and to be secure in you. In Jesus' name, amen.

Behind the Scenes

Since we live by the Spirit, let us keep in step with the Spirit. Let us not become conceited, provoking and envying each other.

GALATIANS 5:25–26

Our social media profiles are usually well manicured. We only share what we want people to see. Don't forget when you browse the lives of others you're seeing something edited, curated, and well-crafted to look good. The same is mostly true of who we are in church. We don't drag ourselves into the meeting halfway through an argument or emotional breakdown. We clean up and put on our best face for the crowds. There's nothing inherently wrong with this—it's natural. Not everyone needs to see our dirty laundry. But it's worth remembering everyone has dirty laundry. As Steven Furtick famously said, "When you compare your life on social media, you're comparing your 'behind the scenes' truth to someone else's 'highlight reel.'" It's okay. You're doing much better than you realize.

REFLECTION

Chances are your "behind the scenes" isn't as bad as you think it is. Today, focus on the truth that we all have maintenance to do in our lives and we all have things to celebrate.

Lord, we all have a "behind the scenes," and we all like to share our best bits with the world. Help me to be mindful of this when I'm on social media. There are no perfect families, relationships, or careers, and there is a price to pay to maintain everything good we have. Let me revert to gratitude for the things I'm able to add to my highlight reel. In Jesus' name, amen.

Humility

Do nothing out of selfish ambition or vain conceit. Rather, in humility value others above yourselves, not looking to your own interests but each of you to the interests of the others.

PHILIPPIANS 2:3–4

When I began my Christian journey, I was very *self*-focused. My life had been filled with all kinds of drama, and I was suffering with depression. Both cause your world to be something of a bubble you struggle to see beyond. I was insecure and struggled to put others first. I resisted sharing opportunities with others, afraid of how that might affect me. When I began my relationship with God, I found I became able to focus less on myself. Knowing his love and favor over my life made it easier to put others first.

Humility leads to a life of blessing for you and others. But the key to practicing humility is knowing your self-worth. When you know who you are and believe your true value, you have no problem allowing someone else to take the credit, attention, and priority over you. You're secure in the knowledge that you are loved, blessed, and highly favored!

REFLECTION

Do you find it hard to put others first? Today, ask God to fill your heart with assurances of your value to him. Think of the cross. Remember that it was *you* he died for and that he cares for you more than you could ever imagine.

Lord, thank you so much for my worth in you. Thank you that you paid the ultimate price for my life. Help me not to focus on what I deserve, but instead focus on how I can put others first as you did for me. In Jesus' name, amen.

People Won't Always Thank You

Serve wholeheartedly, as if you were serving the Lord, not people.

EPHESIANS 6:7

Gratitude should come naturally—manners are usually taught to us as children, after all. But in the real world, people won't always thank you for your help. You could invest a great deal into a person and never hear those two little words. It's important to put yourself in the right frame of mind before you become a Good Samaritan.

We help others because God asks us to—we help as a reflection of God's character and it benefits others. It would be so easy to snatch away our kindness because someone isn't deserving or thankful. But we must decide what kind of person *we* want to be. If we're to be like Jesus, we will pour ourselves out even though people are undeserving, just as he did.

REFLECTION

You might have played an important role in someone's life, and yet that person totally forgets you when he or she tells their story. If that person is making the world a better place, would you take back your positive influence? You may never be mentioned in the church notices for your service, but if people are being saved, will you not play your part?

Lord, help me to remember that when I help people, I am not doing it out of selfishness or vanity; I'm doing it for you. It's nice when people appreciate my efforts, but even if they don't, Lord, I'm still willing to serve you. Help me to overcome that need for approval. In Jesus' name, amen.

It's Okay to Lean on Someone

Carry each other's burdens, and in this way you
will fulfill the law of Christ.

GALATIANS 6:2

There are often extremes when it comes to friendships. Some friends always seem to need support, while others are being supportive. I'm someone who likes to be supportive and doesn't always feel comfortable asking for help. Often, I don't feel like a great friend unless I'm the one coming to the rescue. For each of us, there are bound to be moments in life where we just need to lean on someone's shoulder. That doesn't make us needy or a burden, it just makes us human. It's okay to admit you're struggling and that you don't feel okay. Sometimes we just need each other; sometimes we just need to have a good chat and drink tea.

REFLECTION

Why not take a moment today to thank God for your good friends? Pray a blessing over their lives and give God praise for providing them. If you're really in need of a good friend, pray for one.

Lord, we all need friends. We need to have people we can call upon for help now and again. Help me to find such friends if they aren't in my life already. If I need to build a friendship with someone specific, please show me. Please give me courage and humility if I need to reach out to someone I already know. In Jesus' name, amen.

Making Friends

Jesus grew in wisdom and stature, and in favor with God and man.
LUKE 2:52

The pressure to make instant bonds begins at school. We hope to find companionship on the spot and to have formed a clique on day one. But best friends aren't found; they are made! Meaningful friendships don't grow overnight, and good friendship chemistry is not always instant.

I was so encouraged by this Scripture in Luke. Even Jesus had growing to do in his relationships with people and with God! It takes time to establish yourself and build good rapport with others.

If you're beginning something new—a job or school year—don't pressure yourself to be popular right from the get-go. No one can really get to know a whole group of people in a day or find a friend for life during first period. You might well hit it off with someone at the water fountain before lunch. But the likelihood is that you'll have to invest in a few people and spend a little longer building rapport before a true friendship develops.

REFLECTION

Sometimes in life we meet people who become instant friends. But most of the time that's not the case—we must work for it. Today, take comfort that even the King of kings had to take time to invest in people and build connections. Just breathe, be yourself, and give it time.

Lord, thank you for friendship. I so want to have people in my life that I can count on and connect with. Help me to invest in relationships. Please give me the patience I need to slowly grow alongside others and build something solid. In Jesus' name, amen.

A Good Friend Is Like a Bad Mirror

An open rebuke is better than hidden love! Wounds from a
sincere friend are better than many kisses from an enemy.

PROVERBS 27:5–6 NLT

I stayed in a hotel recently that had terrible lighting in the
bathroom. Between the bad lighting and the magnifying mirror,
I was quite horrified by my appearance when I woke up. I did
my makeup in the terrible mirror and went about my day. I was
amazed to find that when I got into the daylight, my skin looked
flawless! That bad mirror had shown so much detail that I'd done
a better job than ever at my makeup. It gave me the inspiration
for this short poem:

A good friend is like a bad mirror / That shows you the
truth and exposes your flaws / Shows the blue in your eye bags /
Enhances your pores / For you cringe at the details / The redness
much redder / But you deal with what's there / And in daylight
look better.

REFLECTION

It's not always easy to hear the truth. The book of Proverbs is full
of instructions about inviting friends to speak words of truth to
us. Being open to their advice brings wisdom and success. Today,
ask God to give you the patience and strength of character to
absorb instruction from friends.

Lord, help me have ears to hear the truth of a friend. Though
it's not always easy to hear, let me be open and patient when
someone who loves me gives sound but tough advice. In Jesus'
name, amen.

A True Friend Offers Help

Dear children, let us not love with words or speech but with
actions and in truth.

1 John 3:18

A friend that challenges you but isn't willing to help you is no
friend at all. Sometimes, a friend will use the excuse of "truth
spoken in love" to criticize you. The best way for you to tell if that
friend is really on your side is to see if they're willing to help with
the problem. If a friend says you ought to go to church more but
isn't willing to help you get there, what good is that? If a friend
tells you that you drink too much but always reaches to top up
your glass, how are they helping?

I once had a friend in the music industry who constantly
berated my achievements and told me I should be more
successful. He never lifted a finger to help me move forward
even though he was more than able. A person must have a real
relationship with you to earn the right to advise you. Beware of
those who are just using "love" as an excuse to undermine your
confidence.

Reflection

Do you have a friend or family member who is always pulling
you down? Does this person constantly question your ability or
choices? It's worth bringing this to God. Ask him to show you
this person's intentions. If they're not helpful, there is probably
some agenda behind their attitude toward you.

Lord, help me to know the difference between a loving rebuke
and the enemy in disguise. In Jesus' name, amen.

Just Be There

Anxiety in a man's heart weighs it down,
but a good word makes it glad.

PROVERBS 12:25 NASB

When someone you love is going through difficulties, it's easy to feel helpless. Never underestimate the power of just being present—standing in the shadows offering support. It's amazing how easy, important, and underrated that is. It's not your responsibility or within your power to fix everything, but a kind word or two can make all the difference.

Most friendships begin with good times, but friendship really is at its best during the bad times. True friends will step out of their great day to comfort you on your bad day. They'll put down their fun and run to your doctor appointment. They'll call when they sense that tone in your text message that things are not okay. True friends will step out of life's party for you and stand by your side in the lonely corridor of your sadness. They'll help remind you that the fun isn't over, but until you feel ready, they're more than happy to dance with you in the hall.

REFLECTION

If you're truly concerned about a friend today, take a moment to pray for him or her. It's frustrating to feel so out of control, but God surely is not. Lift your friend to God right now, asking him to fill the situation with his peace.

Lord, thank you for those true friends who stand by us through everything. I lift up ___ to you right now. Give my friend peace and comfort, Lord. By your Holy Spirit, help my friend through this time by drawing near to you. In the meantime, teach me how to give the best support I can. In Jesus' name, amen.

Be Generous

"Give, and it will be given to you. A good measure, pressed down, shaken together and running over, will be poured into your lap. For with the measure you use, it will be measured to you."

LUKE 6:38

Sometimes we feel as if people take advantage of our generous nature. We seem to constantly give and never receive. There are certain friends who always seem to have an outstretched hand or have conveniently forgotten their wallet at dinner. Regardless of whether our generosity is appreciated by others or not, God always sees that it is returned to us and then some. You've heard it said that it's impossible to out give God, and it's true! God rewards our giving. When people mistreat us after we've been kind to them, it can be very off-putting. Don't let a miserly friend dissuade you from being the wonderful, giving soul God intends you to be.

REFLECTION

There may be certain people in our lives who indeed are taking advantage of our good nature. This may not be God's intention, so while we aim to practice generosity, we have to make sure people know our boundaries. It's okay to say, "I can't afford to go out this weekend," or "Can you pick up the tab this time?" Pray for wisdom in this today.

Lord, I want to be generous just as you are. Help me to deal with situations where the kindness is one-sided. Please help the people in my life to value me and to contribute to our activities. If there are any awkward conversations that need to be had, I pray you would help me in them. Thank you, above all, that you are my provider. In Jesus' name, amen.

Focus on Who Is with You

A friend loves at all times.

PROVERBS 17:17 NASB

If you've been through hard times recently, chances are you've watched a few peoples' texts dry up. You might have even seen a few faces disappear from around the table. When we're truly at our lowest, there are few people who will love you enough to remain at your side. But I have some good news—you can't lose a *true* friend, because true friends don't disappear. Painful as it can be when friends are absent, don't waste too much time focusing on those empty chairs. Focus on those sitting with you. And make sure you're always ready to go and sit with them!

REFLECTION

It's true that hard times often teach us who our real friends are, but that doesn't make losing those we believed to be true friends any easier. Today, ask for healing in this area.

Lord, thank you for the gift of real friends who stand by me in tough times. Help me to deal with the hurt of losing those who have turned away. Today I release them to you and ask that you bless them. I pray that in due course they would learn the meaning of loyalty—that great blessing you freely promise all of us. In Jesus' name, amen.

Betrayal

Jesus asked him, "Judas, are you betraying the
Son of Man with a kiss?"

LUKE: 22:48

Jesus knew that Judas would betray him. He predicted the
betrayal long before the kiss, but he allowed Judas to remain at
his table. He allowed Judas to walk and serve beside him. Jesus
foretold that Peter would deny him, and still Jesus called Peter
a friend. Jesus held those around him with light hands, never
forcing them to love or serve him.

When we love someone, it's only natural to fear losing them.
There's nothing you can do under the sun to make someone love
you more. Our friends are with us by their own free will. If we
hold on too tightly, they may flee at the first opportunity. If we
keep our hands open, they feel free to stay. Most people feel more
comfortable in a space where they are loved and welcomed but
the door remains open. Sadly, holding a friendship with open
hands doesn't mean we won't face betrayal.

REFLECTION

If you struggle with trust or tend to hold on too tightly to
friends, today is all about you. Let's take a moment to release our
grip on those who aren't ours to own. There's nothing we can do
to make them honor us—all we can do is love.

Lord, I'm thankful for the people you have blessed me with, but
I don't want to hold them too tightly. Let the loved ones in my
world be like the tide—coming and going peacefully. Let them
always feel a sense of peace and freedom in my presence. In
Jesus' name, amen.

Be Reasonable

Bear with each other and forgive one another if any of you has a grievance against someone. Forgive as the Lord forgave you. And over all these virtues put on love, which binds them all together in perfect unity.

Colossians 3:13–14

Some errors in friendship might be nonnegotiable to you, but try to remember that some transgressions are minor and some major. For instance, being late may be a small offense while not showing up might be much larger. Betraying your trust on a small piece of information might be a huge deal to you, but it might not! You might be more careful what you share with your friend next time.

It's good to remember that friends with contrasting personalities are likely to approach friendship differently. Something that you might not *dream* of doing (cancelling last minute for instance), might be something they're prone to for all manner of personal reasons. It doesn't necessarily mean they're terrible people or don't love you; they may simply have grown up in families who regularly cancel and struggle to stick to plans.

Reflection

Are you quite hard on friends who disappoint you? Could you be a little more patient? Or do you have a friend who is quite demanding of you? It's ok to communicate about this and make some changes.

Lord, help me to communicate well my wants and needs in a friendship. Help me to understand that we're all different. In Jesus' name, amen.

Different Views

God is love. Whoever lives in love lives in God, and God in them.
1 JOHN 4:16

The sweetest gift I ever received from a friend was a gold-plated guitar pick with my favorite Bible verse on it. The gift itself was lovely, but what made it extra special was that my friend who gave it is an atheist. Rhian and I have known each other from childhood. Until I was twenty-one I was agnostic, so we never had much cause for disagreement. When I became a Christian, we had lots of late-night debates. In the end, our affection and respect for one another won out.

Rhian has tried to understand my faith. She even took a course with her partner, Leon. We're on a journey together to understand each other's viewpoints. Although we don't have Christianity in common, we do share something very important—we really like each other!

Rhian's gift represented to me the power of love and the blessing of true friendship. A strong and lasting relationship of any kind comes when you're prepared to love each other more than you're prepared to love being right.

REFLECTION

Do you have someone in your life who opposes your faith or viewpoint? Bring your concerns to God today, knowing that he is far bigger, and that love is far more powerful than conflict.

Lord, thank you for the friends I have who don't agree with me. Help me navigate any difficult conflicts that may arise, and above all, protect the love we have for each other. Wherever there is love, you are there, Lord. In Jesus' name, amen.

Manage Expectations

A hot-tempered person starts fights;
a cool-tempered person stops them.

PROVERBS 15:18 NLT

People have different ideas of what a good friend is. Some people expect absolute devotion and attention while others are more casual. Some expect daily phone calls and texts. Others are happy to meet up a couple of times a year, and it's as though no time has passed at all. Considering yesterday's thoughts about being different, perhaps take a moment to discuss what's important to you and make sure your friend knows those things. They might not be able to accommodate your expectations fully, but knowing how you feel could make a difference.

I'm notoriously terrible at remembering special occasions and cards, but when it comes to certain friends, I make the extra effort if I know they count it very important. Those friends have learned to be patient with me over the years because they know I'm trying, even if I sometimes fail. It's all about communication! And don't forget to be kind.

REFLECTION

What we consider the best way is not necessarily the only way to do things. If our expectations are too rigid, we could miss out on adding some people to our lives who would enrich it by their differences.

Lord, help me to manage my own expectations in relationships. Beyond the nonnegotiable aspects of good friendship, help me to have patience and tolerance regarding those things that are not crucial, such as the amount of contact. I don't want to miss out on knowing great people because they approach things differently. In Jesus' name, amen.

Hug

> "I will give you a new heart and put a new spirit within you; and I will remove the heart of stone from your flesh and give you a heart of flesh."
>
> Ezekiel 36:26 NASB

Some of us find physical contact really challenging. But so often where words fail, physical touch speaks. I was really challenged by the training we got the first time I volunteered at a soup kitchen.

The pastor said to us, "Don't be afraid of physical contact. Some of these guys haven't felt the warmth of someone's hand on their back or arm around their shoulder in years." Throughout the night, I tried to serve the guys with a friendly handshake or gentle hand across their arm as we set down their dinner. And I must admit, it looked like the healing they craved.

Touch really does heal. There have been many times where I haven't had the words to comfort a friend. A hug can say a thousand words—*thank you, I love you, sorry, I'm here*—and so much more. A good hug can fix things that words, advice, correction, and even encouragement can't. If someone you love is having a hard time, don't feel bad if you're not able to be the wise old sage. Some situations have no words. On those occasions, just be ready with a hug.

Reflection

God, by his Holy Spirit, gives us an incredible capacity to love. Today, rely on him to give you a warm heart toward the person in your life who needs us most.

Lord, help me to know when to offer physical contact. Help me to be mindful of boundaries but not be afraid to take a risk when necessary. Give me, by the power of the Holy Spirit, a warm and soft heart toward those who need me most. In Jesus' name, amen.

Friendship Can Survive

Above all, love each other deeply,
because love covers over a multitude of sins.
1 PETER 4:8

When I was fourteen, I loved a boy. We'd been dating and became quite close. My best friend and I talked about it a lot. We spent hours talking about how I felt and even plotting together to make this boy more serious about me. But one night in a drunken teenage mistake, my best friend hooked up with my boyfriend. I didn't find out till months later, and when I did, I was utterly devastated. I'd never felt sorrow like it. Not only did my boyfriend hook up with someone else, but my best friend—who *knew* how I felt—had been the one to crush my dreams.

At the time, I never thought we'd speak again. But we did. Twenty years later, we're still best friends. In the end I loved her more than I loved nursing a broken heart. I knew that mistakes weren't beyond me. She knew how close we were to losing that lifelong relationship we'd had since childhood, and I believed that she was truly sorry. Not everything is forgivable in a friendship, but if that friend is more like family, most things are.

REFLECTION

If someone has hurt or betrayed you, maybe it's time to ask, *Is this person important enough for me to let this transgression go?*

Lord, if there is someone in my life who has hurt me, let me forgive. I want to save this relationship and give things another chance. Help me to love in a way that these wrongs are covered. Forgive me, Lord, if I have been the one in the wrong. Friendship is so precious, and I don't want to lose a good one. In Jesus' name, amen.

Do Not Fear Surrender

"Behold, we have left everything and followed You."
MARK 10:28 NASB

At age twenty-one, I started my life over completely. I'd been living in debt, darkness, and a relationship crisis. With nothing left to give or lose in life, I decided to see if God could do a better job than me. I emerged from that long night into a new morning with a simple prayer on my lips: *Your will be done.* It was terrifying. I chose to put my heart, my plans, my thoughts, my relationships, and my future into better hands. This is something I try (imperfectly) to do daily. And though it's still not easy to let go and relinquish control of the details, I've begun to see the most beautiful weaving of light in every aspect of my life. Even in the valleys I'm comforted and protected. Surrender is freedom from self. Say it with me today, "Your will be done, Lord."

REFLECTION

God always does a better job at life than we could do alone. Start this new chapter of the year by opening your hands afresh and letting go.

Lord, your ways will always be higher than mine. It's hard to have the faith to let go and put you in charge. I know you always do a better job than me. Today I relinquish control to you again. In Jesus' name, amen.

Do Not Fear the Unknown

"Have I not commanded you? Be strong and courageous. Do not be afraid; do not be discouraged, for the LORD your God will be with you wherever you go."

JOSHUA 1:9

There can be no true adventure without an element of the unknown. We prepare as best we can, but we will never really know what awaits us on our journey. God promises never to leave nor forsake us. He tells us not to fear because his presence surrounds us always. When we look back at the journey, we can see the tracks that God has left. Somehow, whatever the landscape of our lives, there is an unchanging love that surrounds us.

REFLECTION

Do you feel you are being called into the unknown today? Arm yourself with God's Word—promises from the Father right there in black and white.

Lord, thank you that you promise never to leave me. Whatever happens on this adventure, I know you will be with me. I don't know what is going to happen, but I know your presence surrounds me. Thank you, Lord, for your amazing presence and faithfulness. In Jesus' name, amen.

Do Not Fear Small Beginnings

"Do not despise these small beginnings, for the LORD rejoices to see the work begin."

ZECHARIAH 4:10 NLT

People often ask me, "How did you get where you are?" and I often find it hard to answer with a short response. The truth is, I just came to where I am. One small step at a time.

When I chose to go full-time as a musician, I was terrified. It would have been far easier if I had a guaranteed paycheck or work contract. Instead, I had to make a choice based on how things had been going and where I felt God was leading. I had to be prepared to start small—to take small gigs and fees, to play to small crowds and see small increases.

If we are to attempt an impossible mission, we cannot begin in fear. We can't fear the struggle, the sacrifice, or having less. Everything great begins small, from great businesses to great people. It's not shameful to begin with nothing, to start from zero and build. Simply *begin*.

REFLECTION

The hardest step to take is the first step. Once you have stepped out, every step you take establishes your path a little bit better. Resolve today to keep moving forward.

Lord, help me to respect small beginnings. Give me the courage and the humility to do the small jobs well so I can find myself where I'd like to be in a few years' time. You're faithful to establish my steps when I trust you, Lord, and for that I'm so grateful. To you be the glory. In Jesus' name, amen.

Do Not Fear Being a Beginner

"Though your beginning was insignificant,
yet your end will increase greatly."

JOB 8:7

I'm halfway through my first year as a YouTuber, and already I can see that I've improved a lot. The first few videos were a little awkward and my editing technique was dicey. But I had to start somewhere!

I'm not a fan of learning in front of people—it's one of the reasons I hated piano lessons and later, driving lessons. But, I've learned it's okay to be the beginner in the room; there's no shame in it. Everyone must start somewhere! Even if you're a capable individual, you can't be brilliant at everything right away. You may feel self-conscious as the newcomer at the gym, on the stage, or behind the camera. But as you stand there, new, nervous, and unqualified, you're doing infinitely better than the one who never tried! So go out there today and *try*.

REFLECTION

If you have anxiety about being a beginner, let's deal with that today. It can be overwhelming at first, but don't fear—you won't be a beginner for long!

Lord, give me the courage to start something new. Help me to get over my fear of looking silly or taking up too much time, and help me grab hold of this new opportunity. In Jesus' precious name. Amen.

Don't Fear Just Because You Always Have

Do not be anxious about anything, but in every situation, by prayer and petition, with thanksgiving, present your requests to God.

PHILIPPIANS 4:6

Fear is learned, and fear can be unlearned. Not long ago, I was about to put a spider outside using only my hands. The person I was with recoiled in horror and exclaimed, "You're not going to *touch* it, are you?" I was going to touch it but hesitated. I felt my heart rate increase, then I realized I'd absorbed someone else's fear.

Whatever you're afraid of today, let me tell you—you don't have to be afraid anymore. Maybe you have always struggled with that situational fear or anxiety; that doesn't mean you will always struggle! Just because you had a panic attack last time you flew doesn't mean you will the next time. Just because you've never made conversation with a stranger doesn't mean you cannot!

REFLECTION

Tell yourself today: *I have permission to have a different experience. I am not bound by my past experience.* Today is a new day, a different space, with different people. You are a different person. Some fears have been taking ground in you for a long time, and phobias may not disappear overnight. You can begin to take ground back by thinking, *I can and I will remove this phobia from my bio.*

Lord, you've told us not to be anxious. You've taught us to exchange our anxiety for prayer. So today I want to do that—I turn over to you any fears or phobias right now so you can deal with them. I pray you would miraculously deal with my fears. In Jesus' name, amen.

Do Not Fear Vulnerability

God has chosen the weak things of the world
to shame the things that are strong.

1 Corinthians 1:27 nasb

I was afraid to admit to the public that I sometimes still struggle with fear. I was afraid they wouldn't want to listen to my music anymore or hear what I have to say. But I've found quite the opposite. Only last night at a show, a woman thanked me for my openness, telling me it had helped her overcome her own anxiety.

There is amazing treasure to be found in seasons of vulnerability. Those times give us humility, compassion, and perspective. They give us song, story, and art, and they teach us how to comfort those who are afraid. I used to be petrified of letting people see my weakness, but I've come to view vulnerability as beautiful, universal, and inevitable. Far from being what separates us, it's what connects us. To be vulnerable is to be human, and being human is nothing to fear. I'm thankful that faith makes it possible to find the treasure in every season of struggle.

REFLECTION

The enemy doesn't want you to be honest about your struggles because he knows it helps people. Don't be silenced by a fear of vulnerability. Your vulnerability will put the enemy to shame and begin setting other captives free.

Lord, sometimes the idea of being honest about my internal battles fills me with fear. I know that you can work through it all. Help me to rest in your strength when I feel weak, knowing that you're using everything in my life. In Jesus' name, amen.

Do Not Fear What People Think of You

*If I were still trying to please people,
I would not be a servant of Christ.*

GALATIANS 1:10

I've struggled with what to do with others' opinions of me since I was small. There's a simple fact I can't overcome—despite my best intentions, not everyone will see my heart. Not everyone will understand where I'm coming from, and sadly, not everyone will like me. This can be hard to take if you're a sensitive soul, but it's important to remember that the world's perception of you is *not* you. We view one another through a lens of emotion and personal experience. Other people's cruelty toward you is most certainly a symptom of their own heartache.

REFLECTION

When all is said and done, we must work on how we view ourselves. We must make it a priority to live in peace with who we are and to be authentic. That way, we can always look ourselves in the mirror each day and feel peace.

Lord, help me to be at peace with who I am so if someone doesn't like me, I can handle it. I pray you would protect me from any malicious intentions toward me and help me walk confidently in you. Thank you for your love and favor. In Jesus' name, amen.

Do Not Fear the Worst

"Have I not commanded you? Be strong and courageous. Do not be afraid, and do not be discouraged, for the LORD your God will be with you wherever you go."

JOSHUA 1:9

For a long time, I struggled with what counselors call "catastrophic thinking." When walking down a steep staircase, I would picture falling. If I got a head cold, I would imagine losing my voice forever and being poor. I didn't realize what I was doing until someone else pointed it out.

When in a tough situation, we hope for the best, but all too often fear the worst. When we spend time picturing everything that could go wrong, we're meditating in a negative way. Worry doesn't change the outcome—you can't fix a leaking tap by thinking about it.

REFLECTION

Worrying about the worst-case scenario is a habit, and it can be broken. It's important to realize that we can't change a situation by worrying. The well-known "Serenity Prayer" has truly helped me to overcome this.

"God, grant me the serenity to accept the things I cannot change, courage to change the things I can, and wisdom to know the difference." In Jesus' name, amen.

Do Not Fear Your Enemy's Success

Do not fret when people succeed in their ways, when they carry out their wicked schemes.

PSALM 37:7

We all hope that those who wrong us will eventually receive justice, but we don't always get to see that happen. Reality can often find us watching them succeed instead. We see people who have broken our hearts find love before we do. We see people who have broken the law have successful business ventures. Those we've known to be deceitful and cruel are publicly celebrated.

This can be frustrating, downright painful, and worse still, cause a root of bitterness to grow in our hearts. In those moments, it helps to remember that honesty, kindness, and integrity are their own reward. If you're choosing to do the right thing, live according to what you believe is godly wisdom—you will experience the joy that comes in following God. Being kind, reliable, and loving allows you and others to flourish. That's the kind of fruit we want to bear—fruit that lasts.

REFLECTION

Do you feel ill at ease or bitter toward someone? Take a few minutes today to bring that person to God in prayer. Let the situation go, knowing that your Father in heaven can take care of it.

Lord, it hurts me to see people doing well when they've done me wrong. Help me to remember I can't live anyone's life but my own. It's not my place to decide what they should do or what they deserve. You know everything, Lord. Thank you that you will see the righteous remain rooted and secure. In Jesus' name, amen.

Do Not Fear Pain

Blessed is the one who perseveres under trial because, having stood the test, that person will receive the crown of life that the Lord has promised to those who love him.

JAMES 1:12

"No pain, no gain." There is truth to be found in these words. If you're walking around after the gym with a little pain in your muscles, chances are it was a good workout. Body builders know pain is evidence that you're building muscle. When it comes to the aches and pains of life, I've certainly had my share of broken hearts. Pain is where your power is. It's where your song comes from. It's how you build your muscle. Often, we want out of the pain, but what we need will come from our journey through it.

Pain without faith can make us feel weak and defeated. Add God's power to a painful experience, and we can *Come Back Fighting*, as one of my album titles says. Today, embrace the agony and keep moving forward.

REFLECTION

Pain is never fun—we certainly don't look forward to it. But whenever we look back at painful times, we will always find that we learned something about God being in control. Today, look at the pain you're encountering and begin to get excited about what he can do through it.

Lord, I don't like being in pain. But I know that if I cling to you, you can empower me to get through it. You can build my character and you can give me new songs. You can build my spiritual muscles and make me a better witness for you. Thank you for your comfort in tough times. I know you'll bring me through. In Jesus' name, amen.

Do Not Fear Imperfection

For by grace you have been saved through faith. And this is not
your own doing; it is the gift of God.

EPHESIANS 2:8 ESV

The first time I hosted a bunch of friends for dinner, I wanted it
to be perfect. I spent a week planning and did everything I could
to prepare for a perfect evening. My guests arrived, and I was just
about on top of things. I poured everyone their favorite drink
and served the appetizer, my heart racing and my attention far
from having fun. Then disaster struck. I realized that my oven
had broken and the main course hadn't even begun to cook.

At that moment I could dissolve into a panic and declare the
evening a write-off. I could cover up the problem and attempt to
serve something else. Or I could come clean with my guests and
admit the issue, that dinner was ruined because our oven had
been on the brink for weeks and we didn't have the cash to fix it
at the time. I chose option three. Thankfully, my guests saw the
funny side, and we all shared stories of dinner-party nightmares
over a delicious delivery pizza.

REFLECTION

It's so much more important to be honest than to appear perfect.
The more perfect we appear, the less relatable we become. The
less relatable we become, the more isolated we all feel. Letting
people into the beauty of our flawed lives is a wonderful way to
share life, united in our woes.

Lord, thank you that you don't require perfection of us. We are
saved by your grace. Help me simply to do my best and to know
that you're glorified even through my weaknesses. In Jesus'
name, amen.

Do Not Fear Those Who Are Different

"The LORD does not look at the things people look at. People look
at the outward appearance, but the LORD looks at the heart."

1 SAMUEL 16:7

Judging a book by its cover is something we're programmed
to do. That is why books have covers! We use the information
our eyes give us to make split-second assessments of things and
people—it's part of our survival mechanism. Unfortunately, our
heads have also been filled with stereotypes throughout our lives.
We've learned that hairy bikers are likely satanists. We've learned
that certain ethnic minorities may be associated with terrorism.
We've learned that people who dress a certain way are poor or
rich.

The reflex within you that makes judgments based on
appearances is not an evil reflex. But if we are to be truly like
Jesus and see beyond the appearances to the heart, we must
begin blocking that reflex and being more Christlike with our
responses.

REFLECTION

Some of the most gnarly characters you know may just be the
ones with the most integrity. Just because someone dresses well
and can quote the Bible doesn't mean that person is any holier
than someone whose appearance is disheveled. When it comes to
appearances, we must always keep an open mind.

Lord, thank you that there is so much color and diversity in
this world. Help me to always lead with love and keep my
spiritual eyes open. Teach me to look beyond a person's outward
appearance and be ready to see his or her heart. Thank you that
you always see our hearts. In Jesus' name, amen.

Do Not Fear the Battle

"This is what the LORD says to you: 'Do not be afraid
or discouraged because of this vast army.
For the battle is not yours, but God's.'"

2 CHRONICLES 20:15

If you're discouraged or anxious, you might not feel ready to face the spiritual battle. Don't despair—Jesus can fight that battle for you! Instead of looking at the battleground, look at Jesus.

The day you were born, you were fighting. You fought courageously for that first breath. As you grew, you fought your way through an array of childhood dangers, sicknesses, and a thousand trials. It's no wonder you got used to fighting your battles alone. But the good news is, as a child of the Most High, you are never alone—God promises to fight your battles for you. The day you called out to God and asked for his forgiveness, he sent an army of angels to surround you.

REFLECTION

Whenever the fight of life gets to be too much and I feel the flame of my faith burning low, I need to remember that the King of kings is fighting for me. When my health is under threat, he is fighting for me. When my finances are under fire, he is fighting for me. When I come under attack by an enemy, he is fighting for me. In other words, the battle is not my own.

Lord, I don't always have the spiritual strength to face the warfare. Knowing that you're with me fighting the battle means everything. You are greater than all darkness. No one can defeat you! Thank you for your eternal victory. In Jesus' name, amen.

Do Not Fear Defeat

He has delivered us from the domain of darkness and transferred us to the kingdom of his beloved Son.

COLOSSIANS 1:13 ESV

As someone who has struggled with an anxiety disorder, I know what it's like to wage a battle for my soul. At times, the physical sensations of fear are such that I can almost see shadows. I feel the spiritual warfare taking place—swarms of lies circling my mind, just waiting for a chance to settle and steal whatever faith I have left. Thankfully, I'm no longer in that dark place. But if I ever feel those swarms of lies drawing in, I remind myself of this great promise: *The battle of my soul has already been won. Jesus has already defeated the enemy and purchased my soul for eternity by his blood.*

REFLECTION

Have you felt defeated in the past? Have you encountered situations where you walked away feeling you'd lost? Today, absorb the truth that defeat is off the table when it comes to the battle for your soul—Jesus has already won. Don't let past experiences color your view of today.

Lord, thank you for defeating the enemy. Thank you for winning my soul and placing me securely beside you in heaven. Help me not waste any more time fearing for the well-being of my soul. In Jesus' name, amen.

Believe You Have What It Takes

Such confidence we have through Christ before God. Not that we are competent in ourselves to claim anything for ourselves, but our competence comes from God. He has made us competent as ministers of a new covenant.

2 Corinthians 3:4–6

In this adventure of faith, we regularly feel out of our depth. Since that day back in 2004 when I asked God to come into my life, I've been given assignment after assignment I didn't feel prepared for. Being so late to learn about faith, I didn't feel qualified to talk about Jesus when asked. Having struggled so badly with nerves, I certainly didn't feel prepared to tell arenas full of people that they are loved by God. But somehow, I have managed to accomplish things that are quite clearly beyond my abilities.

Reflection

If ever I feel afraid of the task before me, if I feel unqualified or unready, I remember that God is the one who has sent me and he will accomplish his agenda through me.

Lord, thank you that I am competent in you. You will help me do what you've asked of me. Today I stand against the accuser who tells me I can't, and I speak out the truth: through you I can! In Jesus' mighty name. Amen.

Do Not Fear the Future

"Therefore do not worry about tomorrow, for tomorrow will worry about itself. Each day has enough trouble of its own."

MATTHEW 6:34

It's hard not to be anxious about what the future might hold. The past had so many ups and downs, and most of the time the present is challenging. If you've stepped out in faith to pursue a dream, answer a ministry call, or even begin a family, fear for what comes next is to be expected. But fear is useless. Living with fear for the future is like gathering your own storm clouds over what could be a sunny afternoon—there's every chance that all you love about life lies ahead in spades. If you can muster the fear to dread the worst, then you can muster the faith to believe for the best! In the meantime, trust that God will provide your needs for today and prepare a way for tomorrow!

REFLECTION

God has your future in hand and great things await you! Don't let fear dampen your spirits. You can trust your Father to give you good things.

Lord, thank you for the awesome things you have planned for me. Help me today to exchange my fear for excitement! I'm so grateful for the many adventures ahead. In Jesus' name, amen.

Do Not Fear Being Judged

Whoever dwells in the shelter of the Most High will rest in the shadow of the Almighty.

PSALM 91:1

I light up when people approve of me and can collapse when they misjudge or dislike me. Somehow I've managed to survive as a performer. But fear of judgment has held me back.

A couple of months into my YouTube series, I uploaded a cover of an Ed Sheeran song and altered the lyrics to make them worshipful. It went viral, which was awesome! But the mixture of judgments was daunting. Some presumed I wasn't able to write my own songs. Others presumed I was a thief. But you know what? The more I read, the less it bothered me. I got used to seeing others' opinions and letting them wash over me as the harmless things they are. Had I not stepped out, millions of people wouldn't have heard this material. The risk was every bit worth it! It even led to me writing this book.

REFLECTION

Is the fear of judgment holding you back today? Perhaps you've been wrongly judged in the past and had your fingers burned. Today let's lay that to rest.

Lord, you know I've been humiliated in the past. You know what it felt like for me to hear cruel words. Thank you, Lord, for the healing that is taking place in me right now. You're giving me a new heart so I can step out again. I will not fear the opinions of others. In Jesus' name, amen.

Do Not Fear Losing Your Stuff

Turn my eyes from worthless things,
and give me life through your word.

PSALM 119:37 NLT

Do no fear losing your stuff—because you have nothing to lose!
That might sound grim, but it's true. The things we "own" in this
life are on loan to us at best. When we bought our first house, I
started to feel fear all the time. Being self-employed, I worried
about what might happen if our circumstances changed and
we couldn't keep up with the payments. But I had a light-bulb
moment one day while exploring the history of the house—it's
been here since 1860. It's probably had a dozen families live a
good chunk of life there. Even if that roof is over me till the
day I die, it will outlast me on earth and wind up belonging to
someone else.

We are eternal beings, and all our "things" are perishable.
Things come and go with the seasons. Sometimes people have
plenty, other times they have less. All that matters is, are we
thankful for what we have today?

REFLECTION

The Lord's Prayer gives so much peace when we get anxious
about our lives and the things we place value in:

Our Father in heaven, hallowed be your name, your kingdom
come, your will be done, on earth as in heaven. Give us today
our daily bread. Forgive us our sins, as we have forgiven those
who sin against us. Save us from the time of trial and deliver us
from evil. For the kingdom, the power, and the glory are yours
now and for ever. Amen.

Fear Doesn't Make You a Coward

No, in all these things we are more than conquerors through him
who loved us. For I am convinced that neither death nor life,
neither angels nor demons, neither the present nor the future,
nor any powers, neither height nor depth, nor anything else in all
creation, will be able to separate us from the love of God that is
in Christ Jesus our Lord.

ROMANS 8:37–39

Fear is a human response to threat. It's a biological response to
danger, and turning it off is no easy feat. No matter how many
times I perform in front of a crowd, I still feel fear when the
numbers are large or the songs are new. I used to think I was a
coward. But I've learned that nerves don't make me weak. Getting
onstage when your knees are knocking? That's hardcore.

Feeling fear doesn't make you any more of a coward than
feeling huger makes you a glutton. In fact, continuing in the face
of fear is truly commendable—even heroic. I once heard it said,
"A hero and a coward have one thing in common—fear." It's okay
to be scared. Bravery is feeling the fear and doing it anyway!

REFLECTION

What are you afraid of doing today? Don't let the enemy tell you
that you are a coward when you experience fear. Realize instead
that you're heroic for proceeding despite the fear.

God, thank you that you will go with me today as I face my fears.
Thank you that through you I'm more than a conqueror in all
these things. Help me to have bravery today and simply step out.
In Jesus' name, amen.

Put On the Armor

Stand firm then, with the belt of truth buckled around your
waist, with the breastplate of righteousness in place, and with
your feet fitted with the readiness that comes from the gospel
of peace. In addition to all this, take up the shield of faith, with
which you can extinguish all the flaming arrows of the evil one.
Take the helmet of salvation and the sword of the Spirit,
which is the word of God.

EPHESIANS 6:14–17

Life is warfare. We know that the enemy is a toothless lion who
prowls around trying to intimidate and that God is fighting our
battles for us. To protect ourselves from falling prey to that toothless lion of fear, we must put on the full armor of God. We can
apply these verses directly to handling the symptoms of anxiety.

When we feel that nausea of anxiety, we must speak out
truth. When our hearts race with the adrenaline of terror, we
must guard them with righteous faith. We can continue the fight
knowing that every step of faith is blessed and steadied by God's
peace. Finally, when we're overwhelmed with fearful thoughts, we
must take out the Word of God and protect our minds with his
promises. Our biggest weapon in this spiritual battle is the Bible!

REFLECTION

Take the time to memorize these verses. Whenever you feel anxious, worried, or intimidated, try to imagine the armor of God
that protects every part of you.

Lord, today I'm using Ephesians 6 as my weaponry. I am stand-
ing on your truth and putting on your full armor right now.
Help me to embrace this way of handling tough spiritual battles.
In Jesus' name, amen.

Remember the Time Wasted by Fear

"Who of you by worrying can add a single hour to your life?"
LUKE 12:25

As a child , I was afraid of the dark—the dark never hurt me. At school, I was afraid of not being good enough—school didn't destroy me. At sixteen, I thought I would never overcome anxiety and live a normal life—I'm living a normal life. For the first five years after leaving my parents' home, I was afraid I wouldn't be able to pay my way and survive—I survived. I'm here. And my one regret is the time I wasted being afraid.

Life has not been perfect, but the fear of falling has always been worse than the fall itself. Fear has never changed a single outcome in my life for the better. In fact, all it has done is hold me back from being all I was created to be!

REFLECTION

Let's make this declaration today: "I no longer permit fear to color my enjoyment of a season, be it a season of joy, weeping, sowing, or reaping. Fear, listen up! You're no longer invited to the party."

Lord, I'm sorry for the time I've wasted worrying. I don't want to waste a single hour more on the pointless cycle of fear. I know that you have laid life out for me, and I no longer need to dwell on the scary things in life. Help me overcome this destructive habit today. In Jesus' name, amen.

Fearlessness Is Attractive

Finally, be strong in the Lord and in his mighty power.

EPHESIANS 6:10

Often, we feel that the Christian life is not attractive to an outsider—it's viewed as just a life of boundaries and rules. But the Christian life is not about fencing us in or restricting our inner adventurer. The first thing Jesus said to his disciples was, "Follow me, and I will make you fishers of men" (Matthew 4:19 ESV). The Bible tells us that at the mere sound of his voice, the thrill of this call caused them to throw down everything they depended on for a livelihood and go on a massive adventure. This generation isn't attracted to chaos and hedonism; it's attracted to fearlessness and adventure. Let's be fearlessly good, righteous, and wild at heart!

REFLECTION

Have you ever viewed yourself as a weak little Christian in a loud, intimidating world? Today is the day to shake off that stereotype. You're a revolutionary—a soldier of life and light! As a child of God, you're on the greatest adventure, standing against the evil powers of this world. There is every reason the world should see and admire what we have.

Lord, help me to walk in a new stereotype—the fearless Christian, the one who stands for the weak and oppressed. I want to be an example of your powerful presence and the Spirit that brings down corrupt kingdoms in your name. Draw people to your flame, Lord, as we walk in faith together. In Jesus' name, amen.

Fear Is a Toothless Lion

Little children, you are from God and have overcome them, for he who is in you is greater than he who is in the world.

1 John 4:4 ESV

Fear lies to you. It tells you the worst is about to happen and shows you the bleakest outcome. The father of lies feeds on your fear, stalking its prey like a lion. Though the lion's roar may be impressive, it cannot hurt you. When fear rises up, remind it that the light within you is greater. Tell your fear that God is with you, he has a plan for you, and is working all things for your good. As you begin to separate the truth from the lies, the predator of fear loses ground and runs for the hills.

REFLECTION

Personally, I'm not a confrontational person; I like to live in peace with others. But we are not required to live in peace with the lion of fear. So if you're anything like me, it's important to square up your shoulders and tell the lion where to go. Say with me aloud: "I am not a victim. I am not helpless. I am not defeated. I am *more* than a conqueror. I have been given victory over the darkness of fear!"

Lord, thank you that I am more than a conqueror and that you have overcome the world. Let me stop being afraid of that toothless lion of fear. I know that all he can do is intimidate me. He cannot harm me because you have already overcome him. So help me rise up against that intimidation. In Jesus' name, amen.

The Worry Box, Part 1

Cast all your anxiety on him because he cares for you.

1 PETER 5:7

As an anxiety sufferer, I had a great breakthrough when I created a visual for my struggle and gave it a name—"the worry box" (an imaginary box where I keep my fears).

Picture this with me: The box is made entirely of magnifying glass and is beautifully lit from within, so whatever is inside is magnified beyond all proportion. It makes everything appear more vivid and spotlights our concerns until we can't help but focus on them. For many of us, the box isn't there all the time. The box can emerge during times of stress or lifestyle changes. But when the worry box *is* there, it magnifies our day-to-day concerns. One day it could be finances the next, a relationship. When I identified the worry box and realized that the problems inside were switching daily, the truth hit me—it was the worry box that was my real problem, not the things inside! I began to realize that victory over my fears meant understanding that box and taking time to empty it.

REFLECTION

Anxious? Picture your worry box. Take a few minutes today to look inside and see what's there. One by one, pick up each worry and ask, *Can I do something about this?* If the answer is yes, plan your next practical move. If the answer is no, picture yourself letting it go and handing it over to God.

Lord, help me identify the place inside me that magnifies worry and makes it a negative exaggeration of the truth. Today, Lord, show me that you are bigger than everything inside this worry box. Help me deal with all the fears I've placed inside. In Jesus' name, amen.

The Worry Box, Part 2

"Peace I leave with you; my peace I give you.
I do not give to you as the world gives.
Do not let your hearts be troubled and do not be afraid."

JOHN 14:27

Some people find that physically creating a worry box helps them. Children sometimes benefit from this kind of exercise. Get yourself a box or jar and write down your worries. Now place those worries in the box and say a little prayer. Ask God to give you the wisdom to know what to do with them. Then (this is the important bit), take out each one and sort them into two piles.

My concerns—things I can do something about.

God's concerns—things I can't do anything about.

If you're worried about a sore shoulder, put that one in the "My Concerns" pile. You can make a doctor's appointment and have it examined. If your sore shoulder is a total mystery to the doctors, move it to the "God's Concerns" pile! He is the one who can deal with all those question marks in our heart. To finish, put them all in one pile, give them to God again in prayer, and toss them in the trash! God is more than able to take those burdens so you no longer have to carry them around with you!

REFLECTION

Don't forget God says to cast *all* your anxieties onto him (1 Peter 5:7). Don't leave something out because you think it's too small or ridiculous that he wouldn't be interested. He commands us not to leave anything out.

Lord, take each one of these worries and squash them. I pray you'll take all their power away, in Jesus' name. As I remove each worry from this box, may it be replaced by your peace. Amen.

Switch Fear for Faith

Jesus also did many other things.
If they were all written down, I suppose the whole world
could not contain the books that would be written.

JOHN 21:25 NLT

Worry takes up a lot of time and brain power. If you're used to focusing your attention on the things you're concerned about, that worry box inside you is going to start feeling empty and need filling. Today, why not choose to put faith where fear used to be? Turn your worry box into a faith box.

The way we treat God is quite often the way we regard technical people at events. We only give them attention when things aren't going the way we'd like them to go! They remain quite invisible when all is well. Today, instead of focusing on the bad things that might happen, why not recall some of the great things that have happened and put them under the spotlight? Why not magnify the incredible answers to prayer you've seen? Why not give center stage to the incredible things you're believing God for?

REFLECTION

If you still have that box or jar, take a little time today to write down some of the things you're believing that God can and will accomplish in your life.

Lord, thank you so much for the amazing things you've been doing in my life. Today I remember them and give glory to you for every answered prayer. If ever I feel worried, let me magnify the incredible blessings you've given me over the years and be reminded of your faithfulness. In Jesus' name, amen.

Imagination

Now to him who is able to do immeasurably more than all we ask or imagine, according to his power that is at work within us, to him be the glory in the church and in Christ Jesus throughout all generations, for ever and ever!

EPHESIANS 3:20–21

Worry comes down to imagination. We look at the picture of our circumstances and imagine the worst possible outcomes. But guess what? If your imagination has been doing overtime creating pictures of the worst case scenario, it can be put to work dreaming new dreams instead! And what's more, the Bible verse above says that God can do immeasurably more than we could think, ask, *or imagine*. It's time to put that great imagination of yours to better use! Stretch it as far as it will go. Think outside the box and try to picture things you wouldn't even dream that God could do for and through you.

REFLECTION

Get excited! Write down your requests, dreams, and visions and prepare yourself to be blown away by what God does to better them. When we take a dream and add excitement, we get faith.

Lord, help me to switch all my imaginings for good ones. Help me fix my imagination on the incredible things you are about to do in my life. In Jesus' precious name. Amen.

Pray

Don't worry about anything; instead, pray about everything. Tell
God what you need, and thank him for all he has done.

PHILIPPIANS 4:6 NLT

Prayer is an incredible weapon against fear—the enemy can't
stand in the presence of God. When we call God into the midst of
our issue, the enemy runs away afraid.

Is there something bothering you that you haven't expressed?
Get it off your chest right now in prayer! It doesn't matter how
big or small the problem. If it's big enough to trouble your heart,
then God wants to hear it. If you're an anxiety sufferer and you're
worried about germs, pray about them! If you're worried about
someone's treatment toward you at work, pray about it.

REFLECTION

God says we should cast all our cares onto him (1 Peter 5:7). Not
some, not most, but *all.* So go on, do it now!

Lord, you know my deepest, darkest fear. Today I call you to
occupy that space and bring me freedom from that fear. It
doesn't matter what it is—you can cause the enemy to back
away. He is afraid at the very mention of your name. I speak
your name and declare the power of the blood of Jesus over this
fear today. In Jesus' name, amen.

Fear Changes Shape

"Do not be afraid; you will not be put to shame. Do not fear
disgrace; you will not be humiliated."

ISAIAH 54:4

We need to be on constant guard for fear because it often comes
to us in disguise. No matter your age or stage of life, there'll
always be a new fear to face because fear evolves with us. When I
was five, I was afraid of the dark. When I was fifteen, I was afraid
of death. When I was twenty-five, I was afraid my dreams would
die. My age changed, and my fears changed with it—no amount
of experience prepared me for each one. When we conquer one
area of anxiety, we're bound to be faced with a new one. It's like a
virus that adapts a new strain when we become immune. It's okay
to accept that fear is going to come at you in regular intervals.
The trick is learning to recognize what you're dealing with and
hit back with God's promises!

REFLECTION

Today, why not write out a list of the fears you've had throughout
your life? You may find it interesting. Perhaps there are some
fears that have been with you for most of your life. You might
also notice that your recent fears are actually very similar to your
early fears. Whatever you notice, remember that God instructs us
not to fear, because he is always bigger!

Lord, let me be prepared for each new fear as at arrives. Help
me to know that although my fears may change, you never do!
You're always bigger, you're always victorious, and you're always
the King of kings. In Jesus' name, amen.

Do Not Fear the Reaper

"Thus the saying 'One sows and another reaps' is true. I sent you to reap what you have not worked for. Others have done the hard work, and you have reaped the benefits of their labor."

JOHN 4:37–38

When I first began doing things at church, I was so full of zeal and energy. But it wasn't as easy as I thought it would be. One time, I wanted to do something for the youth, so I organized an event with the help of a few other girls. Together we pulled a great night together, and I was thrilled! Then, right at the last moment, a church member came in through the doors shouting, "How dare you do this without me! I helped build this youth group!"

Being new to the family, I had no idea I'd missed this person when I was setting up the team. I couldn't understand why this person was so mad until years later when a new act was signed to the same management company as me. I began to see this new group benefiting from contacts I'd made and relationships I'd built. They were reaping what they hadn't sown. Finally, I understood why people had felt threatened by me.

REFLECTION

It's never easy to watch others reap the benefits of what we've worked hard for. Remember that at some time we *all* reap what we haven't sown. Those who have gone before us have made a way for us; part of our job is to make a way for others. Remember God will take care of you regardless of who gets the credit.

Lord, help me not to be fearful of others reaping the benefits of my labor—this is the way you've ordered things. We are a team for you here on earth. Thank you that you promise to take care of me and provide for my needs. In Jesus' name, amen.

Love One Another

"A new command I give you: Love one another. As I have loved you, so you must love one another. By this everyone will know that you are my disciples, if you love one another."

JOHN 13:34–35

Can we say too much about loving one another? Jesus seems to think not! In this one verse alone, he says it three times. Jesus typically says things three times when he is creating great emphasis on a truth. He seemed to think this was *very* important. In fact, Jesus says the entire Old Testament can be summed up in these three words: "Love one another." Love should be the key word in our mouths, the key motivation for our actions, and the thing we're best known for.

We can get rather hung up on what we're known for. We can become extremely concerned with how best to witness faith and prove our faith to others. But when all is said and done, love is the great challenge. Love is the greatest commandment. God's character is love. It's who he is. If we're to be known for anything at all, let it be by how we love those who need love and how we treat one another.

REFLECTION

It's easy for our focus as Christians to move away from love. It's crucial we never forget that our entire message hangs upon it. Whatever challenges you're facing as an individual, a family, or a church, the answer will always be based in a response of love.

Lord, whatever happens and whatever is known about me, let me be known for loving others above all else. In Jesus' name, amen.

Love Endures

Be completely humble and gentle; be patient, bearing with one another in love. Make every effort to keep the unity of the Spirit through the bond of peace.

EPHESIANS 4:2–3

It's true what they say: "There's a thin line between love and hate." Most heinous crimes are committed not by strangers but by someone close to the victim. Passion can quickly become fury, and familiarity can breed contempt. When we know others inside out, their actions can drive us to distraction! The people close to us know just how to push our buttons. When we've allowed someone into the sacred space of our own heart, that person has power to do the greatest damage. But as God's love for us endures forever, so must ours!

REFLECTION

Is someone really testing your boundaries right now? Is a loved one really pushing your ability to be patient and loving? It happens to all of us at some time. We must make every effort to maintain unity. If we're to be an example of love to the world, we have to keep displaying that love within our families and wider network.

I thank you, Lord, for your enduring love. Thank you that you loved me so much that you gave your only Son for me. Please Lord, create in me a strong and soft heart that loves in spite of pain, irritation, and even the worst transgressions. Help me develop the strength of character and largeness of heart to love as you do. In Jesus' name, amen.

Don't Condemn

For God did not send his Son into the world to condemn the
world, but to save the world through him.

JOHN 3:17

Before I found my faith, I was very liberal. I never felt the need
to judge anyone's behavior because my approach to life was
very undisciplined. But when my life began to change, I started
to become aware of things other people were doing wrong. I
hated seeing people abuse their bodies or make choices that
were hurting others. But just because we know how to live right
doesn't mean we get to judge other people.

The Bible says there is no condemnation in Jesus. If we're to
be like Jesus, then we *cannot* be condemning of others. We might
be able to see someone else's bad deeds or intentions as clear as
day. We may feel incensed by the way another chooses to live or
act, especially when it's destructive for them or for others. But
our job is never to condemn, only to love. The Holy Spirit is the
one who has the authority and power to convict of wrongdoing.

REFLECTION

Today, let us resign ourselves to the fact that we don't get to
decide who should be condemned. We can't make that decision
and we have no right to. Instead, let us ask for extra resources to
love. And let's pray more for those who disappoint us gravely.

Lord, it's not easy to stand by and watch people living
destructively. But it's not my place to judge, and there is no
condemnation in you, because you give us the free gift of life
through your Spirit. Help me not to judge, and certainly never
to condemn, because it's not your way. In Jesus' name, amen.

God Weighs the Heart

Every man's way is right in his own eyes,
but the LORD weighs the heart.
PROVERBS 16:2 NASB

Our actions don't always reflect the way we feel. People regularly do one thing and say or think another. Quite often, we act aggressively when in fact we are in fear. Sometimes we act aloof when we're really crying out for attention. We block love when we're craving it. This makes relationships extra complicated. We feel justified in our feelings, words, and actions only to find, on reflection, that we caused some damage. This is not a good feeling, but there is hope. God can look at our intentions and not just our actions. When it comes to relationships, it's very helpful to try to do the same.

REFLECTION

Have others wronged you recently? Take a moment to consider what their intentions might have been. Were they doing what they believed was right? Did their actions come from a place of insecurity, brokenness, or pain? Good intentions don't excuse bad behavior, but looking at the heart can help us to understand things better and ultimately forgive.

Lord, help me develop my spiritual sight. Help me take a moment and look beyond a person's behavior to see his or her intentions. Thank you, Lord, that you always do this for us. In Jesus' name, amen.

Open Up

An honest answer is like a kiss on the lips.
PROVERBS 24:26

Ever arrived at a social event tired and stressed and when asked if you're okay, lied through your teeth? It's something we do a lot, especially in church. To a degree it's understandable—we don't need everyone to know our business. But if *no one* knows our business, we can't expect to build much of an authentic connection. People are a lot like flowers in a garden—we blossom together in a relationship when we dare to open up. Opening up is always a risk. We may fear that people won't love what they see or even that they'll use our secrets against us. But a relationship can only go so deep if we don't let one another inside. People need to know they're not the only ones hurting. Honesty and confession are what connects us.

REFLECTION

It's definitely good to use wisdom about whom to open up to. But sometimes, we only find out whom we can trust when we trust them with something. Why not start by sharing something small? It could be the start of something awesome!

Lord, help me to find those few people to whom I can really open up and with whom I can share those authentic bonds. Help me to build real relationships that cause me to blossom. In Jesus' name, amen.

Live by Example

"In the same way, let your light shine before others, so that they may see your good works and give glory to your Father who is in heaven."

MATTHEW 5:16 ESV

When we see others not living in a way we believe is right, we often feel the need to correct them. When we ourselves have been deeply convicted to change our lifestyle, it's hard not to try to persuade others to change too. We might feel the need to enforce our health or spiritual views onto people we love because we believe it can help them. But trying to change a person with a few sharp words of correction is usually futile.

The person you disagree with is looking at life through their own filter. If you want to change a person, or a person's behavior, there is only one good strategy—lead by example.

My husband is a good guy—a real good guy. He likes to do the right thing whether in serving, showing up to support others, keeping his opinions to himself, or simply being a gentleman. But despite being so virtuous, he has hardly ever insisted I do what he does. He's never dragged me kicking and screaming in the right direction. And somehow that has spoken louder than any rebuke.

REFLECTION

When we see others doing what we believe to be wrong, we don't have to shout about their choices. Sometimes quietly doing what you believe to be the right thing sends the most powerful message.

Lord, help my light to shine before others. When those around me are making poor choices, help me to lead by example and inspire others to walk a righteous path. In Jesus' name, amen.

People Are the Best Investment

Therefore, as we have opportunity, let us do good to all people, especially to those who belong to the family of believers.

GALATIANS 6:10

A few years ago, I was hired as a mentor on a talent show looking for members for the world's first Pan-Asian girl group. It was my job to coach and spend time with the girls before their performances in the show. It was so exciting! I thought immediately about all the doors that might open for me in the music world.

Sadly, things didn't go as I had hoped. We had some disagreements during the final judging panel, and the whole thing ended in a cloud of sadness. Such a wonderful opportunity had seemingly come to nothing. But then I remembered the time I had with the girls. We shared our faith. I got to pray for them and speak life into them. I'm in touch with most of them to this day.

The whole experience made me realize that using each moment to invest in people is our best use of time. We can't ever guarantee the success of our work, but people are an investment that will never lose its value.

REFLECTION

Is there anyone you feel called to invest in? Is there someone in your life you need to have a coffee with once a month or so? You are likely to look back years from now and remember the people you invested in more than the things you did.

Holy Spirit, if there are people I need to be spending time with, please show them to me. Help me identify those who could use my input. Help me to use everything I have to raise others up. In Jesus' name, amen.

Let 'Em Walk

"So he got up and went to his father. But while he was still a long way off, his father saw him and was filled with compassion for him; he ran to his son, threw his arms around him and kissed him."

Luke 15:20

There are few things in life more painful than watching someone you love walk away from you. You may throw everything you have at winning them over, but sadly, if someone has decided to walk away, there is often very little we can do about it. Relationships can be tricky, and some things we must take responsibility for. But in so many cases, the decision to walk away is based entirely on someone's own perspective and their personal journey.

Someone I was working with once decided I was no longer valuable. It was painful to hear the words "I'm out," especially as we'd been close friends as well as work partners. But after a little time of trying to make amends, I realized I had to let that person go.

The Bible teaches us to forgive, and I truly believe people are worth a second chance. But life is too short and too precious to spend chasing after those who've rejected you. So instead, keep a soft heart and an open door (like the prodigal son's father) but move on with your life.

Reflection

Do you need to let go of someone in your life? Take a moment to pray for that person and then release him or her. This is not necessarily the end, but for you to be healthy and free, you have to stop pursuing an outcome you can't control.

Lord, I release this person to you right now. I know I cannot attempt to bring that person back. Help me to keep a soft heart and an open door in case you do. In Jesus' name, amen.

Be Kind When Disagreeing

Live in harmony with one another. Do not be proud, but be willing to associate with people of low position. Do not be conceited. Do not repay anyone evil for evil. Be careful to do what is right in the eyes of everyone. If it is possible, as far as it depends on you, live at peace with everyone.

ROMANS 12:16–18

Disagreements are inevitable. Even among Christians there are a million nuances of belief. Though we may agree on the fundamental things, we could spend a lifetime debating the details. It's most disheartening to watch good people become unkind when these differences come to light. The nicest of people can be reduced to mudslinging Neanderthals!

Faith can be uncompromising without being judgmental or inconsiderate. There's nothing more beautiful than to love someone despite differences in viewpoint. We should never forget that while we're up to our elbows in mudslinging, people are watching. They're watching how we do conflict. They're watching to see if we love as well as we argue.

REFLECTION

The computer removes our humanity from the exchange. But remember the heart behind the keyboard. That heart, for the most part, has the same wants and needs as yours—to be heard and to be loved.

Lord, give me patience. I find it hard when people share views that upset me. I struggle to understand how someone I'm friends with could be on the opposing side. But I know that disagreement is inevitable. Help me to live in harmony and peace with others. In Jesus' name, amen.

Watch Your Words

When there are many words, sin is unavoidable,
but the one who controls his lips is wise.

PROVERBS 10:19 HCSB

Our days are filled with many words. When we're in full
conversational flow, our guard quite often comes down and a
thoughtless or cruel comment can roll off the tongue before we
even know it.

As someone who likes to speak a lot, I truly identify with this
issue. There are many times I've looked back on a conversation
and asked myself, *Did I go too far there? Should I have been discussing my personal business with that person? Was I over-sharing?*

There are three things that are helpful for this: 1) *Work on
your confidence as a child of God.* When we know who we are, we
feel less inclined to try to prove ourselves or impress the people
we're with. 2) *Slow down.* The world won't stop spinning if
there's an awkward silence. Far better an awkward silence than a
comment you can't take back. 3) *Pray.*

REFLECTION

If you've said something you shouldn't, take a moment to give it
to God. Thank him for his grace and ask for his covering on your
words. We all make mistakes.

Lord, thank you for your grace. I'm sorry for anything I may
have said recently that was unwise or indiscreet. I know that
sometimes the words come out before I've truly considered
them. If anything has rolled off my tongue that shouldn't have,
I pray that you would cover it by your grace and stop it in its
tracks. Please help me to be more careful next time. In Jesus'
name, amen.

It's Classy to Respect People

Do nothing out of selfish ambition or vain conceit. Rather, in humility value others above yourselves.

PHILIPPIANS 2:3

A couple of years ago, Joel and I took a holiday to Cuba. It was beautiful, and we were *super* blessed to receive a free upgrade! We found ourselves in an exclusive part of the resort with far better facilities and service than the main complex. We were elated!

A group of young people arrived and were having a good time around the pool. They were a little noisy and had had a few drinks, but really they were harmlessly enjoying the place. A more mature lady approached the group and began berating them. She made comments about their accents, their worthiness to be in the posh section, and even their culture and race.

To my amazement, the group of young people handled themselves nobly. They politely corrected the woman on her assumptions and calmly asserted their right to be there. Their gracious response made them look like royalty in comparison to her folly.

REFLECTION

Class has nothing to do with where we come from or what we earn, and everything to do with how we behave and treat people. Don't ever let anyone berate you because of where you come from. You are no more or less valuable than anyone.

Lord, help me not to judge others. I want to walk humbly among my brothers and sisters, never thinking myself to be above anyone. You showed the ultimate humility in sending your son for me. Let me be more like you. In Jesus' name, amen.

Put Down the Flame

How good and pleasant it is when God's people
live together in unity!

PSALM 133:1

Unity is powerful—it empowers our prayers. There is almost nothing we can't achieve when we stand together. That's why the enemy hates it. The enemy will do everything possible to disconnect us and diminish our number. The enemy loves it when we *stop* holding hands with one another and fold our arms—he loves a disagreement. It provides a lovely gap to slip into that can be widened with time.

When we get hurt or frustrated, it's tempting to grab a torch and burn the bridge. We need to realize that every time we do act from our hurt and frustration, we're making our circle smaller. We're saying no to unity and yes to disharmony.

REFLECTION

Some relationships come to an end. We don't have to remain connected to everyone as long as we live. But before you burn a bridge, ask yourself, *Could this be a mistake? Am I just allowing the enemy to win here?* Ask God to give you wisdom to know which bridges to save and which to walk away from.

Lord, please guide me in all my relationships. Help me discern when a friendship is ending and I need to take a step back. Help me also to know when to step up and move things forward in your grace. In Jesus' name, amen.

Mean People Aren't Happy

Better a patient person than a warrior, one with
self-control than the one who takes a city.

PROVERBS 16:32

Sometimes people are mean. They're not just insensitive or impulsive; they're plain cruel. If you're a sensitive soul, cruel words or actions can have a deep and lasting effect, but a little godly perspective can help us move on.

I used to dwell for days on horrible things people had said or done to me. I came to realize something important—I've never met a cruel person who was truly happy. Happy people don't go around hurting people for pleasure; they don't want or need to. Cruelty is a sign that something somewhere is broken within.

Walking through town with my housemate one day, we saw a woman curse at her child. Her words were so harsh that I had to stop myself from running to them and scooping the child up in my arms. I was filled with rage and contempt at this monstrous display. My housemate stopped me and said: "Philippa, people aren't born horrible—something horrible makes them horrible."

REFLECTION

Very often a person's output has come from something that has been inflicted upon them. This doesn't excuse cruelty, but it might go a way to explain things. It can help remind you that someone else's cruel treatment of you is not your fault.

Lord, help us to be gracious when people are cruel. Thank you that you gave your Son so all who believe might find forgiveness and restoration in you. Help us to have wisdom in how to handle these situations correctly so cruelty can be addressed and people protected. In Jesus' name, amen.

Love Your Enemies

Do not be overcome by evil, but overcome evil with good.
ROMANS 12:21

In the wake of so much terror, hatred is certainly prowling. It isn't easy to respond lovingly when we hear of mindless, violent attacks on innocents. But the only way to stop hate in its toxic tracks is to come at it with a great stampede of love. Hate is spreading all over this earth like wildfire between hurt, broken, and deceived hearts. When the enemy attacks innocent lives, it's human nature to feel rage and hate toward those attacks. But hate only breeds hate. Love is the transformative force that changes the tide of darkness. If we can decide to love those who hate, we will hold the cure this world so desperately needs.

REFLECTION

One of the hardest things to do is to repay someone's evil with good. But God is on our side when we do. He cushions and protects us through our kindness and puts out the fire of rage that can turn into even more evil.

Lord, help me overcome the urge to repay hatred with even more hatred. I will not hate the people who persecute me nor those who choose to terrorize us and threaten our freedom. Only by showing love can we break the chains and display your power. I pray you'll make this possible. In Jesus' name, amen.

Grace

Bear with each other and forgive one another if any of you has a grievance against someone. Forgive as the Lord forgave you.

COLOSSIANS 3:13

When people say or do something that offends you, try to remember that they're most likely just doing their best with life. Most people don't wake up in the morning and decide, *Today I will make a mistake and annoy everyone.* Hard as it is to be gracious when people do wrong, grace is vital and commanded by God. We have been forgiven and we must do the same. God gave his only Son for us while we were still sinners. He gave his best for us while we were still at our worst. If we're to be like him, we have to do the same for those who hurt and challenge us.

REFLECTION

Consider the things you've been forgiven. If I make a mental list of every bad word or thought I've had, it's a pretty long list—I made some pretty huge mistakes when I was younger. I'm amazed at God's ability to give me a new beginning. Whenever I feel angry with others, I remind myself of that list.

Lord, thank you for your amazing grace. Thank you for saving me, although I did nothing to deserve it. Whenever I am challenged, whenever I am angry, let me remember what you have done for me. Give me the grace to practice grace. In Jesus' name, amen.

It Could Be Any One of Us

Hatred stirs up conflict, but love covers over all wrongs.

PROVERBS 10:12

Most of us want to believe that we're fundamentally good people. We know we're not perfect but feel we're at least on the right side. We may have a sort of sliding "good and evil" scale in our minds and plot ourselves on the good end. We must remember that within each of us is both the capacity for greatness and the capacity for evil. There is treasure and potential in us all, but no one is immune to the impulses of our humanity.

Before we rush to write someone off as a bad person we should take a moment to consider their life experiences. We may find, on closer inspection, that if we'd walked their path, we too might have fallen onto the wrong side of that spectrum.

REFLECTION

Pray for the humility and wisdom to submit to God's command to love—to choose love over selfishness, rage, and judgment. There has never been a better time or greater need for love to prevail.

Lord, help me to reserve judgment on the behavior of others—I have no idea what they've been through. I have no clue what has led them to the state of heart and behavior they are exhibiting. But Lord, I pray with all my heart you'd begin to reach them. Soften them, Lord. Help them to become a new creation in you so they can lay to rest the behaviors that destroy them. In Jesus' name, amen.

Show Mercy They Didn't Show You

Then Joseph said to his brothers, "Please come closer to me."
And they came closer. And he said, "I am your brother Joseph,
whom you sold into Egypt. Now do not be grieved or angry
with yourselves, because you sold me here, for God sent me
before you to preserve life."

GENESIS 45:4–5 NASB

I recently watched a show about fishing. It was a great show and I
was … *hooked*. This adventurous fisherman was on a free-diving
mission to locate a rare and dangerous that had the power to kill
him. After a long journey told across a whole hour, he found his
prey. And there it was, within point-blank range of his deadly
spear gun. But you know what? He didn't shoot it. "I could have,"
he said, "but in the end it didn't seem fair with him looking down
the barrel like that. Finding him was a win enough for me."

REFLECTION

There may be times when we have the opportunity to take
revenge on our enemies or even just refuse them help. But when
you show your enemy mercy they never showed you, it shows the
true difference between you and them. To show mercy is to show
true strength of character, just as when Joseph gave of his riches
to help the brothers who had sold him into slavery.

Lord, help me be merciful like Joseph. Help me give love when
others don't give it to me. May I have open hands when others
withhold blessing because you have done that for me. You died
for me while I was still mocking you. I want to bring down my
guard and show your mercy to all. Thank you, Lord. Amen.

Give Up the Ghost

"If you forgive others their trespasses, your heavenly Father will also forgive you."

MATTHEW 6:14 ESV

If there's one thing that is guaranteed to steal your joy, it's staying mad or upset with someone. On those rare nights where sleep eludes me, I can find myself replaying old arguments in my head. I find myself reliving those exchanges in detail, wondering what I could have said differently or better. I rewrite my dialogue and deliver it with Hollywood perfection.

One night, I had a revelation. The former enemy, colleague, partner—whoever I was fighting with—was probably fast asleep, enjoying great rest and getting ready to take on the next day. That person was not in the room, sparring with me and hearing my excellent thoughts and well-planned arguments. With that I gave myself permission to sleep.

REFLECTION

We can't change the past simply by replaying it, and we can't change a person's heart with our imagination. The airtime it gets in your mind is wasted. Give up the ghost!

Lord, help me lay to rest past disagreements and issues. Help me not to go over things in my mind, especially when others have clearly moved on. I pray today for your peace and your comfort to bring rest to my soul. In Jesus' name, amen.

The Right People Love the Real You

Beloved, let us love another, for love is from God; and everyone
who loves is born of God and knows God.

1 JOHN 4:7 NASB

I wrote the following poem late one night after contemplating
the concepts within our favorite fairytales. It suddenly struck me
how ridiculous it was that Cinderella's prince didn't recognize
her without the magic. It got me thinking about the filters and
retouching people use on social media. What if one night all our
pictures were reset to their original state? Would people still love
or even *recognize* us? If they don't, are they really "for" us at all?

> If we were Cinderellas in these mirrors on the wall
> And our magic wands were filters that could get us to the ball
> Could software make us over into candidates for love?
> Or would we become so different no one recognizes us?
> If the dreaded strike of midnight was the button for undo
> Would our Princes ever find us in the cinders of our truth?
> If the image was imperfect, something human took its place
> In the pretty light of morning would he love our cindered face?
> This I know—I have no interest in a filtered fairy scam
> Where a prince would pass me over if I'm not in gown
>   and glam
> Where so desperate for acceptance in the cinders of my
>   world
> That my Instagram says "princess" but my heart says "just
>   a girl."
> No. My value isn't measured by my face or clothing tags.
> And we all deserve the kind of love that loves us in our rags.

And I can't avoid the question, what's the good in such
  untruth?
If the prince I plan to marry only knows me … by a shoe?

REFLECTION

One of the ways I knew Joel was good husband material was that
he liked me better without makeup! He displayed love for me at
all times, not just when I was doing everything right. He showed
me a godly kind of love. And that is what we all need.

Lord, I pray to be loved in this way. I pray that the people I
spend my life with will love me despite who I am on the outside.
Let those people love me as you do, in my rags. In Jesus' name,
amen.

Friendship First

Two are better than one, because they have a good return for their labor: If either of them falls down, one can help the other up. But pity anyone who falls and has no one to help them up.

ECCLESIASTES 4:9–10

Modern dating lore has rendered us petrified of establishing a friendship with someone we're attracted to lest we wind up "friend zoned." There's a bit of an urban legend that if you get to the point of feeling that someone is a friend, then you have passed the point at which you could have become something more. I, for one, can testify that this is baloney. Friendship is a really great place to start with love—the best place, in my humble opinion. It allows you to find common ground and become comfortable as your true self in that person's presence. You become concerned for one another and have a deeper level of respect. Chemistry is important, but it isn't always there at the beginning—it can develop over time.

REFLECTION

Chemistry is something that changes throughout the course of a lifetime, but friendship can see us right through. When a relationship is based on true friendship, beautiful things can happen.

Lord, help me to rethink my criteria for a relationship. Chemistry is important, but I want to be with someone who can make me laugh and who will cry with me in hard times—I want a good friend. Lead me toward a partner who can be a true companion. In Jesus' name, amen.

Live Your Message

Set an example for the believers in speech, in conduct, in love, in faith and in purity.

1 TIMOTHY 4:12

When Joel and I started dating, we made a decision not to sleep together before getting married. This was a big deal to me; it was a huge shift in my beliefs and an important part of my healing after years of turbulent relationships. Being adults in a committed relationship, we had plenty of friends and family who wouldn't have had a problem with us sharing a room in their home. In all honesty, there were occasions where our sharing a room would have made life easier for everyone. But when I spoke to Joel about where our boundaries should be on this, he simply said, "I want to be a good witness to your family and friends."

We stuck with our conviction despite cultural and logistical pressures. To this day I thank God for that resolve. It was restorative to me as a person and such a beautiful foundation for our future.

REFLECTION

What do you feel a conviction about? Hold onto it and live it out! Whatever you feel passionate about, your consistent display of an ideal is the best advertisement for what you believe in.

Lord, give me the strength to live what I believe. Help me be a living example of my ideals, even when it's more convenient to go with the flow. In Jesus' name, amen.

Date a Gentleman

Love is patient, love is kind. It does not envy, it does not boast, it is not proud. It does not dishonor others, it is not self-seeking, it is not easily angered, it keeps no record of wrongs. Love does not delight in evil but rejoices with the truth. It always protects, always trusts, always hopes, always perseveres.

1 CORINTHIANS 13:4–7

When I first became a Christian, I had just emerged from two consecutive serious relationships. Those relationships had been very intense; the last one was even quite destructive. I decided I wouldn't date another soul (if at all) until I found the right person. I had no idea that person would come along so soon.

Joel was the son of a pastor and had never dated before. I tried to warn him off, believing that as a new Christian, I probably wasn't worthy of someone so wholesome. But he was convinced we were right for each other, and he gave me the space to take things as slowly as I needed. For four years while we dated, Joel respected my boundaries. He encouraged me to guard my heart and have space from physical intimacy. The way he treated me was exactly the redemptive love I needed. My heart was simply overcome by his loving care and respect that I hadn't experienced from anyone else.

REFLECTION

Find someone who truly values you—body, mind, and soul. You're worthy of that love.

Lord, thank you for those wonderful relationships I see that work. Help me to seek out someone gentle and kind who loves me like you love me. In Jesus' name, amen.

The Love You Deserve

"A new command I give you: Love one another. As I have loved you, so you must love one another."

JOHN 13:34

Our relationships often transform when we resolve to give the love we need. So what kind of love *do* we truly need? We need godly love. And God loves us very well indeed.

> He sees through our anger.
> That holds us in spite of our resistance.
> He comforts us in grief.
> He speaks to our fear with kindness.
> He answers our rage with patience.

He does all these things because this is the love we need to flourish. The next challenge for us is to take all these wonderful lessons in how to love and apply them to our own relationships.

REFLECTION

What kind of love do you really need? Today, write down a list of all the things you feel you need to flourish. Do you need to be heard? To be held? To be forgiven? When you've made that list, flip it around in your head. This is a list of the ways you need to love others.

Lord, I can barely fathom the depths of your love for me. All I can do is thank you for your amazing grace. Help me today to give the kind of love I crave. In Jesus' name, amen.

Find Someone You Admire

His mouth is sweetness itself; he is altogether lovely. This is my beloved, this is my friend, daughters of Jerusalem.

SONG OF SOLOMON 5:16

When I was a teenager, I always used to go for the bad guy, or at least the one who commanded everyone's attention in a room. But something shifted in me when I became a Christian. I'd had enough of the drama and chaos that came with dating egocentric people and became hungry to share my life with someone who had integrity, kindness, and faith. The moment I met Joel, I knew I had found someone special.

My advice for anyone looking for love—marry up. Aim high. Look for someone you consider to be a better person than you. If you find that person and somehow, they hold you in the same regard, do all you can to make that work!

REFLECTION

Dating someone whose morals you admire makes for a really wonderful relationship. If you're still looking for a person with all the moves and talk, it might be worthwhile to edit your checklist!

Lord, help me to look for a partner who will challenge me and push me to be stronger in you. Help me find that special someone who will enable me to grow spiritually. In Jesus' name, amen.

Don't Compromise

Do not be unequally yoked with unbelievers.

2 CORINTHIANS 6:14

A good friend had been on Christian dating websites and spent a few Sundays visiting other churches but hadn't found anyone. Then she met Dave, a successful business person she was connected with through work. She hesitated about dating him but thought she may as well give it a try. They had a great time and found each other attractive! But by date number seven, the cracks were appearing. They had very different thoughts about marriage, having a family, and raising kids. They didn't make it to date number eight.

When we're desperately seeking something, the temptation to compromise is huge. If I'm shopping for something at the last minute, I'll often end up buying pieces that are unsuitable or don't fit well. I always regret these purchases and wind up with more work on my hands returning them. It's the same with love. Don't latch onto the very first thing you see in your hunger for love. You're worthy of a perfect fit!

REFLECTION

What looks like a minor difference of opinion now could look like a vast ocean in a few years' time. Save yourself the heartache and give it some real thought before you begin a relationship with someone who really isn't on the same page as you at all.

Lord, it's hard to be alone. You even say in your Word that it's not good for us. But there's nothing lonelier than being with the wrong person. Help me to be secure and patient so I eventually find someone who is pulling in the same direction as me. In Jesus' name, amen.

Marry a Heart

Husbands, love your wives just as Christ also loved the church and gave Himself up for her.

EPHESIANS 5:25 NASB

Marry a heart. Don't marry someone for their looks or even their sparkling personality. Both tend to change with time. A good heart never ages and gets more attractive every day. If you're looking for love, stop looking for someone who makes your heart race and start looking for someone whose heart captures you with its beauty. Chances are the rest of them will begin to look pretty irresistible too.

REFLECTION

What would you like your partner's heart to look like? We often build a mental picture of what we'd like our future husband or wife to look like physically, but we seldom make a checklist for their inner being. Do you hope they'll be passionate? Strong? Sensitive? Practical? Take a few moments today to write that list.

Lord, help me to focus on the heart. Let me not pass by a really awesome potential partner because they don't look the way I imagined! The right heart will only make a person more attractive. Today, please give me eyes to see beyond the outside. In Jesus' name, amen.

When Things Aren't Perfect

There is no fear in love. But perfect love drives out fear.

1 JOHN 4:18

On this day some years ago, Joel and I had our engagement photo shoot. As I look back at the pictures, I'm reminded of the mixture of excitement and fear I was feeling. I was over the moon to be getting married. I was in love with my fiancé, but I was afraid of growing up. I was nervous about committing my life to someone and saying the words "till death do us part." I was afraid of all the new responsibility and of who I would become as someone's wife. But I had this feeling that we were about to step into a new purpose together. Almost ten years later, I'm amazed at what God has done with us. I've been humbled by his provision, faithfulness, and plan throughout our whole journey together. Of course, it hasn't been easy, and we still have some maturing to do. But I just know we'll grow up at some point … together.

REFLECTION

Do you have concerns that your current relationship isn't perfect? Have you got things to work on as a couple? Don't worry! Every single couple has things to work through. If things are mostly exciting and good, then the rest can be worked on in due time.

Lord, help me to work on the areas of this relationship that need a bit of help. There is so much to be thankful for and it would be tragic to walk away from a good thing. Give me the wisdom to know that if this is a fundamentally good relationship, it's worth the work. In Jesus' name, amen.

REFLECTION

The words and opinions of others can have a profound effect, but we mustn't allow the estimations of others to dictate our confidence and limit our destiny. God has work for you to do, and there is nothing ordinary about his call on your life! Today, be bold enough to say: "I am *amazing*." Confess those words, knowing that they are God's truth. He has a plan for your life that is anything but ordinary. *You* are anything but ordinary.

Lord, I sometimes struggle to really believe that I am amazing. Help me, Lord, to know me as you see me. After all, you are amazing and don't create anything ordinary! Help me guard against the unhelpful words and opinions of others that cause me to feel inadequate. In Jesus' name, amen.

You Are Not a Number

> "Do not fear, for I have redeemed you;
> I have summoned you by name; you are mine."
> ISAIAH 43:1

I was never that good at math, but I do find it fascinating—it's woven inextricably into the fabric of the universe. But if we're not careful, we can give numbers a little too much power. Music, for instance, can all be explained in numbers. You don't have to know what a number is, however, to be moved by a melody. As human beings and children of God, we are more like melodies than math equations.

Numbers help us to make sense of things like time, weight, age, monetary value, and even intelligence, but these numbers should never factor above truth. The truth is, regardless of the numbers that describe you, you're worth more than anyone could ever calculate. If you believe in Jesus, you believe that you were worth dying for. God's decision to love you wasn't based on digits. His act of immeasurable sacrifice was based on the fact that you're his child.

REFLECTION

Today, practice this simple confession: "My calorie intake, my weight, my age, my IQ, and even my number of friends don't define me. I am more than just a number to God, the one who really counts."

Lord, math is amazing. The way you interwove it into creation astounds me. But when you called me, you called me by name—I was more than a number or a statistic. As I go about my life, help me to see numbers as something that help me, but don't define me. In Jesus' name, amen.

Be Partners

The LORD God said, "It is not good for the man to be alone. I will make a helper suitable for him."

GENESIS 2:18

The word that was spoken over us at our wedding was *partners*. That word has come true for us in every sense—partnership is the true purpose of marriage. Dreams need teams. Marriage is an expression of teamwork in every sense! When God created Adam, it wasn't long before Adam recognized the need for a friend. Adam needed help, company, and comfort. Always remember that the purpose of long-term relationships extends beyond romance and attraction. The person who you end up with will be your helper, companion, and comforter. Even if you don't work together like Joel and me, you still have a shared ministry.

REFLECTION

If you're dating someone, why not take a little time to discuss your future mission together? Perhaps you could even write down a mission statement. Do you want to be a safe place for people to fall? Do you want to be wonderful parents who raise leaders of the future? If you're both believers, your job is to be a team. You will accomplish wonderful things if you're dreaming and working together.

Lord, help me to find and be a good partner. If I'm used to being on my own, help me to begin thinking like a team member. I know that two can accomplish far more than one, so let me find someone to work with me in this life. In Jesus' name, amen.

Stay Kind

But the Holy Spirit produces this kind of fruit in our lives: love, joy, peace, patience, kindness, goodness, faithfulness, gentleness, and self-control.

GALATIANS 5:22–23 NLT

Joel and I work, rest, and play together. We spend days at a time in each other's company without so much as a few hours apart. This is great for building memories! But when you spend every hour of the day with a person, it can be challenging. If you're not careful, things can become tense and standards of kindness can drop. We can become impatient with each other's failings and quick to lose our tempers.

A little while ago, I felt God speak to my heart about this. Joel is a gift to me—I'd be quite lost without him. Although he isn't perfect, neither am I. We both must practice patience with one another as best we can, never forgetting to thank God for our relationship.

REFLECTION

Have you been a little impatient with someone you love recently? Has the tone between you gotten a little snappish and strained? It's worth paying attention to this now. Just because things have slipped doesn't mean they have to remain that way. Take time to assess this and make some changes today.

Lord, thank you for this relationship. Help me to be kind and patient, just as you are. It's hard to be nice to one another all the time, and you know that neither of us is perfect. Please help me to try my best and never to take a precious person's love for granted. Help us to always do better. In Jesus' name, amen.

Create Good Habits

I thank my God every time I remember you.

PHILIPPIANS 1:3

Not all habits are bad. To tell someone, "I love you" or "You're beautiful," to give out of habit—these expressions of love are far better than none at all. In the early days of a relationship, it's good to talk about what you need. If you're a person who needs to hear those three little words daily, tell your partner. That way, your partner can plug it into their habits and become great at saying it! Saying something habitually doesn't make it insincere—it just means that we're training ourselves to take a moment to remember how important someone is.

REFLECTION

What good habits would you like to develop in your own relationship? Is it important for you to have physical affection? Are regular dates a thing you'd both enjoy? It takes around twenty-one days for something to become a habit. Start building a new relationship habit today!

Lord, help me to know what good habits I should develop. If I need to be more loving and affectionate, please show me. Help me to look back in a month's time and really see some growth between us. In Jesus' name, amen.

Submission Is Key

Submit to one another out of reverence for Christ.

EPHESIANS 5:21

Submission is probably a terrifying and outdated word for the twenty-first-century person. But submission is not about allowing someone to have control over you. Mutual submission is about allowing both people to be heard and their wishes respected.

Example: When I dated as a teenager, I was very much of the "my way, or the highway" mind-set. I was born around girl power anthems, and I was loath to *imagine* giving another person any kind of reign over my choices. I also (rightly) didn't want to be taken for granted or abused. But when you find the right partner, someone whose opinion and leadership you trust, someone you want to please and make happy, someone you trust feels the same way about you, it's important to agree on and practice mutual submission.

REFLECTION

There's an unwritten rule in our house that Joel doesn't control me but that I won't do something he strongly opposes. As a married couple we're one person, so my choices are a direct reflection onto him. I can't ignore or disrespect that. He does the same for me.

Lord, help me to shake off my stubbornness. You require mutual submission so both people in a marriage can be happy. If there is something in my spirit that is selfish and prefers my own way, help me overcome that. And Lord, please help my partner to do the same. In Jesus' name, amen.

You're Stronger Than You Think

He gives power to the weak and strength to the powerless.

ISAIAH 40:29 NLT

A few months ago, I found a message in my Facebook inbox. It was from a young Christian who was bravely battling chronic illness daily. She was in and out of the hospital on a weekly basis and struggling to make it through even basic tasks without feeling unwell. "I feel like such a failure because I'm just not coping," she wrote. I waited a few hours to respond because I didn't know what to say.

But after a time of prayer, I realized exactly what I must say:

Dear warrior, you might feel weak right now. You might feel unable to accomplish what you did last month or even yesterday. But despite appearances, you *are* handling this, because you're still here. You're even reaching out for support and you're doing everything you can. You might feel weak but let me tell you you're strength is very evident to me right now. Don't underestimate it.

REFLECTION

Struggling and feeling overwhelmed don't make you a failure. Check your pulse—you're still here! That means you're still fighting. Who knows? You might even be an inspiration to others.

Lord, thank you for the inner strength only you can give. I'm still here and that really counts for something. Today, help me not to see myself as someone who is slowly fading, but as someone who is bravely enduring what I'm going through. In Jesus' name, amen.

Your Strength Is in Him

No temptation has overtaken you except what is common to mankind. And God is faithful; he will not let you be tempted beyond what you can bear. But when you are tempted, he will also provide a way out so that you can endure it.

1 Corinthians 10:13

This Scripture is commonly misunderstood. We're led to believe that God won't allow us to go through more than we can handle. Instead, this text is referring to temptation and not to pain or struggle.

God does allow us to be faced with more struggle and pain than we can handle. Not because he is cruel or sadistic, but because God knows that we need him, and that in all things we can reach out for his strong hand. Often, the only time we will open our arms and reach is when the load has become too great to carry on our own. God allows the pain and suffering to drive us to him, showing us our strength lies in him alone.

Reflection

If you feel that your arms are full right now and you simply can't carry the load alone, it's time to reach out and share the load with God. He is there for those times where we can't cope. He is there in the moments where the weight of life brings us to our knees. He is there right now. Open your arms.

Lord, my burdens are just too heavy right now. I can't do this alone. Hard as it is to begin with, I'm choosing to open my arms and share my pain and struggles with you. In Jesus' name, amen.

The Fight Brings out the Fighter in You

On the day I called, you answered me; you made me bold.
PSALM 138:3 NASB

A few years ago, Joel and I had a really tough show. It was one of those events where everything that could go wrong did—there were technical failures, and team members neglected their responsibilities. Every moment was a battle. Despite the issues, I felt up to the challenge. I realized that after years of facing problems in a high pressure setting, the deep end is where I do my best swimming.

Of course, it's natural to wonder why God allows us to be so stretched. But you see, he is a master swimming coach. He knows that where the current is strongest is where we build our stamina. When I prayed about this later, I felt the gentle voice of the Spirit whisper to me, *Whatever it takes to bring out the fighter in you, I'm gonna do it. If a few hard knocks is what it takes to make you throw your whole body into the fight, I will allow those blows to come. You once said to me, "Make me brave. Make me strong." I'm answering your prayers.*

REFLECTION

If you're going through a tough season right now, it might be because God is bringing out the fighter in you. Everyone falls, but not everyone gets back up! Today, make the decision to square up to the opponent of fear and come back fighting.

Lord, thank you for the training you're giving me right now. Help me to rise to the challenge. In Jesus' name, amen.

Diamonds

Give thanks to the LORD, for he is good. His love endures forever.

PSALM 136:1

I don't own many diamonds (one to be exact) that we splurged on to symbolize our engagement. It isn't the crown jewels by any means, but to me it's astonishing and means far more than its monetary value. To me, it signifies a lifelong commitment with someone who loves me. But why do we use diamonds to symbolize enduring love? Because of all the natural substances, diamond is the only one that proverbially endures the way love does—forever.

Diamonds are the hardest natural substance; the only thing that can scratch a diamond is another diamond. Many ancient cultures believed that diamonds gave the wearer strength and courage, and some kings even wore diamonds on their armor as they rode into battle. But what I find most fascinating about them is the way they are formed—under immense heat and pressure almost one hundred miles below the earth's surface.

REFLECTION

Isn't it interesting the hardest natural substance is also considered one of the most dazzling? While the pressure of life can feel unbearable at times, it need not be what breaks us down. By God's grace it can be the very thing that causes is to emerge stronger and more beautiful than ever before.

Lord, thank you that you're making a diamond out of me right now. Under the immense pressure of life, you're making me stronger and more reflective of your glory. Help me to remain filled with your grace throughout this process. In Jesus' name, amen.

Pray for Courage

He gives strength to the weary
and increases the power of the weak.

ISAIAH 40:29

Sometimes we can't muster the courage to do the things we want. We want to face our challenges heroically, but our humanity gets in the way. During those times, prayer can be just what we need to overcome the situation. Sometimes natural strength is not sufficient; we need to throw ourselves into prayer and ask for God's supernatural strength to get us through.

Have you ever looked back on a season and said the words, "I don't know how I did that?" I sure have! I don't know how we made it around fourteen countries in as many days on a European tour with little sleep while battling illness. But we did. And I believe wholeheartedly that it was only possible via a supernatural God-given strength in answer to prayer.

REFLECTION

What are you facing right now that you need courage for? If you don't have anything huge happening, simply pray for the courage to be a great person. There are always challenges for us to face daily. Let's pray to be courageous in everything.

Lord, my prayer today is for simple courage—to give my best when I'm going through my worst. Help me to comfort others while I still hurt and to give in faith even though I'm in need. Because, Lord, you gave your best for me. Amen.

The Battles Are Many

O God the Lord, the strength of my salvation,
you have covered my head in the day of battle.

PSALM 140:7 NASB

Life is not one continuous fight—the battles we face are daily. I recently heard a celebrity interviewed on radio about their depression. This person was speaking soberly, eloquently, and from a very stable place. "This time last year I was a wreck," he said. "Today I'm okay." Sadly, since the interview was aired, the well-loved singer took a downward spiral and ultimately his own life.

To say that this person had lost the battle would be to diminish the courage it took to fight every day for so long. This mental health warrior was an overcomer who had won countless battles, the likes of which we can only imagine. He lost one battle, just one, and sadly the outcome of that was irreversible. There are two things to take from this: First, celebrate every victory and never consider yourself defeated. Second, pray for the strength to face today's battle. Though we have won many, we must never take winning for granted.

REFLECTION

What small victories have you won this week? Have you overcome anxiety or the temptation to gossip? Have you managed to make it into work despite illness? Thank God for all these wins. They may be small, but he is in all of them.

Lord, thank you for the many victories that I have won in life. Thank you that I can hold my head high as a victor because of you. Also help me to seek you and find you in today's battle. Finally, let me never take you for granted. In Jesus' name, amen.

Spiritual Strength

Be strong in the Lord and in his mighty power.

EPHESIANS 6:10

We're taught from an early age that strength is displayed physically. But some of the greatest displays of strength come in keeping our fists by our sides. Sometimes, we even have to hold our tongue in order to calm a situation and win the battle. Remaining calm, respectful, and noble while others rage takes the spiritual strength of a real warrior.

A friend once confided in me that her spouse had been abusive. I was livid, and part of me wanted to go over there and take him on myself. But after the couple had received prayer and counseling, I found myself in an awkward position. The pair were coming to an event of mine, and I wasn't sure I was ready to see my friend's spouse. I prayed about what to do and felt the Lord instruct me to be kind. The evening went okay. But I'll be honest: I had to draw upon every ounce of my spiritual courage to get through it.

REFLECTION

Take a moment to pray for renewed spiritual courage. No one is saying that you shouldn't help a person who needs to be removed from a violent situation, or that an aggressive person shouldn't be disciplined. But the last thing you want is to make the situation worse.

Lord, I pray right now for God's peace to rest over my heart and my choices. Lord, help me to access spiritual strength to treat my enemies and those who have hurt my loved ones with respect and positive regard. In Jesus' name, amen.

Don't Be Ashamed of Weakness

For just as we share abundantly in the sufferings of Christ,
so also our comfort abounds through Christ.

2 CORINTHIANS 1:5

There are two types of people—those who are fragile, and those
who have yet to discover they are fragile. In other words, fragility
is human!

When I first suffered with anxiety, I was ashamed to talk
about it because I thought it made me a weakling. But those
experiences have given me an empathy and humility to connect
with others I never had before. I cannot even count the pairs of
eyes that have met mine in a nod of recognition. I'm so thankful
for that beautiful honesty and connection.

REFLECTION

If you find yourself suffering with addiction, mental health
problems, losing the fight in your relationship, or making choices
you regret, don't let shame overcome you. You are blessed
because you've *seen* your weakness. You've met it; you've named
it; you have weakness in common with others. Tomorrow is a
new day where, by grace, you have permission to begin again.

Lord, thank you that you have shown me my areas of weakness.
Thank you that now I can be aware of the chinks in my armor.
And thank you that you can use my issues to encourage others.
In Jesus' name, amen.

Breakthroughs Can Be Messy

"Do not fear, for I am with you;
do not be dismayed, for I am your God."

ISAIAH 41:10

When we picture a breakthrough, we picture rejoicing—we see ourselves running triumphantly across a finish line to shouts of victory from a cheering crowd. But breakthroughs often feel more like pulling yourself onto the shore after a shipwreck—although you're euphoric, you're also exhausted.

At the beginning of last year, we had a prayer meeting at our church. The phrase that kept emerging was, "This will be a year of breakthrough." But seven months into the year, I was mad at the statement. There had been marriage breakdowns, sickness, and all kinds of other setbacks for the people in my life. *Breakthrough?* I found myself asking. *What kind of a breakthrough is this?*

And that familiar voice in my spirit answered, *Not all breakthroughs look like winning. Some breakthroughs require becoming broken. It's messy and painful but necessary to get to the next level.*

REFLECTION

Breakthroughs require movement—change of any kind can cause a lot of pain. To break through a glass ceiling, sometimes we must punch so hard that our knuckles bleed. If you're tired, hurting, and seeing a lot of broken pieces around your feet, don't be discouraged—you're probably right where you need to be.

Lord, help me deal with being in the center of this mess. It's overwhelming and discouraging to see the broken fragments lying around me. I know that you're working through this chaos to bring a new order to my life. I trust you with this mess. In Jesus' name, amen.

Let Joy Be Your Strength

Nehemiah said, "Go and enjoy choice food and sweet drinks,
and send some to those who have nothing prepared.
This day is holy to our Lord. Do not grieve,
for the joy of the LORD is your strength."

NEHEMIAH 8:10

When times get hard, we sometimes feel guilty for enjoying ourselves. If money is tight, you might feel guilty taking a few hours out of work to enjoy a summer afternoon. If you've just had some bad news, it might seem like a terrible time to go out and enjoy a meal with friends. If you've just lost someone you love, you might feel guilty letting loose and laughing about old times. But the Bible says quite clearly that we should let the joy of the Lord be our strength. This doesn't mean that we shouldn't mourn, but we are encouraged to enjoy life whenever and wherever we can because joy *gives* us life. Without joy, we may not have the spiritual resources to deal with the pain. So go for it, don't hold back!

REFLECTION

What brings your heart the most joy? Do you recharge in nature? Do you get your kicks out of doing something creative or just chilling out? There's no right answer that fits everyone. Whatever it is, make sure you intentionally put more of it into your day.

Lord, thank you for joy. Help me to chase it down. May I seek it in everything—especially in you. In Jesus' name, amen.

Channel Your Anger

Do not be overcome by evil, but overcome evil with good.

ROMANS 12:21

We talked about spiritual strength a few days ago and how important it is to have control over your anger. But anger is not a sin. God displays his anger many times in the Bible, and even Jesus himself was angered by corruption. Being outraged by injustice is righteous, and righteous anger is a powerful force when channeled. Anger is a fire that can make things happen. We just have to take that torch and put it where it can make the most positive difference.

If you find that someone you love has been abused, it's natural to feel anger toward the abuser. But destroying the perpetrator will not fix the problem of abuse nor will it restore what has been taken from the victim. In a situation like that, taking your anger and using it create better resources for victims or better ways of detecting abuse might be truly transformative. Even using your anger to simply shout a message of truth can be a flaming torch that could create a light for many.

REFLECTION

If you feel you have righteous anger about something, why not ask God to begin to give you a strategy? Righteous anger connects us to our intellect like nothing else. It helps us get over ourselves and right to the heart of the matter. Take a few moments today to invite God into your anger so he can direct it to make a positive change.

Lord, thank you for righteous anger that changes things. Help me to channel all of my rage into something productive. In Jesus' name, amen.

Built in a Lifetime—Gone in a Moment

The wise woman builds her house,
but with her own hands the foolish one tears hers down.

PROVERBS 14:1

Many of the magnificent churches in Europe took decades, sometimes even generations, to construct. But during WWII, many were brought tumbling down in mere moments through artillery barrages and explosive charges. Just like these buildings, good marriages, ministries, careers, and reputations can take a lifetime establish. We can invest years of good choices into building something that one lapse in judgment can turn to rubble. In the heat of the moment, a single bad decision might not seem like a big deal. But the harsh reality is, one bad decision is all it takes to ruin a relationship, tarnish a reputation, or end a career. Praying for wisdom is vital to the preservation of these important elements in our lives.

REFLECTION

If ever you are tempted to do something you know will be destructive to the great things you've built, consider this: You may not have the opportunity or the time to rebuild what you're about to bring down. Stop and ask God to give you his wisdom. If you feel you may have made a mistake already, ask God into the situation right away—you might be just in time to diffuse that charge.

Lord, help me to be cautious with my actions. I want to be productive and spontaneous, but I want to make good choices when I do that. I pray you'll protect what I build and everything I set out to do in your name. Amen.

Don't React—Act

Whoever guards his mouth preserves his life;
he who opens wide his lips comes to ruin.
PROVERBS 13:3 ESV

Our humanity makes us quick to react. We're wired to flee from predators and face down enemies. But this is not the Ice Age and we are not Neanderthals.

Of course, there are times when we need to think on our feet and act quickly. But in a tough situation where wisdom is called for, we should be prepared to give the situation a little time and space. If someone opens a tough conversation with you, don't feel obliged to have all the answers immediately. It's okay to say, "I'm not too sure about this and would like to give it some more thought before I respond." If someone challenges or makes an attack on you, you are not obliged to make a knee-jerk reaction.

REFLECTION

Power and wisdom will enter through a little window of time and space. If someone drops a bombshell on you, take a moment to collect your thoughts and opinions without the haze of disappointment and anger.

Lord, help me to remember this advice when those tough moments arrive. Help me have the wisdom and presence of mind to step back and evaluate the situation before I react. May I be intentional rather than impulsive when I respond. In Jesus' name, amen.

Striking Balance with Taming the Tongue

Speak up and judge fairly;
defend the rights of the poor and needy.

PROVERBS 31:9

We know that the power of words is immense—they can cut someone down to size in moments and leave lasting damage. But we also know that words have the power to break terrible silences. Martin Luther King Jr. famously said, "In the end, we will remember not the words of our enemies, but the silence of our friends." There comes a time where silence alone is betrayal. There is clearly a real tension here between knowing when to speak and when to remain silent. Both have their virtues, and both carry a risk. Clearly, we need to call upon godly wisdom to know the difference.

REFLECTION

Is there someone in your world who needs you to speak up on his or her behalf? It might be difficult, especially if what they're going through is controversial. But sometimes we must take that risk and say something. Ask for God's wisdom in this.

Lord, give me the wisdom to know when to hold back and when to speak up. Give me the courage to raise my voice above the crowd when it's right to do so, and show me when to keep my mouth closed and let the moment pass. In Jesus' name, amen.

Be Teachable

Listen to advice and accept instruction,
that you may gain wisdom in the future.
PROVERBS 19:20 ESV

In the first year of my faith journey, my life progressed at a fantastic pace. I made more progress in six months than I had made in the previous five years. I became better at relationships, made strides in my career, and even became a much better musician. There was one key change that made all that possible—I became teachable.

When we reach a certain age or level of experience, we can become quite stubborn and even arrogant about what we think we know. But the greatest masters of a craft only become so by realizing that they will never *completely* master their craft. They remain pliable and they are always keen to learn. They even take advice from people much less experienced, knowing that everyone has a fresh and potentially valuable viewpoint to offer. It's not always easy letting go of the way we used to do things, but being pliable and open-minded means that there are no limits to how far we can progress.

REFLECTION

It's good to have confidence in what you're doing. But no one is immune to mistakes or is above guidance. The Bible mentions teachability and openness to correction many times, so clearly God thinks it's one of the major keys to success and growth.

Lord, help me to be teachable. Help me to be malleable and open to instruction from you. I want to gain wisdom and be successful in all I do for you. Help me to stay flexible. In Jesus' name, amen.

The Correction of a Friend

Timely advice is lovely, like golden apples in a silver basket
PROVERBS 25:11 NLT

Being teachable in your craft is one thing, but hearing truths about your lifestyle or choices can be much harder. It's never easy to hear the words, "You're making a mistake" or "You need to take better care of yourself."

A few years ago, I had to sit down with a friend and tell her she was losing too much weight. She was becoming thinner by the day, and after some time it became clear that she wasn't just dieting but starving herself. I was very nervous to broach the subject as it was highly sensitive for her at the time. For a moment, I feared she might be angry or avoid me. Instead, she began to cry and opened up. Years later, she confided that the conversation was a much-needed wake-up call.

REFLECTION

When someone you consider to be a friend takes the time to lovingly correct you, your initial response can be to defend yourself. Next time that happens, agree to at least listen. Hear the person out, thank the person for sharing, and agree to think on it. When you have a little headspace to reflect, you may find some resonance with what they're saying to you. It could be the reality check you need to finally break a destructive cycle you've been stuck in.

Lord, help me to heed the warnings and loving truth from my friends. Help me to embrace and absorb their words like a gift even when it hurts. I don't want to surround myself only with people who say what I want to hear—I know that won't do me any good. Help me love and value those friends who speak the truth to me in love. In Jesus' name, amen.

Weigh Up Advice

Many are the plans in a person's heart,
but it is the LORD's purpose that prevails.

PROVERBS 19:21

In my twenties, I learned to take advice. In my thirties, I learned I wasn't bound to take all the advice I was offered. It's great to become more open to criticism and to embrace a friend's loving rebuke, but there are also times in life where our friends our wrong. Consider the book of Job—when Job went through the darkest time of his life losing almost everything, he received a broad range of advice from his friends. They may have meant well, but they were all wrong! Not all advice is sound, and not everyone deserves to be a voice in your decisions.

REFLECTION

Job had faith, and he felt he'd been promised good things by God. Sometimes, while your friends might be right from a practical point of view, their absence during your intimate conversations with God means that they don't see the big picture. They may lack the faith for your situation that you've been given by grace. If they are advising you not to do something that you feel called to do, clearly wisdom is needed. Time to pray again.

Lord, I pray for the wisdom to follow the right voice. If I am misguided and my friends and family are right, please open my eyes to the truth. If I should ignore their well-intentioned advice, please give me the grace and the strength to do so lovingly. Protect all my relationships. In Jesus' name, amen.

To Act or Not to Act?

Desire without knowledge is not good—
how much more will hasty feet miss the way!
PROVERBS 19:2

Some say the time is always right to do the right thing: to speak up, to protect the oppressed, to seek justice. And to a degree this is true. But strategy is crucial, and a good strategy always includes impeccable timing.

You might have been given a great message to share with the world but not feel strong enough to deal with the response just now. You might have a great idea, but you know that if you share it before you have protected the idea, it will be stolen! Waiting is sometimes exactly the right thing to do with a great plan. In the meantime, take the time to arm yourself with as much knowledge as possible. If you have a business idea, make sure you research the market. If you want to go and bless another nation with your talents, learn about the culture! Knowledge undergirds our enthusiasm with a good foundation.

REFLECTION

Is there something you'd like to take on in the next few months? Maybe it's time to arm yourself with more knowledge through research. Make sure you have everything you need to dive right into the new challenge when the time is right. It might set your plans back a little, but chances are it'll save you time in the future.

Lord, give me the wisdom to know when to move and when to stay still. Help me to know the difference between a fear of acting and choosing to stay put in faith. Lord, please cover these decisions so that whatever happens I glorify you. In Jesus' name, amen.

Consequences

"I have the right to do anything," you say—but not
everything is beneficial. "I have the right to do anything"—
but not everything is constructive.

1 CORINTHIANS 10:23

The twenty-first century is very much the age of the individual.
We are encouraged to do whatever satisfies and makes us happy
in the moment. Some of this comes from a very good place;
however, no amount of good intention can change the truth that
our actions have consequences. What we choose can and does
affect others.

Our choices are contagious! People are up to 30 percent
more likely to choose something on the menu if they see another
choose it first. It's important to remember that while we have
the freedom to do anything we like within law and reason, not
everything will benefit us. Not everything we choose to do will
move us forward and help us to grow. Some things will hold us
back and have a negative influence on those we love.

REFLECTION

Are you doing things that don't benefit you? Are you maintain-
ing habits or keeping company that might be holding you back?
It's important to be honest with yourself about these things.
You're free to do as you wish! But not all your wishes will lead to
blessings.

Lord, thank you for the gift of free will. Help me to use it wisely,
being sensitive to what will benefit me and what will not. May I
not be selfish with my choices but always seek the best outcome
for everyone concerned. Give me the strength, wisdom, and
capacity of love to make this happen. In Jesus' name, amen.

Beware of Gossip

Without wood a fire goes out; without a gossip a quarrel dies down.

PROVERBS 26:20

Most of us have been there—we relax in the company of friends and our guard comes right down. We catch up, exchange stories, and our tongues become very relaxed. It's in these moments we can find ourselves idly discussing business that isn't ours—spreading gossip to eager listeners.

There are lots of reasons we might end up talking about others and their personal business when they're not present. Sometimes, we are genuinely concerned about a person in our lives. At other times, we may be offloading about someone out of frustration. Sometimes talking about someone else's bad behavior helps *us* to feel better about our own transgressions. And sometimes, gossip comes out of simple social awkwardness—it fills a silence and helps create a bond between those chatting.

REFLECTION

Gossip is a quiet killer. Highly toxic, it spreads like wildfire that's hard to contain. Of this you can be almost sure: gossip shared in confidence has a way of finding its way back to the person it concerns. Don't be surprised if you become the villain of the drama. If you don't want to be the villain and you wouldn't want the person to hear what you're saying with their own ears, button that lip.

Lord, it's so hard to always say the right thing. Help me to have wisdom and self-control when it comes to chatting, sharing information, and bonding with others. Give me great things to say. I want people to come to me and feel better when they leave. In Jesus' name, amen.

Take Care What You Share

Let no corrupting talk come out of your mouths, but only such
as is good for building up, as fits the occasion, that it may give
grace to those who hear.

EPHESIANS 4:29 ESV

Sharing posts is a social media phenomenon. As a big Facebook
user, I browse daily and see all kinds of viral posts. Sometimes a
post so upsets me that my thumb hovers over the share button
almost instantly. Where I would have clicked to share the post
immediately, I now hesitate, made wiser by my experiences.

C. H. Spurgeon once said, "A lie will go round the world
while truth is putting its boots on." The sad fact is, a good deal
of what appears on social media is made up. You'll see things,
especially around the time of an election or the breaking of a big
story, and presume them to be completely true. But if you take
a second to investigate the source, you'll find that it's just satire,
propaganda, or slander. People have been wrongly accused of
crimes and even thought to be dead! Before you share, check the
source.

REFLECTION

As lovers of the truth, we have to make sure we aren't just
perpetuating lies. People's lives and reputations are at stake.
Don't be a part of the reason someone's world collapses.

God, I pray that you would awaken my spiritual senses online.
There is so much dark material circulating, and I don't want to
let it. Help me not to draw attention to bad deeds and situations
by commenting on them or sharing. Empower me to squash the
enemy's schemes by scrolling past the darkness and sharing the
light. In Jesus' name, amen.

Beware What You Promote

Whatever is true, whatever is noble, whatever is right, whatever is pure, whatever is lovely, whatever is admirable—if anything is excellent or praiseworthy—think about such things

PHILIPPIANS 4:8

When we kick and scream about something that offends us, we often draw more attention to it. Sometimes there *is* a time to speak up, but by shining the spotlight on someone's horrible Facebook post, we're often just making more people see it.

The same is sadly true of coming to someone's rescue in the comments section. Recently, I had a video of mine go viral, and there were thousands of lovely comments! But one person dared to put something negative, and the crowd swarmed. The comment got over five hundred responses, and guess what happened then? It went right to the top of all the comments and stayed there—it was the first thing people would see if they commented on the video.

It's upsetting to see any kind of hate directed toward others, but I can't help but wonder if sharing on social media does anything more than keep those negative messages in the air.

REFLECTION

Have you felt tempted to comment on someone's hate or correct someone who is being negative? By engaging with them you're actually drawing more traffic to their comments and their hate! Stop and think before you tap out a response. Instead, why not try commenting in the affirmative or sharing something beautiful?

Lord, I pray for your discernment. Let me not give the bullies a megaphone by engaging with them. I want to promote life. So please, Lord, help me to do that always. In Jesus' name, amen.

Pruning Produces Fruit

"I am the true vine, and my Father is the vineyard keeper.
Every branch in me that does not produce fruit He removes,
and He prunes every branch that produces fruit so that
it will produce even more fruit."

JOHN 15:2 HCSB

We spend lots of time praying for God to add great things to our lives, but sometimes we need to remove some things. One of my favorite songs by Kenny Rogers captures this sentiment perfectly, talking about a gambler's secret to survival is knowing which cards to throw away and which to keep.

When we look at the hand life deals us, it can be hard to know what to throw away and what to keep—you might well be looking at a great hand. But God sometimes asks us to throw away a high card. In other words, he asks us to let go of something that is working to make room for something else.

REFLECTION

You might well be looking at what you think is a losing hand. But with God all things are possible, and he can work through even through those low numbers. We need wisdom to know what to play next.

Lord, help me to know when to let go and when to hold on. Help me to have faith for things in life that look like poor cards. If it's your will, help me to have faith to let go of my high cards and trust your plan. You are the only one that can make sense of these cards, Lord. And you can make any hand I am dealt a winning one. Thank you for what you are about to do. In Jesus' name, amen.

Take the Narrow Road

"Enter through the narrow gate. For wide is the gate and broad is the road that leads to destruction, and many enter through it."

MATTHEW 7:13

If I was to tell you that you had a choice of two roads on your journey—one a bumpy dirt road lined with trees, the other a newly paved road with an ocean view—which would you choose? It's a no-brainer, right? But what if I was to tell you that the dirt road was the only one that would lead you to your chosen destination? I'm sure that would change things, but I'm guessing you'd *still* be tempted to take the easy road.

Doing the right thing in life is harder than doing what comes easily. It isn't called the narrow road without reason. It's a path with more obstacles and struggles, but ultimately, it's the road home. If you're faced with doing what's easy versus doing what's right, *always* remember that the easy option will leave you stranded in the end.

REFLECTION

Have you been struggling with a decision or a behavior recently? Do you feel tempted to take the easy road? Just remind yourself today that the easy road is only easy at the start—where it ends up taking you is not where you want to be.

God, keep me on the path of righteousness. Please show me the way you would have me to walk. Keep me blameless and upright as I follow you—I want to end up where you want me. Even if something looks like the easy option today, help me have the wisdom and courage to go by the narrow road. In Jesus' name, amen.

Don't Follow the Crowd

When he saw the crowds, he had compassion on them, because
they were harassed and helpless, like sheep without a shepherd.

MATTHEW 9:36

Last year, my husband, my parents, and I went to a local festival
for families. It was a glorious sunny day (a rarity in England),
and we took the dog along for extra fun. When it came time for
lunch, we looked to where all the food vans were parked. There
were dozens of them, but the van with the longest queue of people grabbed our attention. The line was three times longer than
the others, so we agreed it must be the best. We joined the line.
It was a nightmare. By the time we reached the front, we were
tired and irritated and the dog was too hot and needed water.
The van was out of most of the items we wanted. They got our
order wrong and even gave me the wrong change. As we sat down
to eat, we realized our foolishness. The place next door had less
choice, but the people walking away looked calm, comfortably
munching away in the shade while I fretted about our situation.

REFLECTION

Following the crowd is an instinct, but beware—too often the
crowd is going the wrong way! They don't really know *why*
they're going that way; they just know it's popular and therefore
the easier choice. Don't follow the crowd. Take the road less traveled and you might just get fed after all.

Lord, give me the strength of character to buck the trend and do
something new, since the crowd isn't always going the right way.
Instead of following the majority, let me follow you at all times,
because you always lead me to greener pastures. In Jesus' name,
amen.

Discernment

"The Lord does not look at the things people look at. People look
at the outward appearance, but the LORD looks at the heart."

1 SAMUEL 16:7

I consider myself to be quite open-minded and want always to
see the good in others. But now and again my human nature
causes me to make wrong judgments. A few days ago in town,
I saw two teenage boys in hoodies running down the grass
embankment. A split-second judgment had me presuming they
were running from someone, perhaps a fight with some other
kids, or maybe they were fleeing from a police officer. My heart
was arrested by the Holy Spirit when I realized they were running
to pick up a homeless man who had just fallen. The whole thing
happened in a matter of seconds, and it moved me because my
eyes were opened in the Spirit.

REFLECTION

What we perceive with our senses and what is truth can be very
different. Ask God to elevate your spiritual sight so you will be
ready to see the full picture. Even if those two boys had been
troublesome, it wouldn't have meant that they are not precious to
God and made in his image.

Lord, thank you that you're able to see beneath the surface. Help
me to look harder too. Help me to be kind always while keeping
my wits about me and giving people the benefit of the doubt. In
Jesus' name, amen.

The Fear of the Lord

The fear of the LORD is the beginning of wisdom,
and knowledge of the Holy One is understanding.

PROVERBS 9:10

I didn't used to like the idea of the passage above, and it put me off reading the Bible for a while. As an anxiety sufferer, I wanted God to be a comfort, not a tyrant. I wanted God to be a safe place, not a monster. But the more I lived with the Word and got to know God, the more I understood this kind of fear was different.

I was a bit of a rebel as a kid. My dad was quite easy going and didn't come down too hard on me about anything. The kids I knew who stayed on track were mainly the kids who had a fear of their dad's reaction—not a hide-under-the-table fear, but a healthy respect and an awareness of the consequences. That fear prevented them from doing the wrong thing and ultimately protected them. Fear is not always a bad thing.

REFLECTION

Our fear of the Lord comes from a place of knowing that he is the best Father in the world. He is always right. He always loves and protects us. We know disobeying him will lead to our own destruction. We understand that actions have natural consequences, and he sees those consequences before we do. We love him and want make him proud. Welcome that healthy fear—it's a beautiful, holy fear that will keep you from falling.

Father, I want to fear you in a righteous way—the way a child fears the reaction of a good father. You act out of your love for me, and you discipline me so I don't get into trouble or danger. Help me today to deepen my respect for your Word and my reverence for you. In Jesus' name, amen.

Sleep on It

My dear brothers and sisters, take note of this: Everyone should
be quick to listen, slow to speak and slow to become angry.

JAMES 1:19

I'm both impatient and impulsive. If I have what I think is a great
idea, I want to tell everyone *now*. If someone sends me a snarky
message or email, I want to respond *now*. But some experience
(including a few mistakes) has taught me it's good to sleep on it.
Even a big purchase decision—the wedding dress, a new couch,
that cell phone contract—it's best to delay our decision, to sleep
on it. There may be times in life where we must think on our feet
and make a snap decision, but for the most part there's no rush.
Salespeople can be pushy, but they'll be there tomorrow.

REFLECTION

Have you had an upsetting email or message from someone? Do
you have a decision to make but lack the peace about what to do?
Give it the night. Tomorrow you'll be calmer and your head will
be clearer. Trust me, it can wait.

Lord, help me be slow to anger just as you are. Thank you that
you are rich in love and full of wisdom. When someone speaks
out of turn to me, help me be patient and not quick to react. In
Jesus' name, amen.

Avoid Temptation

On reaching the place, he said to them,
"Pray that you will not fall into temptation."

LUKE 22:40

I have a saying in our house: "To buy cookies is to eat cookies." In other words, if you want to avoid the calories in a box of Oreos, walk past them in the supermarket—you're far less likely to walk past them at home!

I like to think I have pretty good self-control, so sometimes I will buy cookies and intend to eat them over a couple of weeks. So far, a package of cookies hasn't lasted longer than a few days in my possession. We must learn to take care of our future selves by removing temptation. I'm not suggesting you never buy cookies. But be realistic about what's going to happen.

If you're an impulsive spender and need to save cash, don't plan a trip to the mall during a sale. If you're a recovering alcoholic, don't rent an apartment above a bar. Just play the movie of how future you will have to deal with the consequences!

REFLECTION

The Lord's Prayer doesn't say, "Lord, help me deal with temptation." It says, "Lead me not into temptation." Today, be realistic about the temptations you're about to face. Don't overestimate your own self-control, even if you're feeling strong.

Lord, help me be wise when it comes to the things that tempt me—you know everything I grapple with. I pray you would be right there in the midst of those things. Show me how to avoid them rather than just resisting them, which is so much harder! In Jesus' name, amen.

Age Is Just a Number

"Is not wisdom found among the aged?
Does not long life bring understanding?"

JOB 12:12

Joel and I play in over a hundred churches a year and often stay in host accommodations. Often we have a great time, enjoying delicious home-cooked meals, and find ourselves really blessed by the company. But occasionally, our hearts will drop when the family is elderly, and they don't know about the internet. One incident taught me not to stereotype quite so harshly.

We came in through the doors of the quaint 1920s house to find a charming old couple. They were eighty-two and seventy-seven years old, and their house was filled with heirlooms and memories from their kids and grandkids. After a lovely cup of tea, Joel and I exchanged a glance. "There's no way they have Wi-Fi," I whispered.

It turned out the old couple *did* have Wi-Fi. In fact, they were internet entrepreneurs! They'd created a website for children's resources that was getting thousands of visitors per month—more than my website at the time.

REFLECTION

It's unwise to make presumptions about people because of their age. A lot of people in their golden years have a great deal of wisdom we can draw from!

Lord, thank you for the older, accomplished people in my life. Bless and protect them. Help me to draw from their knowledge and wisdom and not overlook them. May I be productive and fruitful all the days of my life. In Jesus' name, amen.

Freedom Is Contagious

Now the Lord is the Spirit, and where the
Spirit of the Lord is, there is freedom.

2 CORINTHIANS 3:17

We've all broken into song when we think no one can hear, but I had a slightly embarrassing moment while on holiday last year. Lost in my own little world on the sun lounger, I found myself singing along to a Bon Jovi song that was playing via the hotel radio. When I removed my hat, I realized that a couple had set up nearby and could hear me. Highly embarrassed, I stopped singing immediately. However, my heart did a little dance when that chap on the nearby lounger began singing too! I realized that my silliness had been mistaken for freedom and it had been contagious.

Singing is not the only thing that catches on with others. Dancing, laughing, and dressing the way you want to dress all give others silent permission to do the same. Being who you really are without apology helps others find their freedom.

REFLECTION

Today, be who you really are. Sing, dance, laugh, and watch the world slowly find their voices and join your chorus.

Lord, set my spirit free! Let me be unapologetically who I am so others are given permission to let go and be themselves too. In Jesus' name, amen.

You Don't Have to Win All the Time

The horse is made ready for the day of battle,
but victory rests with the LORD.

PROVERBS 21:31

It's been a busy year. Between January and today, you did a *lot* of different things. You had some new experiences and chased down some new dreams. You faced some new hurdles and nursed some new bruises. Did it all work out perfectly? Did you win every battle? It's unlikely. But freedom doesn't come from seeing all your dreams come true. True freedom is freedom even from the relentless stirring of your dreams. We're free when we can passionately pursue our goals while understanding that they don't define us. We find freedom when our failures begin to look simply like lessons to learn from. Losing doesn't define us.

REFLECTION

It's as important to be free *not* to dream as well as to dream. Have you felt that you always need to be running like the wind—moving mountains in the process? Take some time today to enjoy the liberty of simply sitting and watching the world go by. Be free just to live in God's presence.

Lord, thank you that you've put a winning spirit and attitude in me. Help me not to be bound by it. I want to enjoy the freedom that comes from not always needing to be at the top of the leaderboard. My worth doesn't come from getting it right all the time or collecting awards—it comes directly from you. In Jesus' name, amen.

Be Truthful with Yourself

"Then you will know the truth, and the truth will set you free."
JOHN 8:32

We all put on a bit of a performance for the world, and we like to think that behind closed doors we are real and come clean with ourselves. Sadly, this isn't always so. The deepest secrets are the ones we keep from ourselves. Addiction, disorders, and even sin can be secrets we won't admit even when it's just us, alone with our thoughts. We often won't face up to our struggles, addictions, loneliness, or temptations because we're afraid if we say them out loud they'll become real. This is why families and friends stage interventions. This is why small debts become bankruptcies. The secrets we keep from ourselves are like weeds growing in our lounge rooms. Eventually they take over and we have to move out.

REFLECTION

To finish out this year with freedom, take some time to be honest with yourself. You owe yourself that much.

Lord, if there is something in my life I need to face up to, let me face up to it now. Let me be truly transparent in my own intentions so I can fully see myself. I don't want to live in denial or suppress a feeling that something needs to change. I want to be set free, so let me know the truth about myself even if it isn't always easy for me to take. In Jesus' name, amen.

You're Not Bound by This World

Everyone born of God overcomes the world. This is the victory
that has overcome the world, even our faith.

1 JOHN 5:4

At the age of twenty, I was in all kinds of chains. I was in financial
debt and an unhappy, controlling relationship. I was enslaved to a
cycle of bad choices that seemed to repeat on an annual basis. But
the moment I gave my life to Jesus, I laid down who I was and
received a new life in Christ. Freedom comes from knowing that
your old life of slavery is gone and your new life is hidden in him.

You're not your body or your reputation. You're not
your face, your family, or your job. You're not the sum of the
presumptions of others. You don't belong to the things of the
world—you're free!

God has forgotten that old life of yours, so let the world say
and think what they will.

REFLECTION

Have you been holding on to something from your past? Have
you had a hard time forgiving yourself or letting go of former
things? The enemy wants to remind you that you've made
mistakes. But the Lord tells you over and over, *The past has gone!
You're a new creation, and I've set you free. The old you doesn't
even exist anymore.*

Lord, help me guard against the lies of the enemy that say I'm
still in chains. If ever the darkness tries to remind me of my past,
help me to simply declare the victory of the cross. What Jesus
did for me was enough. He set me free, and I'm forever grateful.
In his name. Amen.

Worship

> "God is spirit, and his worshipers must worship
> in the Spirit and in truth."
>
> JOHN 4:24

We are always called to worship. No matter what our jobs or our callings are, worship is the silver thread that runs through everything and keeps it together. So what is worship, and how do we make sure we're doing it? It's certainly not summed up solely in the singing of songs. Though it can be a musical offering, true worship is so much more—it costs us something. It's sacrifice. It's the best and most precious thing we have surrendered. When you know you've been forgiven, healed, and changed, you'll pour your best out for him. Like the woman who poured out her most precious perfume on the feet of Jesus or like the widow who gave her only two copper coins, true worship says, *Nothing I could give you is enough to express my love for you, and yet you accept me regardless of what I give.*

REFLECTION

Worship keeps us on track with our dreams. It keeps God at the top, which aligns everything beneath according to his will. Take some time today to consider your lifestyle of worship and fully commit everything deeply important to you to God's kingdom.

Lord, I want to worship you in Spirit and in truth. I want to put you first and keep you above everything in my life so everything else can follow. Today I commit everything dear to me into your hands once again. In Jesus' name, amen.

Inner World Peace

> "Leave your gift there in front of the altar. First go and be reconciled to them; then come and offer your gift."
>
> Matthew 5:24

Peace—it's what we all need. We crave and pray for it in our troubled world, especially at this wonderful time of year. But peace is a principle we must apply to the innermost corners of our own lives before we can demand it elsewhere. It's a contradiction to crave peace in the world yet remain at odds with someone we love.

World peace begins with our inner world. We must seek personal peace before we can put on our shoes of peace and take it outward. It's true, we can't force the opposition to put down their weapons and call a truce, but we can lay down ours and declare that we are no longer on the warpath.

Reflection

If there is someone in your life you need to make peace with, now is a perfect time to do it. It might mean saying sorry, even if you're not solely to blame. It might mean letting go of something that has yet to be resolved. But the inner peace will be worth that sacrifice.

Lord, I want the freedom that comes from laying quarrels to rest. It's not always easy or even possible to make peace with an adversary in person, but as far as I'm able, help me make peace with everyone in my heart. If it's possible to make amends with a handshake or hug, please allow that healing to take place. In Jesus' name, amen.

There Is Enough Time

"Therefore do not worry about tomorrow, for tomorrow will worry about itself. Each day has enough trouble of its own."
MATTHEW 6:34

We all feel added pressure at this hectic time of year. It can often feel as if there truly aren't enough hours in the day—but there are! God created a day that is more than sufficient. If you don't have time to do everything today, then quite frankly some of it will have to wait!

Instead of making yourself an impossible to-do list and struggling to check it all off before the sun comes up, make a habit of resigning to the clock. When it becomes too late for you to function well, put down your to-do list and go to bed. Make a new list tomorrow and start over. Prioritize what is most crucial, and don't forget to include self-care! If trying to get life perfect before Christmas makes you stressed, it's not at all worth the effort.

REFLECTION

Stop for a moment. Have you been stressing out over the holiday season? Is your to-do list out of control? Give it to God! He has given you every hour you need to lead a full life. Today, ask for his strength to accomplish the lovely things you'd like to do for your friends and family, but also to accept that you're only human.

Lord, thank you for designing the perfect day. When you ordered time, you knew that the twenty-first century was coming. Though the pace of life has increased, what matters most has never changed. You know our needs and you will provide. Thank you, Lord. Amen.

Give Yourself a Break

> "Take my yoke upon you and learn from me, for I am gentle and humble in heart, and you will find rest for your souls. For my yoke is easy and my burden is light."
>
> MATTHEW 11:29–30

Perfectionism is one of the greatest enemies of our joy. The holiday season can cause it to rear its ugly head. There is so much pressure to be the perfect host and give the perfect gifts, even to rock the perfect festive look. But guess what? You. Are. Human. And humans aren't capable of perfection. If there's one swift way to destroy your own peace, it's to constantly strive for it. Your high standards are a good thing! It means you care. But don't set yourself up to feel like a failure by expecting to get everything right 100 percent of the time. Your house and outfits might not be perfect. Christmas Day might not be perfectly planned, and when dinnertime comes, the turkey might not be perfectly moist. But you're doing your best, and guess what? That's enough!

REFLECTION

When we feel as if we're missing the mark or even just straining to hit it, prayer is the answer. We need to ask for his help and thank him for his faithfulness in all circumstances. That way, when we feel overwhelmed we can find our balance again by the anchor of his presence in everything we do.

Lord, today I'm shaking off the spirit of perfectionism and giving thanks for you, the perfect Savior. I can do all things through you, and I don't need to rely on my own flawed human hands. Thank you for everything you're giving me in this season and for everything you are. In Jesus' name, amen.

Holiness

Flee the evil desires of youth and pursue righteousness,
faith, love and peace, along with those
who call on the Lord out of pure heart.

2 Timothy 2:22

Diets are challenging because they involve constantly avoiding and depriving ourselves of what we want. But what if there were a way to make dieting a joy?

When Joel and I were dating, we went through what most Christian couples go through. We wanted to save sex for our wedding night, but we also craved intimacy with each other. I began to feel quite upset with myself for struggling with this and began to feel as if I was battling against God. I discussed this with a friend, and he said something that changed my state of mind: "It might help if you stop focusing on avoiding sin and start desiring holiness." My faith walk has been based on this ever since. When we focus on eating food that boosts our energy levels and gives us life, it takes our minds off avoiding junk. When Joel and I made the choice to desire holiness, it enriched our future marriage, giving us an incredible foundation of trust.

REFLECTION

Picture yourself reaching out for light rather than avoiding darkness. Instead of focusing on what you have to give up, imagine your reward, which is far greater and far more satisfying in the long term.

Lord, let me not be deceived into believing I'm missing something by doing things your way. You always have something better. Help me eagerly desire holiness in every area of my life. In Jesus' name, amen.

Just Enjoy the Ride

No one can comprehend what goes on under the sun. Despite all
their efforts to search it out, no one can discover its meaning.

ECCLESIASTES 8:17

Even when you do a sterling job of planning, things can go
wrong. You could plan the perfect trip, but when it comes down
to it, most elements are outside of your control.

A little while back, I did a big tour through Norway. It was
a fourteen-date tour, and I had to be very organized with my
packing and travel. I went out of my way to prepare well for
this one. I began over a week before washing and packing all
the outfits I would wear. I remembered all my adapters and
chargers and even got a great exchange rate on my currency. But
perfection wasn't mine to demand. The flights to Norway were
delayed, my luggage was lost, and we ended up paying high prices
for emergency supplies. I just had to surrender and take comfort
in the fact that I did my best. And you know what? The trip
turned out pretty good regardless.

REFLECTION

There are some things in life you can't really plan for—so much
is outside of our control. You can plan a picnic, but in the end the
weather will always be out of your control. Faith comes in very
handy for those times when it rains on your picnic.

Lord, help me always accept it graciously when things go wrong.
There are so many things out of my control in this life. Help me
to switch faith gears when it all comes crashing down. I know
that you're with me even in the chaos. In Jesus' name, amen.

Promises, Promises

> Above all, my brothers and sisters, do not swear—not by heaven or earth or by anything else. All you need to say is a simple "Yes" or "No." Otherwise you will be condemned.
>
> JAMES 5:12

Enthusiastic people often agree to things on the spot. Hands up on this one—I'm totally guilty! Whether agreeing to a night out or helping at an event, I have so often found myself having to go back on a promise or flake out on a commitment because I hadn't really thought it through. This has been bad for my relationships and self-esteem. It's so good to realize that you don't have to say yes to everything, and you don't have to respond on the spot! Taking an extra couple of minutes to check your schedule will save you trouble and awkwardness later.

REFLECTION

If you're a people pleaser, have a little word with yourself today. You really don't have to say yes to everything! People will get over you saying no far more quickly than you realize. And if you don't keep a calendar, start one! Then make sure you check it before you say yes to things.

Lord, help me to be a person of integrity. Help me to think before I commit to something and learn to say no when I need to. In Jesus' name, amen.

What Do You Really Need?

"Take care, and be on your guard against all covetousness, for one's life does not consist of the abundance of his possessions."

LUKE 12:15 ESV

Our tour in Norway caused me to reevaluate where my security comes from. To find myself without my usual comforts was daunting to begin with. I'm used to having and doing certain things to make me comfortable in life. But being stripped of some of those things was quite liberating. I remembered that I don't actually need a full face of makeup and a pretty shirt to play to a crowd, and I got to experience the helpfulness of others. We had to accept the generosity of strangers because we had no choice. It made me realize some of the things I thought I needed were more of a burden than an essential. Through the experience I realized I'm thirstier than ever for peace in my life.

REFLECTION

This time of year is an especially materialistic one. We all begin to think about what we might ask for as a gift, and the post-holiday sales begin as soon as we clear away the wrapping paper. Today is a good time to ask yourself: *Do I really need the things I own? Or are they just adding to my stress?* You might find a way to a new level of peace in your life.

Lord, help me get rid of my attachment to things. I know I need clothing and other provisions, and in once in a while, it's helpful to dress impressively, but I want to fit in with your plans for me. Please give me your perspective. In Jesus' name, amen.

You Can't Take It with You

For we brought nothing into the world,
and we can take nothing out of it.

1 TIMOTHY 6:7

We spend a lot of time and energy working on our earthly comfort. Joel and I have really enjoyed doing up our first home. It has become a place where we feel peaceful and enjoy rest. But it can also be a source of stress. On those days where we find a leak or a damp patch, or something expensive breaks, we can feel an impending sense of doom. These things that we collect can be dear and sentimental to us, but when all is said and done, it really isn't worth our grief. We can't take these treasures with us, and giving them so much heart space is a recipe for sadness—unlike us, they're not built to last.

REFLECTION

This season focuses a lot on giving and having. It's the best time to bless the people we love but try not to get too attached to the material element of the holidays. Don't forget we're celebrating the birth of a child, born of a virgin, who is the King of kings. He gave away everything he owned to be near to us.

Lord, during this season of plenty let your light and sacrifice remain the focus. You were born with nothing and died the death of criminal to redeem me from my sins. Whatever happens though December, let our focus be on you, Jesus! Amen.

Don't Get Hung Up on the Unknowable

It is not good to eat too much honey, nor is it honorable to search out matters that are too deep.

PROVERBS 25:27

I looked in on a friend of mine on Facebook a few weeks ago. A theological debate had broken out on their wall and went on for some time. The debate was about heaven and hell—whether salvation could be altered by a change in beliefs. The more I read, the sadder I felt. It was so disheartening to see people delving so deeply into the unknowable, so deeply that they were losing faith. I started to type my comment saying as much, but then stopped. I realized I didn't want to get lost in an online debate that could never be won.

REFLECTION

It doesn't matter how learned or intellectual you are. There are certain mysteries you'll never unravel in this life. If you spend too long swimming the depths of the unknowable, you're likely to become lost and exhausted. It's good to talk, debate, and study. It's good to discuss difficult subjects. But it isn't good to get hung up or angry about things we'll never comprehend.

Lord, help me be okay with not knowing things. Help me have peace about the vast wealth of knowledge I'll never have. I believe you'll supply me with all the knowledge I need in this lifetime. In Jesus' name, amen.

Be Your Authentic Self

Let us therefore make every effort to do what leads to peace
and to mutual edification.

ROMANS 14:19

Putting on a brave face for others is exhausting. As you dip in
and out of different surroundings this week, you'll feel all kinds
of pressure to be what people expect, but it's not worth it. Being
all things to all people is bound to disturb your peace. So don't
do it—be you. Say no to the things you don't want to do. Don't
wear clothes you dislike just to impress your partner or friends,
and don't pretend you like horses to impress the moms at dance
club. Learning how to be authentically you might cost you some
opportunities and maybe even some friends, but everything left
behind will fit you like a glove. You'll look around and see a life
that feels like your own.

REFLECTION

Spending time with challenging family members or even just
putting on a hosting face for others can be stressful. If you're
feeling the added anxiety of holiday visits, today's prayer is for
you. Remember that it's okay to be yourself. You don't have
to become a domestic goddess overnight. Christmas is about
togetherness and joy, not impressing your relatives.

Lord, give me peace during this hectic season. Help me create a
warm and easy atmosphere so everyone can feel at ease in my
company. Help me not to get hung up on being the life and soul
of the party but to take time out to be still and enjoy the people
who matter most to me. In Jesus' name, amen.

Stop

"Come to me, all you who are weary and burdened,
and I will give you rest."
MATTHEW 11:28

Feeling emotional? Tearful? Stressed? Maybe, just maybe you need to get some rest. Exhaustion makes us sensitive. Babies cry when they're tired. A simple task can seem impossible and outrageous to a sleepy toddler. Just because we're grown up and have learned to better control our emotions doesn't mean they're not there. You must make time to stop and take care of yourself. So much of what life has for you is in the here and now, and being too busy means that we can miss it.

REFLECTION

Schedule an early night for yourself. It's possible. If you can make time for all the things you're doing right now, then you can make time for this. Get yourself a wonderful night's sleep so you can wake up feeling like a well-rested toddler, cheerful and eager to explore the world.

Lord, I'm tired. I need to stop and rest. Help me to be disciplined enough to make this happen. You command it. You designated times to be involved and times to sit out and recharge. In Jesus' name, amen.

You Don't Need to Prove Yourself

The devil said to him, "If you are the Son of God, tell this stone to become bread." Jesus answered, "It is written: 'Man shall not live on bread alone.'"

JOHN 4:3–4

When Jesus went out to the desert for forty days, he was greatly tempted and tested by the enemy. In preparation for his incredible mission on earth, he went through this season of temptation. He was asked to prove himself, and he was tempted with false promises. The same is very likely to happen to us. As we prepare to assume our true calling and step out in our true God given identity, the enemy will taunt us. We will be tempted to try to prove our identity, worth, and skills. But we don't need to do that. God at the right time will give us our vindication.

REFLECTION

When you feel the need to prove yourself in some way, take a moment to consider Jesus. While knowing he was God's Son and that his was the name above all names, he endured cynics and accusers. He always retained his dignity and declared truth in the face of his enemies' taunts.

Lord, make me strong. Help me to be dignified when others doubt or accuse me, knowing that in due course you'll bring the truth to light. In Jesus' name, amen.

Money Worries

Keep your lives free from the love of money and be content with what you have, because God has said, "Never will I leave you; never will I forsake you."

HEBREWS 13:5

I truly believe money is a principle—an energy that affects every family, individual, and life. Whether you're born with a silver spoon in your mouth or find yourself in poverty, there are issues surrounding finance, need, loss, and gain in every life. With every penny comes responsibility. The more you have, the more you have to lose. And as you move forward with your business, ministry, project, or household, you'll face challenges. You'll have to make decisions, and sometimes you'll need help.

The bottom line? No matter where we are on our financial journey, there will be times when we realize we're walking a fine line. As a couple, Joel and I regularly ask God into our finances. We thank him for his provision, and we ask him to meet our needs and guide our decisions. I do the same thing with my music manager, who is also a Christian. When we feel called to do something good, we call God into the financial needs we have there.

REFLECTION

Pray for financial peace and for God's provision wherever it's needed. Ask for wisdom and guidance whenever you need to make decisions, knowing that God has promised to take care of you.

Lord, thank you for your constant provision in my life. Help my relationship with money to be healthy. Help me to not love money or fear poverty. Guide me to make wise decisions. In Jesus' name, amen.

You're in Training

Everyone who competes in the games goes into strict training.
They do it to get a crown that will not last, but we do it to get a
crown that will last forever.

1 CORINTHIANS 9:25

What Jesus went through in the wilderness was tough. It was
hardcore temptation and trial. But he went toward it willingly
because he knew it was necessary. The Holy Spirit led Jesus into
the wilderness because Jesus needed to build spiritual muscle and
practice self-control while vulnerable. He knew the great strength
of character and will that would be needed later. Having had
nothing to eat or drink for forty days, his resolve was tested. But
he remained strong. When we go through seasons in the wilderness, we too are in training. God is teaching us how to trust him
and remain faithful to his calling, even when we're desperate.

REFLECTION

If you feel you're in the wilderness right now, don't let go of your
identity. The enemy will whisper to you, *Where is God now?* He
will show you the successes of others and ask you, *Where are your
kingdoms? Where are your awards and accolades?* In these times,
you must come back with God's truth. Tell the enemy that God
has a plan to prosper you and not to harm you, a sure plan to
give you a hope and a future.

Lord, thank you that your resolve was strong when tested. Help
me to be as single-minded as you. Keep me focused on your
truth and your promises when life seems dry and I'm starving
for success. In Jesus' name, amen.

Don't Get Overwhelmed by Ideas

The plans of the diligent lead surely to abundance,
but everyone who is hasty comes to poverty.

PROVERBS 21:5 ESV

If you're like me, ideas can be both your best friend and your
worst enemy. You have them at all hours of the day and night,
and they're like little puppies that jump up and paw at you for
attention. They pull you away from your current tasks, including
sleeping, and you find it hard to ignore them because you know
how great they can turn out. Ideas can be found everywhere:
from an encouraging email or the perfect birthday gift to creative
projects, Facebook statuses, and business plans. If you're like me,
you'll sometimes suffer idea overload.

Why not create a wish list of ideas? Put everything on there
from cleaning out the shed to scuba diving in Australia. Realize
that you can't do them all today, this week, or even this year. And
you don't have to. Just because you imagined something doesn't
mean you have to accomplish it right away.

REFLECTION

Set yourself a short list of goals for the week. Decide on *two*
things you want to accomplish today. For more long-term items
(like writing novels and winning the Nobel Peace Prize), give
yourself a few years. Perhaps you'll decide you want to write a
chapter a month or save a little each a month toward a dream
trip. You may find you accomplish a whole lot more this way.

Lord, in due time help me to tackle all of things that matter to
me. Today I'm downloading all my plans and desires and trusting that you'll help me to get to them at the right time. In Jesus'
name, amen.

Don't Stick Your Head in the Sand

Instead, let us test and examine our ways.
Let us turn back to the LORD.

LAMENTATIONS 3:40

The most natural thing to do if you get into a difficulty in life is to stick your head in the sand and pretend it's not happening. Whether its debt, addiction, or depression, trust me—it's not going away just because you stop looking at it. The more you ignore it, the worse the problem is likely to become. By being open and honest with the people in your world—your friends, family, and even your creditors—you'll find there are lots of practical ways to deal with problems.

The enemy wants us to hide from our issues until they're out of control. But there is no pit too deep for God to reach in and retrieve you from!

REFLECTION

There is no shame in financial difficulty. Addiction is something we all encounter to a degree. Today, decide not to stick your head in the sand because of shame. We're all the same, and the sooner you come up for air, the quicker God can begin restoration.

Lord, today I'm praying for courage to face the issues in my life. Help me to know that I'm not alone and that shame is an illusion. I trust you today, Lord, knowing that you're mighty to save. In Jesus' name, amen.

Focus

The LORD's lovingkindnesses indeed never cease,
for His compassions never fail. They are new every morning;
great is Your faithfulness.

LAMENTATIONS 3:22–23 NASB

Sometimes I get overwhelmed by the uncertainty of the future—there's so much I don't know. I've learned instead to focus on what I *do* know:

I know that *somehow* I've made it this far.

I know I have survived every tough day I've ever had.

I know the odds I've beaten are greater than the odds I face.

I know that while resources are sometimes stretched, I have always had enough.

I know that everything I *do* have has been an answer to prayer—from the clothes on my back to the roof over my head and the people under it.

I know that every trial and heartbreak I've ever faced has been temporary.

That's what I know. I believe in a God who knows the rest.

REFLECTION

As we approach the end of the year, let's commit the future to God. We all feel nervous about the unknown, but the God who brought us this far will lead us into a new season.

Lord, thank you for what you're about to do. You've always been so faithful and have brought me this far. I know I have nothing to fear in my future because you will be there every step of the way, blessing and guiding me as always. In Jesus' name, amen.

The Promise of Hope

Three things will last forever—faith, hope, and love.
1 CORINTHIANS 13:13 NLT

Depression is described in many ways, but I describe it as a feeling of sheer hopelessness. It's more than sadness, grief, loss, or loneliness—all of those things can live alongside hope. Depression is the feeling that all the doors inside you that used to lead to hope are closed. It's the feeling that every time your heart searches for joy, it can't find it.

Today I want to tell you that even if you can't *feel* hope, hope is still there. It's anchored to your pulse. While your heart is beating, hope remains. Though hope may be sleeping, it will awaken—that is its very nature. So don't fear. Though you may be out of breath, resources, and ideas, hope searches the emptiness for a way and always finds it. If hope can't fix what you're facing today, it will cause you to adapt tomorrow. You may not feel it right now, but you better believe the eternal light of hope is fiercer than your despair.

REFLECTION

Today, let go of all that pressure to *feel* hope; that will come. Because hope is not just an emotion—it's a promise.

Thank you, Lord, for eternal hope. Thank you that your promise is to us and it's not going anywhere. The story is never over while you're still in the middle of it, Lord. I invite you to be central to my life again right now and forever. In Jesus' name, amen.

Today Is a New Day

The LORD's lovingkindnesses indeed never cease, for His compassions never fail. They are new every morning; great is Your faithfulness. "The LORD is my portion," says my soul, "Therefore I have hope in Him."

LAMENTATIONS 3:22–24 NASB

In a TED talk, Glennon Doyle Melton said: "I like to think of hope like the sunrise. It comes up every day … to shine on everybody … equally. You can spend your whole life in darkness, yet if one day you decide to come out, it'll be there. I used to think of the sunrise as accusatory and searching. But now I see it as hope's daily invitation to come back to life."

This year might be an old year now, but today is still a *new day*. Every sunrise is a new chance to live again, and God's mercies are new every morning. Just like the sunrise, hope doesn't discriminate. No matter how far gone you feel, hope holds out its hand to you today. Today the sun rose for you—it's every bit as much yours as anyone else's.

REFLECTION

Find a quiet, private space and sit or kneel. Close your eyes and hold out your hands. Now picture yourself receiving the free, brand-new, and unopened gift of hope. You're invited to that party of hope all over again. Reach out and receive that gift from him right now.

Lord, thank you again for the gift of hope, which I receive now in your name. Thank you that your mercies are always fresh and new and that you're making me new too. Great is your faithfulness, Lord. In Jesus' name, amen.

Forgiveness

"When you stand praying, if you hold anything against anyone, forgive them, so that your Father in heaven may forgive you your sins."

MARK 11:25

Throughout this year we've mentioned forgiveness several times. But being that the New Year is on the horizon, it's a great time to revisit this tough subject.

There's no question, people will have disappointed you this year. People may have failed or even abandoned you. You may have had cross words with someone, or you may have even crossed swords with someone. There might have been breakdowns in your relationships and offenses committed against you. But to take *any* of those things with you into the next year would be an offense against yourself.

REFLECTION

If you've been hurt or wronged this year, call it to mind now. What happened? Who was in the wrong? While you consider this, thank God for his mercy and forgiveness. He has covered your wrongs. And now he must cover theirs. Trust that he is a just and kind God and that he will take care of this situation.

Lord, thank you for your grace and forgiveness. Help me to let go of all of this right now. I don't want to take this feeling or this offense with me into the next chapter of my life, so I pray you'd remove all anger and offense from my spirit. In Jesus' name, amen.

Payoff for the Pain

Do not be surprised at the fiery ordeal that has come on you to test you, as though something strange were happening to you. But rejoice inasmuch as you participate in the sufferings of Christ, so that you may be overjoyed when his glory is revealed.

1 PETER 4:12–13

A couple of years ago, my guitar was wrecked by an airline halfway through my tour. Not only was this upsetting, but it impacted the already hectic schedule. Struggling to find something to borrow was very unsettling and stressful. Allowing team members to speak on my behalf to airlines and guitar shops because I don't speak the language was tough. The final blow was finding out my beloved instrument was beyond repair. I'm pleased to say, however, we had a beautiful resolution, which has taught me a valuable lesson.

Not only did the manufacturer reach out and offer to replace my guitar as a gift, but they were able to fix other guitars using parts from the broken one I had donated back to them. So much payoff for that bit of pain!

REFLECTION

My hope message for the day is this: There is hidden treasure in the fragments of our tragedy. Not only can we have faith for our own restoration, but through our suffering there is healing for others. God wastes nothing.

Thank you, Lord, for your resourcefulness. You're able to take my mess and make it a message. You're able to take my broken instruments in life and turn them into even more music. And for this reason, I will trust you even when things are shattered in my life. In Jesus' name, amen.

You Are Not a Hopeless Case

And so, Lord, where do I put my hope? My only hope is in you.
PSALM 39:7 NLT

As we near the end of this year, I wanted to tackle another sort of hopeless—being labeled as hopeless by others. Let me tell you, I spent my entire young life forgetting things, losing things, struggling to be organized, and failing to measure up academically. I knew I had potential, but I felt the regular demands of life didn't fit me. "I'm not cut out for this," I would say. To a degree, I was right. Structure is hard for me and most of life requires it. But now I know—I may not be cut out for the boxes life tries to squash us into, but that's okay. It means I'm able to live an unpredictable and flexible life with a silly schedule. If you've been told you're hopeless, it's time to shake off that label and replace it. Thanks to God's amazing grace you are now hopeful!

REFLECTION

Have you ever felt hopeless? Have others labeled you as hopeless? Today is the day to lay that to rest. God has promised you his unfailing hope that lasts forever. He's promised that his power is made perfect in your weakness. He has promised to take what was intended for evil and repurpose it for good. You are a new creation and a child of God. There is nothing to feel any guilt, shame, or fear about, so let it go!

Lord, thank you that you designed me for certain purposes. Though I have weaknesses, I also have strengths. I, like everyone else, am a work in progress. Thank you that you're working in and through me right now and that you'll never give up on me. In Jesus' name, amen.

When the Miracle Doesn't Happen

He brought me out into a spacious place;
he rescued me because he delighted in me.

2 SAMUEL 22:20

I've seen lots of miraculous answers to prayer over the years. But I've also seen many prayers go unanswered (or at least not answered in the way we hoped). It's easy to look at a situation like that and ask, *Where was my miracle?* But in hindsight, we often find that something miraculous *has* taken place—broken hearts have found a way to carry on. God has somehow carried us through the valley and out into the clearing.

Sometimes the miracle is that we keep going, keep believing, and somehow become stronger. That's truly something to thank God for.

REFLECTION

Have you been carrying around any anger about a miracle that didn't seem to come? Don't forget that you're still standing! You might feel that you're defeated, but your very heartbeat tells a different story. You made it through the storm, and that alone is a miracle. As for everyone else, we're in the same boat. We must keep our eyes and hands raised toward God, knowing he is still good.

Lord, thank you that you have been able to give us the peace that surpasses all understanding. Thank you that you have been able to turn weeping into joy. You are the God of miracles, even when our prayers aren't answered as we first expected. Help me to fix my heart and my eyes on you even when my answer or my healing doesn't come. Help me to know and believe that you're always good, because you are God. In Jesus' name, amen.

Your Story Isn't Over Yet

You have turned my mourning into joyful dancing. You have taken away my clothes of mourning and clothed me with joy.
PSALM 30:11 NLT

When P. L. Travers wrote *Mary Poppins*, she was in fact rewriting her own story with a sweeter ending. In the classic children's novel and blockbuster movie, the charismatic nanny redeems a slightly aloof father figure and stitches a family back together in the nick of time. In the author's own life, redemption didn't quite come the way she'd written it for her treasured father. But she did something amazing—she wrote something beautiful, redemptive, and uplifting from her pain.

As I watched *Saving Mr. Banks*, the story behind bringing *Mary Poppins* to the silver screen, I was moved. I felt God reminding me in my spirit that we can all seek out a better ending for our story. With God's grace our mourning can become dancing and beauty can come from our ashes.

REFLECTION

If you didn't get the breakthrough you've been asking for this year, you have my sympathy. But the end of the year is not the end of your story. Keep writing. And may next year be the beginning of a new chapter that changes everything for the better.

Lord, thank you that you're the author and perfecter of our faith. Thank you that you can take a tragedy and cause it to become an adventure story. You can turn the character who is on a losing streak into a winner and a hero. Thank you that you're able and willing to do this for me at all times. In Jesus' name, amen.

Strength to Strength

Blessed are those whose strength is in you, whose hearts
are set on pilgrimage. As they pass through the Valley of Baka,
they make it a place of springs; the autumn rains also cover it
with pools. They go from strength to strength,
till each appears before God in Zion.

PSALM 84:5–7

After my first year as a Christian, a strange anxiety came over me.
I'd had such a great year! Almost everything in my life had done a
180-degree turnaround. I came out of a horrible relationship and
managed to quit smoking, began a career in music and ministry,
and was free from depression for the first time in years. But I
couldn't shake the nagging feeling it was all about to fall apart!
I'd grown so used to things collapsing throughout my life that I
feared the blessings would dissolve into chaos.

We had a visiting speaker at our church—a pastor and
church network leader named Dave Gilpin. He was so positive
and faith filled, I felt I had to speak to him afterward. One phrase
has stuck with me from that conversation: "Philippa, you're going
to go from strength to strength."

REFLECTION

When we remain in Jesus, he takes us on a good journey. There
are moments of weakness, peaks, and troughs. But ultimately, he
is renewing us and moving us from strength to strength in him!

Lord, thank you for all the great things you've done for me.
You're so good and faithful. I'm excited for all the wonderful
things to come. Thank you that you're promising to move me
from strength to strength. In Jesus' name, amen.

Gratitude

Give thanks in all circumstances;
for this is God's will for you in Christ Jesus.

1 Thessalonians 5:18

We made it! If you're reading this then you've gone through this year and stayed on a journey of soul-searching and seeking God's perfect will for your life. There is no better way to celebrate this awesome year than by saying thank you!

Take a few minutes out of the celebrations today to make a list of all the key things that have happened. Take time to reflect on the awesome ways God has sustained and provided for you. And don't forget to congratulate yourself too! You've survived trials, faced fears, and begun adventures. You've learned things, and you've laid old troubles to rest. All that remains is to say a prayer of thanks.

REFLECTION

What have been the high and the low points of your journey this year? What are you most thankful for and what have you learned? Write it all down and hand it all over to God in gratitude. He got you through this! And you're not where you were on January 1.

Lord, thank you for all that you have done this year. Thank you for the blessings and the triumphs and for your faithfulness during our hard days. Thank you that I have made this journey and emerged whole. I give glory to you for all you've achieved through me. I ask that you would forgive anything I did that may have fallen short, and I give you the year ahead. May your awesome, pleasing, and perfect will be done in and through me. In Jesus' name, amen.

About the Author

PHILIPPA HANNA is a singer/ songwriter, author, and YouTuber based in the UK where she lives and works with her husband, Joel. Together they perform up to 150 events a year, visiting over twenty-five countries sharing their moving music and testimony.

Philippa was born into a musical family with Irish roots, and since finding faith in 2004, she has been using songs, videos, and the written word to encourage others and share her faith. She is best known for songs such as "I Am Amazing" and "Raggedy Doll," which document her journey with self-esteem and encourage fans of all ages throughout the world. She has been invited to open tours for the likes of Lionel Richie and Leona Lewis. Her openness on the subjects of mental health and identity has helped win hearts worldwide and given her opportunities to play anywhere—from eating disorder clinics to arenas.

With the help of crowdfunding, Philippa's supporters have helped fund five studio albums, two books, and a live DVD, as well as several international tours. Philippa has been a proud ambassador for the child sponsorship organization Compassion for over a decade and recently joined the team at Compassion UK as Official Artist in Residence.

Her ambition and vision in life is to see others redeemed and released into their unique God-given dreams.

For more on Philippa, go to her website:
PhilippaHanna.com
For press and event enquiries, please contact:
info@storm5management.com